Competitiveness, Convergence, and International Specialization

Competitiveness, Convergence, and International Specialization

David Dollar and
Edward N. Wolff

The MIT Press
Cambridge, Massachusetts
London, England

This book was set in Palatino by Asco Trade Typesetting Ltd., Hong Kong and printed and bound in the United States of America.

Library of Congress Cataloging-in-Publication Data

Dollar, David.
Competitiveness, convergence, and international specialization / David Dollar, Edward N. Wolff.
p. cm.
Includes bibliographical references and index.
ISBN 0-262-04135-9
1. Competition, International. 2. Competition—United States. 3. Industrial productivity. 4. Industrial productivity—United States. 5. International trade. I. Wolff, Edward N. II. Title.
HF1414.D65 1993
338.6′048—dc20 92-27958
CIP

To our parents, John and Muriel Dollar and Arthur and Ethel Wolff

Contents

Acknowledgments

We would like to express our appreciation to the Division of Information Science and Technology of the National Science Foundation, the C. V. Starr Center for Applied Economics at New York University, and the Alfred P. Sloan Foundation, which funded various parts of the research. We are also indebted to Maury Gittleman for his very valuable assistance. It should be noted that the views expressed in this book are those of the authors and do not necessarily reflect the views of the World Bank. Many helpful comments were supplied by our colleagues, including William Baumol, Magnus Blomstrom, Hans Ehrbar, Angus Maddison, Richard Nelson, Tom Michl, Willi Semmler, Kenneth Sokoloff, Bart van Ark, and several anonymous referees.

We also benefited from comments and discussion at various seminars and conferences over the years, including the NBER Conference on Empirical Methods for International Trade, Cambridge, Massachusetts, April 1986; Conference on Demographic Change and Economic Development, Hagen, West Germany, September 1986; Center for Economic Research, Tilburg University, the Netherlands, October 1988; Jerome Levy Economics Institute Conference on Profits and Instability, Annandale-on-Hudson, New York, March 1989; University of Valencia, Valencia, Spain, September 1990; Stockholm School of Economics, Stockholm, Sweden, February 1991; and Workshop on "Historical Perspectives on the International Convergence of Productivity," Columbia University, New York, New York, November 1991.

1 The Scope of the Book

1.1 The Public Debate on Competitiveness

Has America been surpassed by Japan and Germany as an industrial and trading power? Has it lost its competitiveness and entered a period of steady decline? These questions are very much part of the public debate in the United States. They are fueled by massive fiscal and trade deficits that have persisted longer than anyone thought possible, Japan's ongoing export success, and U.S. productivity growth that has been well below levels achieved in other major industrial economies.

Other important questions are related to this alleged decline in competitiveness. How can we account for the extraordinary industrial expansion in Japan, and to a lesser extent in European economies like Germany and Italy? What has been the role of international trade? Have Japan and other nations followed mercantilist policies of import protection at home and export promotion abroad, at the expense of a naively free-trade America? And what is the role of government? Is America lagging behind because its government has not developed a sufficiently close partnership with business? Should the government play a more active role in creating new technologies and products and in promoting U.S. production and export of these items?

These are the broad questions addressed by this book. They are large ones, and the potential answers are not susceptible to rigorous proof or disproof. It would be disingenuous to suggest that there are simple answers to the questions of whether the United States is in decline and what kind of government policy might reverse such a trend. Our goal is not to provide definitive answers, but to bring new information to bear on the questions so as to inform the debate more fully. On the weight of this information, we feel comfortable making a number of recommendations.

However, we admit that there is plenty of room for debate about the implications of our research results.

We should also say at the beginning that the book is not just about the United States. Although the public debate about competitiveness is probably most intense in the United States, there are similar debates in all of the advanced economies. Even in Japan, which is perceived to be so successful by the American public, there is considerable self-doubt about the nation's future. The issues addressed here are relevant to all of the developed economies and, to a lesser extent, to developing economies in the Third World as well. Nevertheless, it is useful to take the United States as a benchmark, as that country has clearly been the preeminent industrial economy in the postwar period and now must adjust to a new economic world order in which it is, at best, first among equals.

1.2 What Is Competitiveness?

Even the simple question, has the United States lost its competitiveness, is difficult to answer because the competitiveness of a country is not a well-defined economic term. Competitiveness is a meaningful concept when applied to firms in particular subindustries. For example, Japanese firms are very competitive in the production of midsize automobiles. What competitiveness means in this context is that firms produce high-quality, low-cost items. This statement could be substantiated by data on worldwide sales or exports of this product. It is impossible, however, for one nation's firms to be competitive in all industries. Japanese firms are not particularly competitive in the production of heavy-duty trucks, as well as in a wide range of other manufactured and nonmanufactured products. The same can be said of the United States, Germany, and the other advanced economies: there are some subindustries in which their firms are competitive, and others in which they are not. U.S. firms remain highly competitive in the production of aircraft, computer software, and motion pictures, just to name a few examples. Concerning the overall competitiveness of a nation, it is often defined implicitly in terms of the country's trade balance. In the popular press, the large U.S. trade deficit during the 1980s and the large surpluses in Japan and Germany have been cited as evidence of relative competitiveness. There is a certain intuitive logic to this approach. If a nation has competitive firms in many subindustries, then it should have a trade surplus. A nation with only a few competitive firms, on the other hand, would have a trade deficit. The problem with this approach, however, is that trade imbalances tend to be temporary. Certainly the U.S. deficit has persisted for nearly a decade. But over long periods of time there are solid economic reasons why a nation's trade roughly balances. Having taken on a large amount of international debt in the 1980s, the United States will almost certainly shift in the future to a position of trade surplus as it pays interest on that debt and perhaps repays some of it.

In the late 1980s the U.S. trade position improved because the currency devalued, reducing U.S. wages relative to wages in other industrial countries. Suppose this trend continues: further devaluation of the U.S. dollar and further declines in U.S. wages. If the United States moves into a position of trade surplus with lower real wages, would anyone take this as a sign of improved competitiveness? Certainly not. It is always possible to compete internationally through a devalued currency and lower wages. Clearly this is not what is meant by competitiveness. Hence the overall trade balance per se is not going to be the proper measure.

We are not convinced that competitiveness is a useful term to apply to nations. Nevertheless, since it is likely to be continually used in public debate, we will offer our own general definition: a competitive nation is one that can succeed in international trade via high technology and productivity, with accompanying high income and wages. Given this definition, the best overall measure of competitiveness is one that has long been used in international comparisons: productivity. Labor productivity, in particular, indicates the extent to which a nation can be a competitive, low-cost producer while maintaining high wages. Another measure of productivity is informative as well: total factor productivity (TFP) measures the output produced by given amounts of labor and capital together. High TFP indicates a high level of technology and means that both capital and labor can earn large returns while the cost of production remains low. A nation with high labor and total factor productivity is one that can compete internationally with high incomes and a high standard of living.

It should be noted that this definition does relate back to the concept of competitiveness at the level of the firm. In the case of midsize cars, for example, the competitiveness of Japanese firms will be reflected in high levels of labor and total factor productivity, compared to other nations, for this subindustry. If Japanese firms are strong in all subindustries of the broader industry called transport equipment, then that country will be found to have high labor and total factor productivity for the whole industry. On the other hand, if Japan is competitive in midsize cars, Germany in luxury cars, Sweden in heavy-duty trucks, and the United States in aircraft, then differences in labor and total factor productivity for the transport equipment industry will tend to be small among these countries.

If one nation has a productivity advantage over other countries in all industries, it will necessarily have a higher per capita income. Even in this unusual case, however, the "competitive" nation would not be exporting in all industries. Rather, it would tend to export from the sectors in which its *relative* productivity advantage was greatest, and to import in areas in which its productivity lead was small. The United States in the early postwar period, for instance, was the productivity leader in virtually all sectors. But its exports were concentrated in subindustries such as aircraft in which its productivity lead was very high. In other industries, like textiles, the country also had a productivity lead, but only a modest one, and as a result was an importer.

In practice, price levels and exchange rates adjust to ensure that each country is a low-cost producer of some goods. If one nation has an absolute productivity lead in all or most activities, these adjustments will result in that country having the highest wages and incomes. Loosely stated, countries can be competitive either on the basis of low wages and devalued exchange rates or as a result of high absolute productivity. For this reason, export success per se, or even a trade surplus, is a misleading measure of national competitiveness. The ability to compete in international trade with high productivity and hence high incomes is worth aspiring to.

It should also be noted that one nation having absolute productivity advantages in all industries is unusual. It is possible, and more likely, that countries will have absolute advantages in different sectors. In this case it makes sense to look at overall productivity for the whole economy and per capita income for the nation to measure one country's competitiveness against others'.

1.3 Productivity Convergence

Among advanced economies there has been a marked tendency for aggregate productivity levels to converge. Abramovitz (1986) and Baumol (1986) demonstrate that this convergence has been occurring for at least a century, and that the process has been particularly rapid during the postwar period.[1] Figure 1.1 shows real output per capita for the whole economy in the six largest market economies over the period 1950–85.[2] The United States had a large labor productivity advantage over all other countries as the world emerged from World War II. This advantage was partly the result of the destruction of the capital stock in Europe and Japan during the war. In addition, as part of the war effort, U.S. industries had pioneered a wide range of new technologies in chemicals, aerospace, elec-

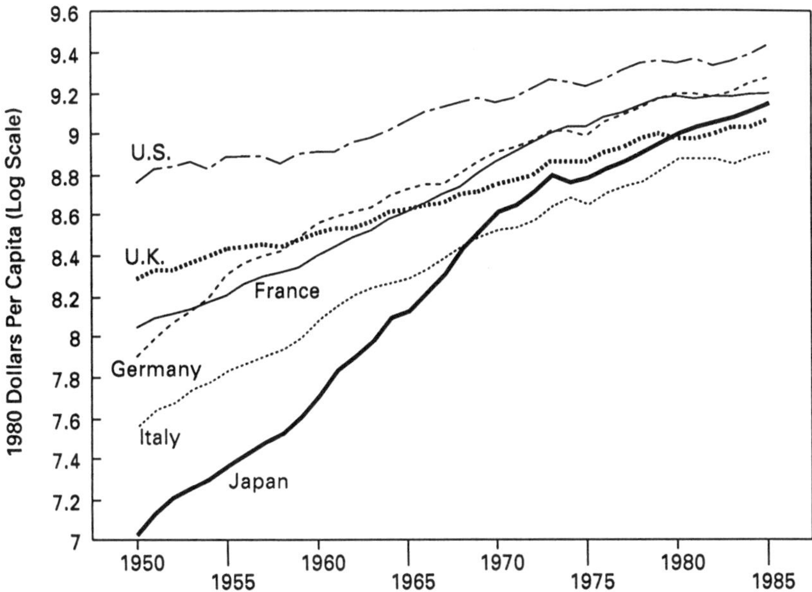

Figure 1.1
Real per capita GDP in the six largest OECD economies, 1950–1985

tronics, and other sectors. The rapid convergence of the other countries' productivity on the U.S. level in the 1950s partly reflects postwar reconstruction of the capital stock. Reconstruction had largely been completed by the end of the 1950s; however, it can be seen that convergence on the United States continued, though at a less rapid pace.

By the end of the 1980s the aggregate productivity levels of the industrial countries were close together. Note, though, that the United States was still on top. That result may surprise some readers. In the popular press one often reads that per capita income in Japan is now far higher than in the United States. That conclusion, however, is arrived at by comparing per capita gross domestic product (GDP) through the current exchange rate. But at the current exchange rate many goods and services are far more expensive in Japan than in the United States. Services that are not traded internationally—such as housing and restaurant meals—are particularly expensive. If these differences in price level are controlled for, so as to arrive at an estimate of real per capita output, the comparison that emerges is the one indicated in figure 1.1: real output per capita has risen rapidly in Japan, but remains well below the level of the United States and of the leading European economies.

The debate about declining U.S. competitiveness really concerns the extrapolation of this picture into the future. At the extremes, two basic predictions can be made. The first possibility is that the rapid growth of productivity in Japan and a few other nations will continue, so that those nations will soon surpass the U.S. productivity level and leave the United States behind. The second alternative is that, having converged on the U.S. level, countries like Japan and Germany will experience slower growth, so that all of the advanced economies will progress together, with differences in productivity levels contained within a narrow band. Obvious variations can be played on these two basic themes. For example, Japanese growth could slow down, relative to its recent history, and yet still remain higher than U.S. growth, with the result that Japan would gradually develop a productivity lead. Or, most of the advanced economies might proceed together, with one or more laggards falling further behind.

It is implausible that these complicated relationships are fueled by simple mechanical forces. But it is useful analytically to frame the debate in terms of the extremes: convergence to a world in which there are a group of advanced economies with similar levels of productivity, or divergence, with Japan and perhaps one or two other countries putting more and more distance between themselves and the laggards. It should also be noted that there are several variants of the divergence argument. One of the more highly publicized is the notion that the United States is becoming deindustrialized; that is, Japan and Germany are taking over key manufacturing industries while the United States is left to produce in low-paying service industries.[3]

Our contribution to this debate is to delve, more deeply than in any previous work, into the sources of the productivity convergence that had been observed up through the end of the 1980s. A more thorough understanding of the sources of productivity convergence should enable us to assess better the probability that the trend will continue. Furthermore, this knowledge should also be useful in shaping public policy aimed at improving a nation's productivity and competitive standing. As part of this work, we will examine whether the United States in fact is becoming deindustrialized.

Before proceeding, it should be noted that there is considerable debate as to whether productivity convergence is a general phenomenon, or one confined to only a small number of countries. The economies depicted in figure 1.1 were not randomly chosen. These are the successful countries that are rich today. There are other economies that were relatively rich in 1950 that have not grown well and have not converged on the productivity leaders. Argentina and Venezuela are the best examples. They had higher productivity than Japan in 1950, but have largely stagnated in the postwar period.

Furthermore, across all economies—rich and poor—there is no clear trend toward convergence in the postwar period. Convergence requires that countries with low levels of productivity at the beginning of the period grow more rapidly than the high-productivity countries, reducing the cross-country dispersion. In fact, the dispersion in productivity levels across all economies is about the same today as in 1950. On the basis of this evidence some economists have questioned whether there is any tendency toward convergence, or whether the appearance of convergence among advanced countries is merely a statistical artifact achieved by selecting certain countries for the analysis and omitting others.[4]

Some recent literature has examined these issues in a more sophisticated way.[5] This literature demonstrates that there is a general trend toward convergence across all economies—even the poorest—after controlling for several key variables. The most important control variable is the level of investment. Poor countries tend to have low levels of savings and investment, and this deficiency is one of the key factors holding them back from rapid growth and from convergence on more advanced economies.

A second important factor is trade orientation. There is a growing body of evidence that outward-oriented economies develop more rapidly. Outward orientation is achieved through a relatively liberal regime for foreign trade and investment and through good exchange rate management. These policies facilitate technological advance by allowing firms to import machinery and materials and by providing a large export market for output. A final important factor that shows up in recent studies of convergence is education, particularly at the primary and secondary level.

After controlling for investment, trade orientation, and education, backward countries grow more rapidly than more developed ones. That is generally true across all countries, and it is a very interesting and important result. This convergence tendency is consistent with Gerschenkron's (1952) celebrated notion that there are advantages to being backward. The basic idea is that backward economies can benefit from the innovations of more advanced nations in order to grow rapidly. The benefit can come through importing machinery that embodies the frontier technologies or by borrowing ideas that are not embodied in machinery. The latter can occur in many ways: by sending students to engineering school in advanced countries, by reverse engineering of final products, and by subcontracting to produce for firms in advanced nations.

That these advantages of backwardness exist is well established in the recent literature. In practice, however, they can easily be swamped by other factors that affect growth: low investment rate, inward orientation, and/or a weak educational base. These results imply that it is difficult for extremely poor countries to exploit the advantages of backwardness because their poverty has a large effect on savings and investment and on the education of the next generation. Middle-income developing countries are in a much better position to exploit the advantages of backwardness, because of their higher levels of savings and education. It is from this middle-income group that the successful newly industrialized countries (NICs) have emerged.

Many middle-income countries have not lived up to these prospects, however. Argentina, for example, was not able to take advantage of its relative backwardness. The country has been plagued by low savings and a highly inward-oriented trade policy that have overwhelmed the potential advantages of its position.

Thus, across all countries, convergence can be viewed as an opportunity whose realization depends on several other factors. The countries that today make up the Organization for Economic Cooperation and Development (OECD) all had sufficient savings rates, outward orientation, and educational base to form the "convergence club" of the postwar period.

Although the recent studies of convergence have indicated what policies and factors influence a country's inclusion in or exclusion from the club, they have not provided much information about the details of convergence at a more micro level. That is where we begin our investigation.

1.4 Deindustrialization

In conjunction with the aggregate convergence that is now well documented, has the United States experienced a significant loss of its industrial core in comparison to other advanced economies, notably Japan and Germany? This is the fear raised by the deindustrialization school. The following chapter investigates this question in detail and finds that there is scant evidence of any such industrial decline. Among OECD countries the U.S. share of manufacturing output has not declined; rather, it has increased slightly since the early 1970s.

By 1985 the U.S. share of OECD manufacturing production was 36.7%, slightly higher than the country's share of OECD population, 35.3%. In fact, as shown in figure 1.2, the distribution of manufacturing output across the developed countries broadly mirrors the distribution of population. Japan has a few percentage points more of the output than its population

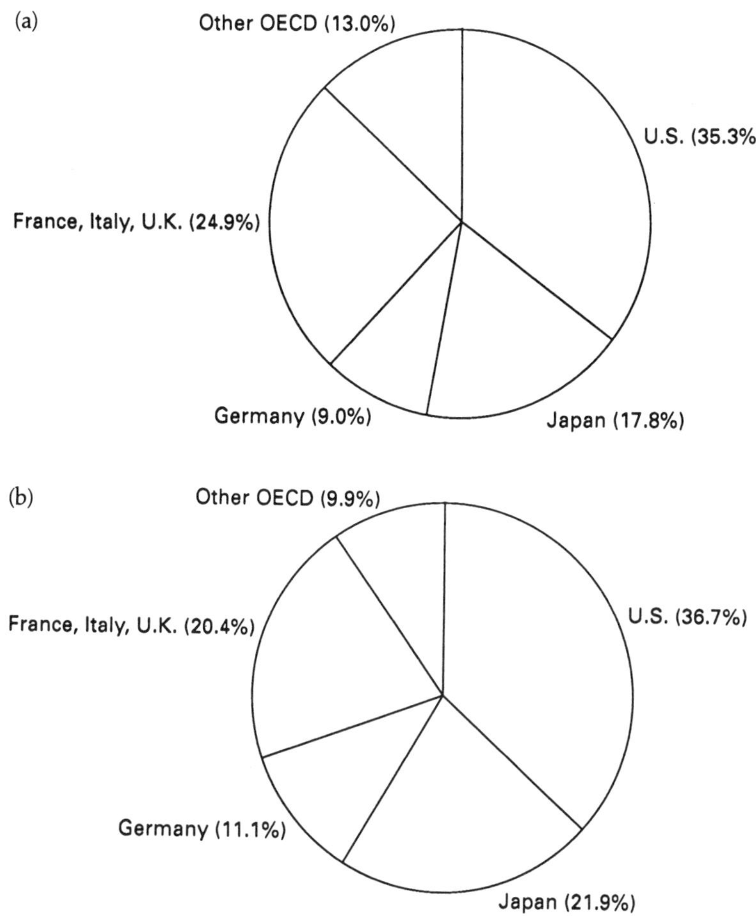

Figure 1.2
(a) Distribution of population among OECD countries, 1985; (b) distribution of manufacturing output among OECD countries, 1985

would justify, but the difference is minor. Germany and the United States also have larger shares of output than of population. To a first order of approximation, however, variation in the amount of industrial production among countries today corresponds closely to differences in size, as measured by population.

The trends in output shares at the industry level reveal some interesting patterns. The industries in which the U.S. share of OECD output has risen are generally ones closely connected to natural resources. Examples are textiles, in which U.S. cotton production provides an advantage, and wood products, in which there is also a resource base for production. The industries in which the U.S. share has declined sharply are the very capital-intensive sectors: chemicals and basic metals. The United States has also lost ground in machinery and equipment—a classification that includes automobiles, machine tools, computers, and aircraft—but the change has been minor: from 43% of OECD output in 1961 to 40% in 1987. Given that the latter category includes most high-technology products, these data provide a strong case for the stability of the U.S. position, rather than for its relative decline. Japan has certainly made impressive gains relative to the rest of the OECD group, from 14% of total manufacturing production in 1970 to 23% in 1987. Japan's gains, however, have come more at the expense of Europe than of the United States. The United Kingdom experienced a large decline in its share of OECD production, and even Germany's share decreased, from 14% in 1970 to 11% in 1987.

Trends in manufactured exports are broadly similar. The U.S. share of OECD manufacturing exports declined from 18% in 1970 to 16% in 1985. Germany experienced a similar decline, while Japan registered a large gain (from 11% to 18%). Note that export shares do not closely match population shares. The reason for this is that countries that are large in terms of area and population tend to export less of their GNP than smaller countries. The important point is that the U.S. position within overall OECD exports has been fairly stable.

That overall stability, however, masks a number of trends at the industry and subindustry level that raise some concern about U.S. competitiveness. The U.S. share of high-technology exports has declined steadily from 28% in 1965 to 24% in 1976 and 21% in 1986. High-technology goods are defined as those produced by industries in which research and development expenditures are above a certain threshold. By 1986 Germany's and Japan's positions in high-technology markets were close to that of the United States, with the former accounting for 16% of high-tech exports and the latter, 20%. Note, however, that the United States still remained the leading exporter.

From America's point of view, there are reasons to be concerned about a downward trend in its export performance, but no evidence of wholesale deindustrialization.[6]

1.5 Sources of Convergence

What have been the mechanisms through which Japan and other nations have caught up with the United States in terms of overall productivity? We address this question from a number of different points of view, the first of which concerns industrial composition. There are two reasons why the aggregate productivity of nations may differ: first, one country may have higher productivity at the industry and subindustry level; second, one country may have its work force concentrated in high-productivity industries and subindustries.

The second possibility arises because some industries produce far more value added per worker than others. Aircraft production, for example, has higher labor productivity than the making of footwear. This results from the former activity requiring more capital and/or higher skills and technology than the latter. It is a curious fact that, in principle, two countries can have the same level of productivity in every industry and yet have different overall levels of productivity, provided one has a labor force concentrated in the high-value-added sectors.

In practice, differences in overall productivity are likely to be the result of both factors, higher productivity in individual industries and distribution of employment among sectors. Nevertheless, it is interesting to investigate the relative importance of these two sources of productivity differences. Some of the literature on the alleged decline of U.S. competitiveness focuses on the importance of high-value-added sectors, with the implicit or explicit message that improving competitiveness requires support for these key subindustries.[7] In addition, much of the American obsession with Japan arises from that country's success in some highly visible product lines: automobiles, televisions, VCRs, and computers.

Has Japan's aggregate productivity convergence been achieved by gradually edging the United States out of key high-value-added sectors? Our research answers this question with a resounding no. To an amazing extent, productivity convergence among OECD countries has nothing to do with shifts of employment at the industry level. Figure 1.3 provides a clear visual image of this result, in the case of Japan. The figure shows Japan's labor productivity relative to the United States for the whole manufacturing sector in 1963 and 1986. During this period Japan caught up very impressively with the United States, its relative productivity in manufacturing rising from 26% to 65%.

The figure also indicates relative productivity for the twenty-eight distinct industries that make up manufacturing. In 1963 Japan was well behind the United States in all of these industries. The average relative productivity at the industry level was 27%, almost exactly the same as for all manufacturing. There was no substantial difference between the industrial mix of the two economies at that time. This does not mean that the distribution

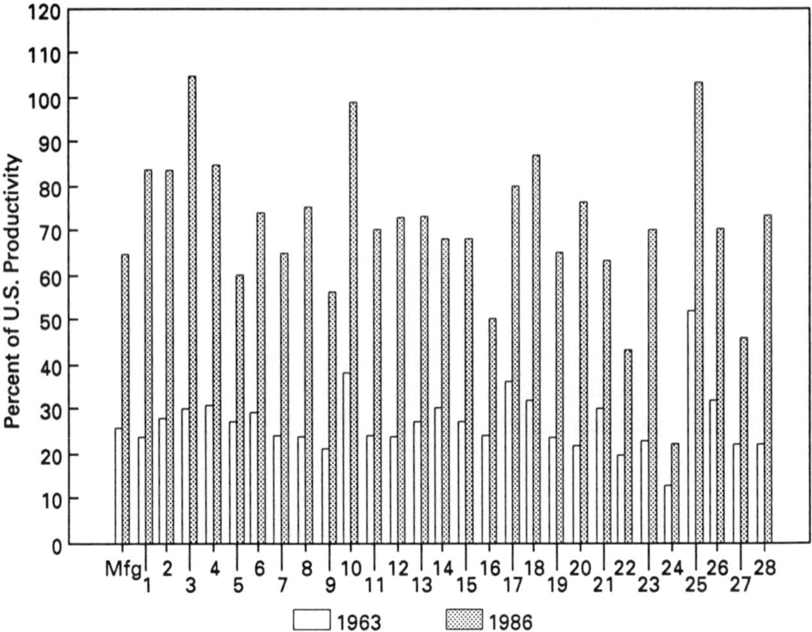

Figure 1.3
Japan's relative productivity in twenty-eight manufacturing industries, 1963 and 1986

of output and employment across industries was the same in the two countries; rather, the differences could not be characterized as the United States having an employment mix that favored high-productivity sectors. Similarly, changes in Japan's industrial mix played virtually no role in the catch-up of its relative productivity for all manufacturing. Japan caught up with the United States because its relative productivity increased in every industry. The same basic result holds for the other OECD countries.

Another interesting feature of figure 1.3 is that the extent of catch-up varied quite considerably among Japanese industries. In a few sectors Japanese productivity had surpassed or come very close to the U.S. level by 1986: iron and steel (no. 3 in the figure), glass products (no. 10), and petroleum refining (no. 25). In other areas the convergence was not nearly so strong. The extreme examples are natural-resource-related items, such as food and tobacco products. But relative productivity remained low in other sectors as well, such as clothing, professional goods, and pottery. (See chapter 3 for the details of productivity convergence in the twenty-eight industries.)

This same basic pattern of convergence can be observed in all of the OECD countries. Aggregate productivity converged on the U.S. level because relative productivity increased in virtually all industries. Nevertheless, the catch-up was stronger in some industries than in others. Finally, shifts in the industrial mix played no role in the convergence.

Another intriguing part of this story is that different countries had their strongest convergence in different industries. As a result, the cross-country dispersion in productivity is today considerably higher at the industry level than at the level of all manufacturing. By 1986 the dispersion in overall manufacturing productivity among industrial countries, as measured by the coefficient of variation (the ratio of the standard deviation to the mean), had declined to 0.22. The variation was typically greater for individual industries, with some of the extreme examples being industrial chemicals (0.41), transport equipment (0.39), and electrical goods (0.61). What these results imply is that in different countries productivity growth has been concentrated in different industries. Japan has done well in iron and steel, France and Italy in textiles, clothing, and leather products, and Germany in transport equipment and machinery.

Thus, there is not some key industry or product line that has to be captured as the means to economic success. OECD countries are rich because they have good productivity performance across a wide range of sectors and then excel in particular in a few activities.

1.6 Sources of Productivity Growth

One approach to investigating aggregate productivity convergence is to examine in which industries countries' convergence has been concentrated, as discussed above. An alternative, and complementary, approach is to inquire into sources of productivity growth at the industry level. The U.S. labor productivity advantage at the end of World War II was rooted in two factors: the use of more capital per worker at the industry level and superior technology in virtually every industry. Better U.S. technology was reflected in higher total factor productivity in individual industries, compared to other advanced economies.

We show in chapter 4 that both capital accumulation and technological advance played important roles in labor productivity convergence within industries. Technology catch-up was particularly important until the mid-1970s: up to that point technology convergence among advanced economies was the main driving force for labor productivity convergence. Furthermore, technology convergence was especially strong in industries and countries which lagged particularly far behind the United States. That result is consistent with Gerschenkron's notion of the advantage of backwardness. Within the OECD group, countries and industries that lagged far behind had the most promising opportunity to borrow advanced technology and to improve rapidly.

Most of the technology catch-up had been completed by the mid-1970s. By that time Japan and Germany had achieved roughly 90% of the TFP level of U.S. manufacturing, and the dispersion among all OECD countries was minor. Since the mid-1970s there has continued to be further convergence of labor productivity, at a modest rate, and this has largely been the result of capital accumulation.

Concerning convergence of TFP and capital intensity, we find the same pattern that we discovered for labor productivity: there is more cross-country dispersion at the industry level than for all manufacturing. Again, this result implies that in different countries investment and technological advance are concentrated in different industries. It is this focus of investment and technological development in particular industries that explains the especially strong labor productivity growth of those industries.

In addition, technology catch-up and capital accumulation at the industry level are highly correlated. This correlation is difficult to interpret. One possibility is that new technology is embodied in machinery, so that a large level of investment occasions a sharp rise in measured TFP. The alternative hypothesis is that disembodied technical improvement makes an industry particularly profitable, thus attracting new investment. The reality probably encompasses both possibilities.

The important point is that technological advance and investment tend to go hand in hand and are the sources of rapid labor productivity growth at the industry level. We observe the same pattern of convergence in all of the OECD economies: there has been sufficient TFP growth and capital accumulation in all industries to achieve gradual convergence toward the U.S. level. Nevertheless, each country typically has a few star performing industries, and these tend to be different in each country.

1.7 International Specialization

Two basic metaphors dominate current debates about international trade policy: trade as war and trade as mutually beneficial exchange. The trade-as-war metaphor views specific markets as territory to be captured and has as a necessary concomitant the notion that some export lines are of strategic importance. (It is perhaps no coincidence that political scientists who cross over into the analysis of international economic relations tend to like the trade-as-war metaphor.) The alternative vision (more common to economists) emphasizes the benefits of specialization per se, without much regard for the products in which particular nations specialize.

The results of our research shed some light on the relative value of these two metaphors. If the productivity advance of different nations is concentrated in different industries, then there is clear evidence of specialization among the advanced economies. That fact may appear to contradict an earlier statement: that variations in industrial composition cannot explain differences in aggregate productivity or the convergence of aggregate productivity. In reality, there is no contradiction. Industrial mixes are different, but they cannot be characterized as specializing in high-value-added versus low-value-added industries.

There is no one magic sector that is better than other sectors, and hence it is not useful to view trade as war. There is, rather, a wide range of high-productivity activities, and they are dispersed across all of the manufacturing (and nonmanufacturing) industries. Why does a nation specialize in just a few of these activities? Why not excel in all of them? The basic answer to this question appears to be economies of scale, especially in the production of new technology.[8] It takes a lot of research and development to create state-of-the-art medical machinery, for example. This R & D expenditure is a fixed cost: once a particular item has been designed and patented, it can be produced in any volume without additional R & D spending. Thus, the average cost of production (including the fixed R & D cost) declines as the volume of production increases. In this type of market one expects to find a small number of firms producing differentiated products.

Trade among rich countries is increasingly concentrated in high-technology areas in which R & D is important. As all of the OECD countries have the financial and human resources to conduct some sophisticated R & D, it makes sense that each country is the home for some firms that are leaders in their fields. It is mutually advantageous for all of the rich countries that their firms tend to specialize in different subindustries and product lines and that there is a large volume of trade among these countries.

It should be noted that the firms that sell internationally are also, in general, the firms that have become truly multinational, with production in a wide range of countries. It is interesting that the bulk of foreign investment by these OECD firms is in other OECD countries, not in low-wage locations in the Third World. Overseas investment is another way of exploiting a firm's technology edge. Since the broad availability of productive factors such as skilled labor and capital do not differ much among the rich countries, there is no strong reason to produce only at home. Furthermore, there may be advantages to locating production close to the market, such as proximity to consumers or getting behind trade barriers. These overseas investments are probably another reason why productivity at the industry level does not vary too much among countries. Even with overseas investment, though, there will continue to be some variation. Suppose, for example, that a Swedish firm is the world leader in production of a special kind of machinery. It may locate production plants in a variety of advanced countries, raising the subindustry's productivity level in those locations. However, it will typically reserve its research activities and often production of its most advanced items to its home country, making that country the productivity leader for the subindustry.

In chapters 5, 6, and 7 we provide some empirical support for this general view of international trade among advanced economies. Most important, we present evidence that shifts in comparative advantage parallel advances in total factor productivity. In the case of Japan, increases in its share of OECD exports have come in industries in which its technological growth has been particularly rapid. For the United States, on the other hand, the loss of export shares in a number of sectors mirrors the fact that the country has been overtaken technologically in those areas.

It is also interesting that the rate of technological advance and the rate of technology convergence on the U.S. level have been more rapid for manufacturing than for the other broad sectors of the economy, though there has been some convergence for them as well. There are a number of possible factors that may explain this result; one of them no doubt is that manufactured goods are widely traded internationally, whereas many services are not. This means on the one hand that manufacturing firms face a virtually limitless market, increasing the financial incentive to innovate new products and processes. On the other hand, the active international trade is also likely to lead more rapidly to dissemination of new ideas and technology, bringing about convergence.[9]

These two views may appear contradictory, but they are not. The large international market spurs the creation of new technology; but that same market, with its wide diffusion of products, leads quickly to the destruction of the temporary monopoly that goes with any specific technological innovation. This rapid dissemination of new technology is another factor encouraging firms to develop new products continually, so as to stay ahead of competitors.

1.8 What Should America Do?

Evidence for the more extreme versions of the America-in-decline thesis is scant. The industrial core of the country has not disappeared. America remains the productivity leader, both overall and in many industries. U.S. firms continue to be successful in international trade. The share of exports originating from U.S. firms—out of locations both at home and abroad—is virtually unchanged over the past few decades.

Nevertheless, we would not want the results of our research to be interpreted as a call to complacency. Developments to date are highly consistent with the notion of convergence: the large U.S. productivity lead after World War II was something of an aberration, and the world has now returned to a more normal state, in which there are a number of advanced economies whose productivity levels are close together. As Japan and Germany have approached the U.S. level, their growth rates have slowed down, which is further evidence in support of the convergence hypothesis.

Today, industrial production is distributed among OECD countries more or less in proportion to population. Recent history gives us good reason to expect that the advanced economies will grow at similar rates, so that aggregate productivity differences among them will remain small. However, there is nothing automatic about this process. The source of productivity growth at the industry and subindustry level is innovation and investment. For a nation to remain a member of the convergence club, its firms will have to continue to create new technologies and make new investments at a rapid rate.

Although we have not examined the institutional structures that support (or retard) innovation and investment, nevertheless we feel that our research is very relevant to some of the public debates about which institutions are likely to support successful growth. Most important, we find our results a strong endorsement for maintaining an open door to foreign trade and investment. If it turned out that there were a small number of subindustries that were the key to advanced productivity, some might interpret that as a good argument for protecting or subsidizing the development of these crucial sectors (trade as war).

Our finding that advanced countries have leading sectors—but that they differ among nations—supports the notion that open trade is an important institutional support to growth. Without trade this kind of specialization is impossible. And without the large and competitive international market the incentives to innovate would not be so great. In principle, there might be an argument for protecting one's own leading sectors as they develop new products—if, a crucial caveat, there were no threat of retaliation. In reality, the advanced economies cannot afford to play this game. There is too great a danger that what is purported to be selective and temporary protection will result in the permanent erection of trade barriers all around, with detrimental consequences for growth in all of the rich countries.

The fact that different nations have their advanced production concentrated in different product lines also suggests something about what kind of government intervention is desirable. Again, if there were a few key technologies that were the secret to success, then a strong case could be made for ex ante promotion of these activities. In reality, the progress of nations is focused on highly specialized subindustries that are different in each country. It is difficult for anyone, in government or not, to predict in which areas new innovations are going to occur. Furthermore, once a particular country has pioneered some new technology, the best strategy for other nations is not necessarily to try to catch up in that exact product line. Rather, it may be preferable for other countries' firms to take off in related—or even in totally different—directions. What all this means is that it is generally not a good idea for a government to target the development of particular technologies. There is ample evidence that this kind of targeting has not worked well in a wide range of countries.

Instead of promoting particular technologies, governments would do better to work on improving the overall environment for innovation, without concern for the direction in which their firms choose to go. The same can be said about investment: governments should be less concerned about the sectors in which investment occurs than about the overall climate for investment. Another thing that our research demonstrates is that innovation and investment tend to go together, so that institutional support to one will have spillover effects on the other.

Our research does not examine in detail what makes a good environment for research and development, and hence we do not have a lot of specific recommendations in this area. Nevertheless, a number of general points can be made about the current situation of the United States. An important part of the environment for innovation and investment is the basic social and economic infrastructure of the nation, which is to a large extent provided by the government. In America today, this infrastructure has many problems. The public school system at the primary and secondary levels is deteriorating, as evidenced by declining student performance and falling teacher morale. Much of the physical infrastructure—roads, bridges, railways, ports—is also deteriorating. It seems likely to us that no other measures to improve innovation and investment in America will have much impact unless these basic problems are addressed.

Not only is it necessary for the government to provide much of the investment to build up the social and economic infrastructure, but it is preferable for it to do so with its own savings, not through borrowing from the public. The massive fiscal deficits of recent years have been a serious drain on private savings that could otherwise have gone to productive investment. The end of the Cold War presents the United States with a unique opportunity to reorient its expenditure priorities, reducing military spending and employing the savings to (1) improve education, (2) invest in physical infrastructure, (3) provide increased support for research and development, and (4) reduce the fiscal deficit. It may be possible to accomplish all of these tasks by slashing military spending.

In addition to basic infrastructure, there are a host of institutions that can support or retard innovation and investment. The land grant colleges in America, for instance, have been an important source of agricultural innovations that have been disseminated to farmers through extension services of the government. Venture capital markets are another institution that can have a beneficial effect in bringing innovations to the production stage. There are also institutions that are alleged to have a detrimental effect on innovation and investment in the United States, such as the practice of taxing short- and long-term capital gains at the same rate. Such taxation means that no preference is given to long-term productive investment over short-term speculative activities, as is the case in many other countries. There is an interesting, recent literature on how these kinds of institutions differ among countries, giving rise to different national systems of innovation.[10] Government can do much to improve the environment for innovation and investment, and we return to this important issue in the concluding chapter.

It is tempting to think that there is some quick fix that the government can implement to make the economy perform better in the long run: tinkering with the tax code; protecting the semiconductor industry; promoting the development of high-definition TV. In reality, however, there is no quick fix. The prosperity of the nation depends primarily on innovation and investments made by private individuals and firms. In the increasingly competitive world market, U.S. firms are doing quite well, as are Japanese, German, and Italian firms. Much of what is perceived as the decline of the United States is simply the convergence of advanced economies into a fairly homogeneous group.

If there is a cloud on the horizon for the United States, it results from lax fiscal policies during the 1980s. Ill-conceived tax cuts combined with a large military buildup have drained resources away from public investment in education, research, and infrastructure. Excessive public borrowing has crowded out private investment as well. The government needs to deal with these imbalances, or else the prospects for long-term growth will be threatened.

1.9 The Plan of the Book

This introductory chapter has set forth the main ideas and issues that our book addresses. Chapter 2 examines the issue of deindustrialization by investigating trends in industrial output and exports among OECD countries. Chapter 3 takes up labor productivity convergence in the manufacturing sector and in specific manufacturing industries. Chapter 4 then decomposes labor productivity convergence at the industry level into a part attributable to capital accumulation and a part attributable to technological advance. The main empirical findings of our research concentrated in these three chapters raise a host of related questions, which we then address in the second half of the book.

Most of our detailed research focuses on the manufacturing sector and its individual industries. The justification for this focus is partly the better availability of data for this sector; but, in addition, manufactures make up the bulk of international trade, and much of the concern about competitiveness of nations is tied up with the manufacturing sector. Chapter 5 investigates whether the convergence trends that we find in manufacturing are typical for the whole economy or something of an aberration. Chapter 6 then looks at how the pattern of productivity convergence has affected wages, as well as the return to capital, in different industries and different countries. In chapter 7 we make a tentative effort to relate the productivity changes that we document to shifts in the pattern of international trade, focusing in particular on U.S. and Japanese exports. All of the work up to that point deals with OECD countries, that is, ones that are rich today. In chapter 8 we go beyond the developed world to examine the pattern of productivity convergence for the newly industrialized countries, some of which are catching up with the advanced economies, albeit from a starting point that was far, far behind. The concluding chapter focuses on the implications of our work and returns to the question of what kind of public policy is likely to aid the United States, as well as other industrial countries, in maintaining its status as a high-productivity, high-income economy.

2 Deindustrialization and the Changing Pattern of Industry Output and Trade

2.1 The Decline of U.S. Manufacturing?

Two themes in particular have received widespread attention in the U.S. press in recent years. The first concerns fears about the deindustrialization of the American economy. Has the United States experienced a significant loss of its industrial core in comparison to other advanced economies, most notably Japan and Germany? Has the United States lost ground relative to other countries in the volume of its manufacturing output? The second relates to concerns about America's declining competitiveness in the international marketplace. Are U.S. exports holding their own on the world market, or are they being displaced, either rapidly or gradually, by the products of other countries? In manufacturing—particularly high-technology manufacturing—how have U.S. exports fared relative to those of other industrialized and semi-industrialized economies?

This chapter documents the changing composition of industry output and exports among OECD economies from the early 1960s to the mid-1980s. It demonstrates that the U.S. share of OECD manufacturing output has not declined but has actually increased slightly since the early 1970s. Moreover, there are several sectors in which the United States has made considerable gains on its major competitors, while it has sustained losses in others. U.S. merchandise exports, on the other hand, have declined as a share of both OECD and world exports. Losses have occurred among a broad range of commodity lines. However, somewhat surprisingly, U.S. exports of high-technology products have declined only moderately, and they were actually increasing during the early and mid-1980s.

2.2 Trends in Output and Employment Shares

We begin our documentary evidence with the record of the shares of total manufacturing output produced by various member nations of the OECD.

Table 2.1
Percentage shares of total fourteen-country OECD manufacturing output by country, for selected years, 1961–87

	1961[a]	1970	1975	1980	1983	1985	1987[b]
Germany (FRG)	13.6	13.7	13.0	12.5	11.8	11.1	10.8
Japan	—	13.7	15.1	17.9	20.8	21.9	22.7
United States	39.8	36.9	35.8	35.9	35.4	36.7	37.5
Other OECD	—	35.6	36.1	33.7	32.1	30.3	29.1
Australia	—	1.9	1.9	1.7	1.6	1.6	—
Belgium	1.1	1.2	1.3	1.3	1.3	1.2	1.4
Canada	2.8	3.0	3.3	3.1	2.9	3.1	3.2
Denmark	—	0.5	0.6	0.5	0.5	0.5	0.5
Finland	0.5	0.6	0.6	0.7	0.7	0.7	0.7
France	6.4	7.6	8.4	8.1	8.0	7.1	6.4
Italy	6.4	7.6	7.6	8.3	7.7	7.2	8.1
Netherlands	1.5	1.5	1.5	1.4	1.3	1.3	—
Norway	0.6	0.5	0.6	0.5	0.4	0.4	0.4
Sweden	—	1.5	1.5	1.2	1.2	1.2	1.2
United Kingdom	—	9.6	8.8	6.9	6.4	6.1	—
OECD total		100.0	100.0	100.0	100.0	100.0	

Sources: 1960–86—OECD International Sectoral Databank (ISDB), 1989. 1987—*National Accounts, Detailed Tables*, vol. 2, 1987, OECD, Department of Economics and Statistics. GDP by kind of activity, constant currency; GDP converted into 1980 US$ by the conversion rate implicit in the ISDB.
a. Estimated under the assumption that countries with missing data have same share of total OECD output in 1961 as in 1970.
b. Estimated under the assumption that countries with missing data have same share of total OECD output in 1987 as in 1985.

Our main data source is the OECD International Sectoral Database (ISDB), available on computer diskette (see the Appendix for details). Data are available for only fourteen OECD countries, so that we confine our analysis to them. According to the deindustrialization thesis, the U.S. share of total OECD manufacturing output should have shown a rapid decline in the years after 1960. As shown in table 2.1 (and illustrated in figure 2.1), the U.S. share did decline from 40% in 1961 to 36% in 1975 and then remained steady until about 1983, when it actually began to increase. By 1987, according to our estimates, the U.S. share of OECD manufactures had risen to almost 38%. These figures hardly constitute a strong argument in support of deindustrialization.

Japan, as all the popular evidence indicates, did experience a rapid growth in its share of OECD manufacturing output, from 14% in 1970 to 23% in 1987. The Federal Republic of Germany, somewhat surprisingly, had the opposite experience, with its share falling from 14% in 1970, the same

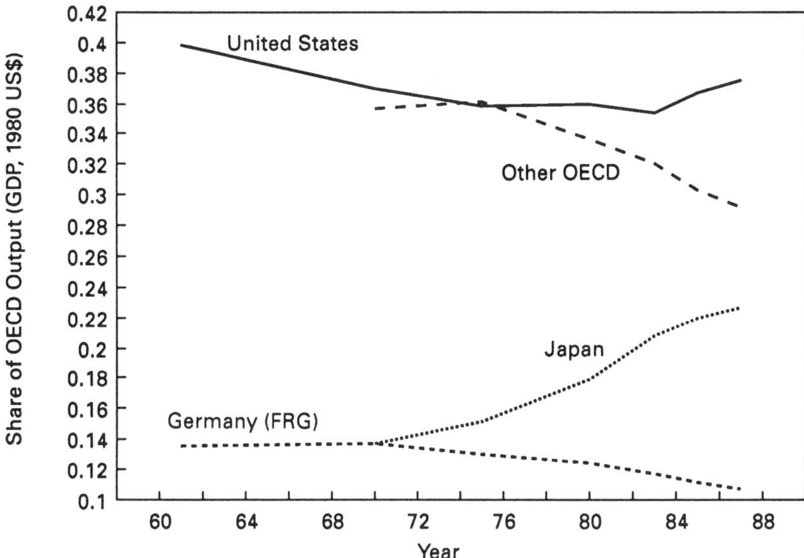

Figure 2.1
Shares of total OECD manufacturing GDP by country, 1961–1987

level as Japan, to 11% in 1987. The share of total manufactures produced by the other OECD countries also fell, from 36% in 1970 to 29% in 1987. The most precipitous decline was recorded by the U.K. Interestingly, France's share held steady between 1961 and 1987, while Italy's increased, and in both 1985 and 1987 Italy ranked fourth among the OECD countries in manufacturing output.

Output Shares on the Industry Level

Though the United States has not lost out in terms of total manufacturing, it is of interest to determine in which sectors the United States may have gained on its rivals, and in which it may have lost. We begin again with the OECD data base, which provides rather broad industry aggregations. The figures are shown in table 2.2, and the U.S. shares are illustrated in figures 2.2 and 2.3.

It is first of interest to see where the United States has been gaining on its chief manufacturing rivals. Two broad sectors stand out in particular: textiles, where the U.S. share of total OECD output increased from 26% in 1961 to 34% in 1987, and wood and wood products, where the U.S. share

Table 2.2
Percentage shares of fourteen-country OECD manufacturing output by industry, for selected years, 1961–87

	1961[a]	1970	1975	1980	1983	1985	1987[b]
1. *Food, beverages, and tobacco*							
Germany (FRG)	13.3	13.1	11.9	12.3	11.6	11.7	—
Japan	—	14.0	16.6	16.5	16.0	14.3	13.7
United States	32.7	31.2	29.9	30.1	31.1	31.3	33.9
Other OECD	—	41.7	41.6	41.1	41.2	42.8	—
2. *Textiles*							
Germany (FRG)	14.1	13.0	11.2	9.9	9.0	9.2	—
Japan	—	9.3	10.8	9.7	11.4	11.2	10.4
United States	26.4	28.6	29.2	33.2	34.3	33.3	34.4
Other OECD	—	49.0	48.8	47.3	45.3	46.3	—
3. *Wood and wood products*							
Germany (FRG)	17.9	17.1	17.3	14.4	13.4	12.0	—
Japan	—	—	—	—	—	—	—
United States	50.3	51.3	51.7	51.6	52.7	54.9	56.0
Other OECD	—	31.6	31.0	34.0	33.9	33.1	—
4. *Paper, printing, and publishing*							
Germany (FRG)	7.5	8.3	7.5	7.4	7.0	6.9	—
Japan	—	5.7	7.0	7.2	8.7	8.4	8.2
United States	47.8	46.8	48.3	47.6	49.7	49.7	48.5
Other OECD	—	39.2	37.2	37.8	34.7	35.0	—
5. *Chemicals*							
Germany (FRG)	14.4	18.5	16.8	16.9	15.5	15.6	—
Japan	—	12.4	15.4	15.6	17.5	18.9	20.0
United States	45.6	40.6	38.7	37.9	38.2	36.2	35.9
Other OECD	—	28.5	29.1	29.6	28.7	29.3	—
6. *Nonmetal mineral products*							
Germany (FRG)	12.5	13.1	12.1	12.9	12.3	11.3	—
Japan	—	18.0	17.9	16.4	18.6	19.6	19.3
United States	30.9	27.8	27.2	27.5	27.4	29.3	29.5
Other OECD	—	41.1	42.8	43.2	41.6	39.9	—
7. *Basic metal products*							
Germany (FRG)	11.3	11.2	11.3	10.5	10.9	10.6	—
Japan	—	14.9	17.4	23.7	23.6	27.5	33.1
United States	36.3	33.4	30.7	28.5	22.3	22.0	25.4
Other OECD	—	40.5	40.6	37.3	43.2	39.9	—
8. *Machinery and equipment*							
Germany (FRG)	15.6	16.2	15.5	14.2	13.3	11.8	—
Japan	—	11.5	12.7	18.5	23.6	25.1	24.7
United States	43.4	40.4	40.4	40.4	38.7	41.5	39.9
Other OECD	—	30.0	31.4	26.9	24.4	21.7	—
9. *Other manufactured products*							
Germany (FRG)	3.0	2.6	2.0	1.9	1.6	1.4	—
Japan	—	58.6	56.2	62.0	66.7	64.6	67.9
United States	18.3	17.1	17.9	14.0	12.7	17.1	16.0
Other OECD	—	21.6	23.8	22.1	19.0	16.9	—

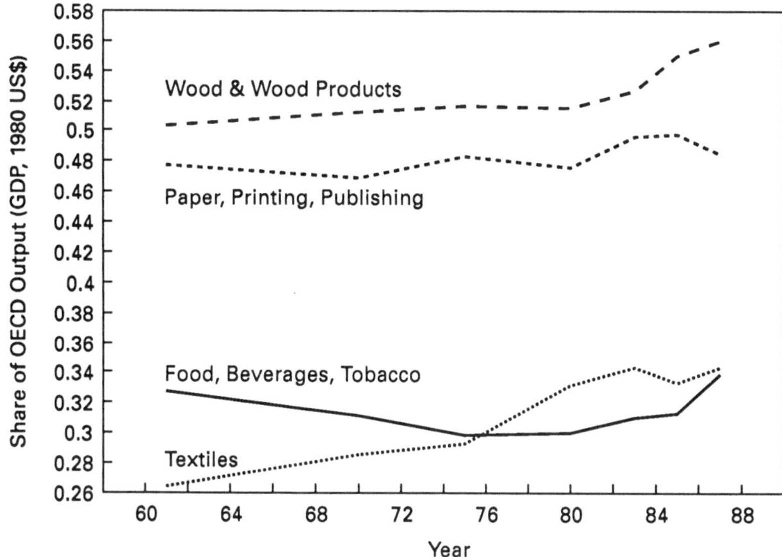

Figure 2.2
Shares of U.S. manufacturing industries in total OECD output (industries with rising shares)

grew from 50% to 56%. In both of these industries, the United States has a particular advantage in terms of the resource base: cotton for the former and forestry for the latter. In a third resource-based sector, food, beverages, and tobacco products, the United States held its share over the period 1961–87. Interestingly, Japan made only modest gains in textiles and held its own in food and related products,[1] while Germany's share fell in all three categories.

The U.S. share also remained relatively constant in paper, printing, and publishing (an unfortunate mix of industries, which are classified separately in the U.N. data); in nonmetal mineral products, including glass, cement, and the like; and in other (miscellaneous) manufacturing products. Japan made gains in all three sectors, while Germany fell back in all three.

Table 2.2 (continued)
Sources: 1960–86—OECD International Sectoral Databank (ISDB), 1989. 1987—*National Accounts, Detailed Tables,* vol. 2, 1987, OECD, Department of Economics and Statistics. GDP by kind of activity, constant currency; GDP converted into 1980 US$ by the conversion rate implicit in the ISDB.
a. Estimated under the assumption that countries with missing data have same share of total OECD output in 1961 as in 1970.
b. Estimated under the assumption that countries with missing data have same share of total OECD output in 1987 as in 1985.

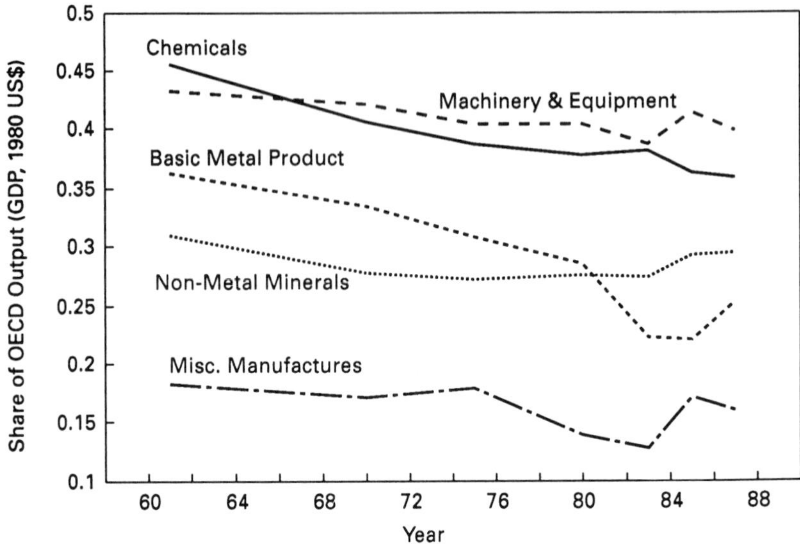

Figure 2.3
Shares of U.S. manufacturing industries in total OECD output (industries with declining shares)

The United States lost ground in machinery and equipment—a classification that includes automobiles, machine tools, and aircraft—but perhaps by not as much as many people have feared. The U.S. share declined from 43% in 1961 to 40% in 1987. Japan's share more than doubled, from 12% in 1970 to 25% in 1987, but even in 1987, Japan was still considerably behind the United States. Germany and the other OECD countries also showed considerable declines in their shares.

The two biggest losses for the United States were chemicals and basic metal products, including steel. The U.S. share of OECD chemical output declined from 46% in 1961 to 36% in 1987. Japan's share increased substantially, from 12% in 1970 to 20% in 1987, but, still, by 1987, the United States was by far the largest producer of chemicals in the world. Interestingly, Germany lost a little ground over the period, while other OECD countries showed a modest increase in their shares. The U.S. share of basic metals fell from 36% in 1961 to 25% in 1987, while Japan's increased from 15% in 1970 to 33% in 1987. By the late 1980s, Japan was considerably ahead of the United States in this industry. Germany's share held its own, as did that of the other OECD countries.

Employment Shares on the Industry Level

As will be our practice throughout this volume, we will also look at similar figures from other data sources. Our other major data source is the United Nations *Yearbook of Industrial Statistics* for various years. The data are available from 1963 through 1986 for twelve countries: Australia, Austria, Canada, Denmark, Finland, Germany (FRG), Italy, Japan, Norway, Sweden, the United Kingdom, and the United States. The main advantage of this source is that the U.N. industry classification is much more detailed than the OECD ISDB data. The output data are rather spotty for earlier years, but luckily, the employment data are relatively complete. As a result, we will base our industry shares on country employment as a proportion of total employment for the twelve countries.

Trends in employment shares for the United States and Japan are shown in table 2.3. Some of them are very illuminating. Over the 1963–86 period, the United States made exceptional gains with regard to the share of industrial employment in the following industries: beverages and tobacco products; wood products (as noted above); paper and paper products, as well as printing and publishing; plastic products; glass and glass products; shipbuilding and repair; and professional goods, including scientific instruments. With a few exceptions, the major gains were made by the United States in either resource-based industries (beverages, tobacco, and wood) or in so-called light, labor-intensive industries (see chapter 3 below). Shipbuilding and repair appears as a surprise on this list, particularly since U.S. employment in this industry declined from 218,000 in 1979 to 169,000 in 1986. However, the anomaly is due to the fact that total twelve-country employment declined even faster in that sector, from 709,000 to 550,000.

Heavy losses were sustained by the United States in only three industries: leather and leather products, footwear, and petroleum refinery. Interestingly, over the 1963–86 period the United States does not appear to have done too badly in iron and steel, although between 1979 and 1986 its employment share did fall from 31% to 25%. Likewise, the U.S. employment share in general machinery (n.e.c.), office and computing equipment, electrical machinery, and even radio and televisions actually increased between 1972 and 1986; but in each case its share fell between 1979 and 1986, and for all except electrical machinery the decline was quite steep. In the other sectors, the U.S. employment shares remained relatively constant. This group includes the motor vehicle sector, in which the U.S. share

Table 2.3
Percentage shares of twelve-country total employment by detailed industry, for the United States and Japan, selected years, 1963–86

	U.S. percentage shares				Japan percentage shares			
	1963	1972	1979	1986	1963	1972	1979	1986
Food products	36.3	34.1	33.5	32.0	23.3	22.8	23.6	27.3
Beverages	25.9	27.8	29.7	30.5	18.8	16.8	15.9	13.9
Tobacco products	29.0	29.3	29.5	33.0	15.8	18.6	20.0	11.5
Textiles	22.8	29.0	32.8	34.2	30.8	27.2	25.1	26.9
Wearing apparel	43.1	42.4	44.9	40.2	10.2	13.1	17.0	21.9
Leather and products	29.0	30.5	33.5	24.9	12.8	14.9	16.8	22.8
Footwear	36.4	34.3	32.9	23.8	4.8	5.6	7.6	9.2
Wood products	27.2	28.3	31.8	33.6	32.3	29.0	25.1	21.7
Furniture, fixtures	—	44.4	46.3	46.0	—	19.1	18.1	17.3
Paper and products	34.8	35.8	39.0	40.6	18.9	17.8	16.7	16.7
Printing, publishing	41.7	42.7	46.9	48.9	18.2	19.0	18.2	19.2
Industrial chemicals	23.5	23.2	25.1	23.4	16.2	13.5	11.3	11.5
Petroleum refineries	48.3	44.3	46.2	43.4	8.2	11.9	12.4	11.9
Rubber products	32.0	33.0	35.8	31.9	20.8	16.9	17.1	23.5
Plastic products, n.e.c.	28.8	31.6	36.9	35.9	27.1	27.2	23.9	26.8
Pottery, china, etc.	8.0	8.9	9.7	8.9	17.0	16.3	17.2	19.4
Glass and products	34.6	37.3	42.5	39.4	16.7	16.4	14.9	18.8
Nonmetal products, n.e.c.	31.2	30.2	33.9	32.7	24.5	28.5	27.9	29.4
Iron and steel	28.4	27.9	31.2	25.2	16.5	18.3	16.4	22.5
Nonferrous metals	32.1	33.6	36.8	34.7	16.3	19.5	17.3	17.4
Metal products	34.6	33.1	37.9	35.9	19.5	21.4	19.2	22.1
Machinery, n.e.c.	31.2	32.4	39.6	33.8	18.0	20.3	17.5	22.0
Office, computing, etc.	—	40.7	51.6	43.3	—	24.9	21.7	30.9
Electrical machinery	32.0	30.7	35.7	33.2	19.7	23.9	22.4	29.8
Radios, televisions, etc.	—	42.2	49.6	45.7	—	31.8	27.7	36.5
Transport equipment	34.4	35.2	36.9	37.5	14.0	16.7	15.0	17.6
Shipbuilding, repair	15.9	18.8	26.1	30.7	20.6	24.2	16.7	15.6
Motor vehicles	37.4	37.5	38.2	35.7	20.4	24.0	24.0	31.6
Professional goods	39.1	40.7	46.9	51.5	16.2	18.5	17.2	19.7

Source: United Nations, *Yearbook of Industrial Statistics,* various years. The data are available for twelve countries: Australia, Austria, Canada, Denmark, Finland, Germany (FRG), Italy, Japan, Norway, Sweden, the United Kingdom, and the United States. Exceptions are as follows (see the Appendix for details on industry codes):

Australia: For 1963, codes 3511 and 3513 are combined; code 3825 is missing. For 1972, code 3825 is missing. 1985 data are used for 1986.

Austria: For 1963, all data are missing. For 1972, 1979, and 1986, codes 3511 and 3825 are missing.

Denmark: For 1963, codes 351 and 352 are combined, code 3513 is combined with 356; and the other mining sector is combined with 369.

Finland: For 1963, code 3825 is missing.

actually increased slightly from 37% to 38% between 1963 and 1979, and then declined somewhat, to 36% in 1986.

The picture for Japan is surprisingly mixed. Between 1963 and 1986, Japan suffered relative employment losses in beverages and tobacco products separately (although, as reported above, it did gain in food products as a group); in textiles as a whole (although, as noted above, its share was relatively constant between the early 1970s and the mid-1980s); in wood products and furniture; in paper and paper products; in industrial chemicals; and in shipbuilding. Its most spectacular gains were in wearing apparel (its share more than doubled from 10% in 1963 to 22% in 1986); in leather and leather products (from 13% to 23% over the 1963–86 period); in footwear (from 5% to 9%); in iron and steel (from 17% to 23%); in office and computing equipment, particularly between 1979 and 1986 (from 22% to 31%); in electrical machinery (from 20% to 30%), particularly radios and televisions between 1979 and 1986 (from 28% to 37%); and in motor vehicles (from 20% in 1963 to 32% in 1986). Modest gains were also made in petroleum refineries; rubber products; pottery, china, glass and glass products, and other nonmetal products; general machinery; transport equipment; and professional goods.

It is interesting to note, however, that even in 1986 the United States led Japan in terms of employment in every sector listed in table 2.3, with the exception of pottery and china. Japan had drawn close to the United States in food products, leather and leather products, iron and steel, electrical machinery, and motor vehicles, but U.S. employment was still consid-

---

Table 2.3 (continued)

Germany: For 1963, codes 331 and 332 are combined; codes 351 and 352 are combined; codes 341, 353, 354, 372, 381, 382, 384, 3211, 3511, 3513, 3522, 3825, 3832, 3843 are missing. For 1972, 1979, and 1986, codes 331 and 332 are combined; codes 351 and 352 are combined; codes 353 and 354 are combined; codes 3211, 3511, 3513, 3522, 3832, and 3843 are missing. For 1986, data refer to persons engaged in production, not number of employees.

Italy: 1967 data are used for 1963. For 1967, 1972, 1979, and 1986, codes 351 and 352 are combined; codes 353 and 354 are combined; codes 361, 362, and 369 are combined. For 1967, 1972, and 1979, codes 3211, 3411, 3511, 3513, 3522, 3825, 3832, 3841, and 3843 are missing. For 1986, codes 3511, 3513, 3522 are missing.

Norway: For 1963, codes 331 and 332 are combined; codes 353 and 354 are combined; and code 3825 is missing.

Sweden: For 1963, codes 3511, 3513, 3825, and 3832 are missing.

In cases where data for one or two countries are missing, employment shares for a given industry and year are estimated under the assumption that countries with missing data have same share of total employment in that year as in the succeeding year.

Table 2.4
Percentage shares of world and OECD exports for Germany, Japan, the United States, and non-OECD countries, 1963–85

	1963	1967	1970	1976	1979	1982	1985
A. *Total world exports*							
Total OECD	77.1	77.5	78.7	71.1	70.9	71.2	79.5
Germany (FRG)	11.3	11.6	12.2	11.5	11.6	10.9	11.6
Japan	4.2	5.6	6.9	7.6	7.0	8.6	11.2
United States	17.7	16.6	15.2	12.8	11.7	12.7	13.0
Other OECD	44.0	43.9	44.3	39.3	40.7	39.0	43.7
Non-OECD	22.9	22.5	21.3	28.9	29.1	28.8	20.5
B. *Total OECD exports*							
Germany (FRG)	14.6	14.9	15.5	16.2	16.3	15.3	14.6
Japan	5.5	7.2	8.8	10.6	9.8	12.0	14.0
United States	22.9	21.4	19.4	17.9	16.5	17.9	16.4
Other OECD	57.0	56.6	56.3	55.3	57.3	54.8	55.0
C. *World manufacturing exports*							
Total OECD	92.4	90.6	90.6	88.2	87.2	84.9	85.5
Germany (FRG)	16.7	16.1	16.3	16.5	16.3	15.0	14.3
Japan	6.4	8.1	9.6	11.7	10.7	13.1	15.0
United States	19.7	18.2	16.3	14.5	13.1	14.3	13.3
Other OECD	49.6	48.2	48.3	45.6	47.2	42.6	42.8
Non-OECD	7.6	9.4	9.4	11.8	12.8	15.1	14.5
D. *OECD manufacturing exports*							
Germany (FRG)	18.1	17.8	18.0	18.7	18.7	17.6	16.8
Japan	6.9	8.9	10.6	13.2	12.2	15.4	17.6
United States	21.3	20.1	18.0	16.4	15.0	16.8	15.6
Other OECD	53.7	53.2	53.3	51.7	54.1	50.1	50.1

Source: United Nations, World Trade Data Tapes. Exports are recorded in current U.S. dollars. World totals are the sum of exports recorded by countries reporting to the United Nations Statistical Office. Key (see the Appendix for detailed U.N. trade commodity codes):

Manufacturing: beverages (U.N. trade code 11), tobacco, raw and manufactured (U.N. trade code 12), war firearms and ammunition (95), and other manufactures (U.N. trade codes 50–89).

Table 2.4 (continued)

	1963	1967	1970	1976	1979	1982	1985
E. *World agricultural exports*							
Total OECD	58.1	60.2	62.2	65.1	65.4	68.8	69.7
Germany (FRG)	1.5	2.1	2.9	3.9	4.4	4.8	5.2
Japan	1.3	1.3	1.8	1.2	1.0	1.1	1.2
United States	16.4	15.8	15.1	17.9	17.8	18.4	16.0
Other OECD	38.8	41.0	42.3	42.1	42.2	44.4	47.4
Non-OECD	41.9	39.8	37.8	34.9	34.6	31.2	30.3
F. *OECD agricultural exports*							
Germany (FRG)	2.7	3.5	4.7	6.0	6.7	7.0	7.4
Japan	2.3	2.2	2.9	1.8	1.5	1.6	1.7
United States	28.2	26.2	24.4	27.5	27.3	26.8	22.9
Other OECD	66.9	68.0	68.1	64.7	64.5	64.6	68.1
G. *World minerals and energy exports*							
Total OECD	43.1	39.1	38.8	23.8	26.0	33.0	56.1
Germany (FRG)	6.2	4.3	3.8	2.0	2.3	2.2	3.0
Japan	0.1	0.2	0.2	0.1	0.2	0.2	0.3
United States	9.6	8.8	8.3	3.4	3.3	4.7	6.6
Other OECD	27.2	25.8	26.5	18.2	20.3	25.9	46.2
Non-OECD	56.9	60.9	61.2	76.2	74.0	67.0	43.9
H. *OECD minerals and energy exports*							
Germany (FRG)	14.3	11.1	9.9	8.5	8.8	6.7	5.4
Japan	0.3	0.5	0.5	0.4	0.6	0.5	0.6
United States	22.2	22.6	21.5	14.4	12.5	14.2	11.7
Other OECD	63.2	65.9	68.2	76.6	78.0	78.6	82.3

Agriculture: unprocessed foods (U.N. trade codes 00–10, 21, 22, 29, and 94); crude and synthetic rubber (U.N. trade code 23); wood, lumber, and cork (U.N. trade code 24); pulp and waste paper (U.N. trade code 25); textile fibres (U.N. trade code 26); and animal and vegetable oils (U.N. trade codes 41–43).

Minerals and Energy: crude fertilizers and minerals (U.N. trade code 27); metalliferous ores and scrap (U.N. trade code 28); coal, coke, and briquettes (U.N. trade code 32); petroleum and products (U.N. trade code 33); natural and manufactured gas (U.N. trade code 34); and electrical energy (U.N. trade code 35).

erably above Japan's in textiles, wearing apparel, footwear, industrial chemicals, metal products, general machinery, professional goods, and, most notably, office and computing equipment.

A word about Germany (whose employment shares are not included in table 2.3) is also in order. German employment shares showed declines in all sectors, except six. In food products, wood products, and rubber products, Germany held its own. Increases were recorded in only three sectors: industrial chemicals (from 28% in 1963 to 35% in 1986), nonferrous metals (from 14% in 1972 to 16% in 1986), and transport equipment (from 14% in 1972 to 18% in 1986). However, it should be noted that there was no separate breakdown of German employment in motor vehicles or radio and televisions.

It should also be noted that if industry labor productivity differs among countries, employment shares are not an unbiased indicator of output shares (which are really our concern in this chapter). In general, as we shall see in chapter 3, labor productivity growth rates were higher in Japan and Germany (as well as in most other OECD countries) than in the United States over the period from 1963 to 1986. As a result, employment shares of the United States could have remained constant or increased, even if its output shares had declined. For Japan (and Germany), the opposite is the case.

2.3 Export Shares

Another important indicator of a country's competitiveness at the industry or subindustry level is the behavior of its exports over time. If a country is becoming more efficient in the production of a particular commodity, or if its product is improving in quality, then we should expect this to be reflected in a rising share of world exports.

Table 2.4 (as well as figures 2.4 and 2.5) documents the relative success of Germany, Japan, and the United States in export performance over the 1963–85 period. The data source for this analysis is the United Nations Trade Data Tapes. Panel A shows relative shares in total world exports, including manufactures, agricultural products, and mineral, petroleum, and other mining products. The most dramatic story is the rapidly rising share of Japan's exports in the world economy, from 4% in 1963 to 11% in 1986. Equally important is the falling share of U.S. exports, from 18% to 13%. German exports remained relatively constant over time as a proportion of total world exports. By 1985, the United States was still the leading exporter in the world, but Japan and Germany had closed the gap consider-

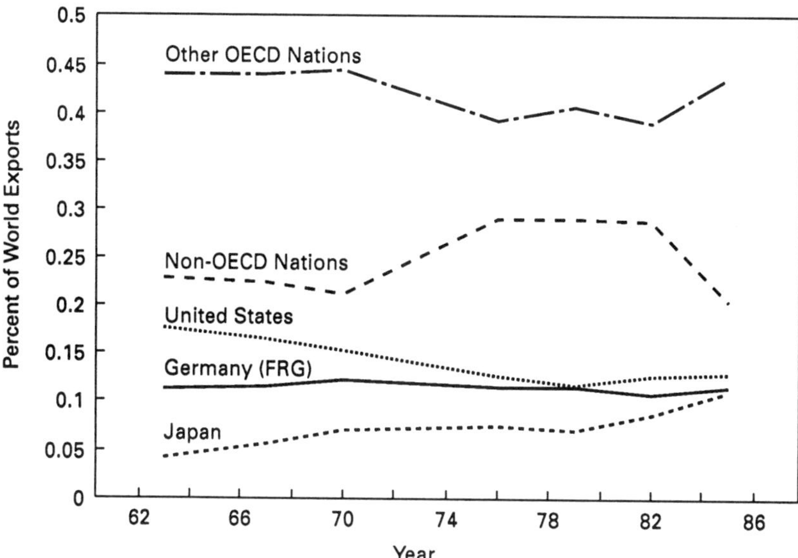

Figure 2.4
World export shares by country, 1963–1985 (UN trade data)

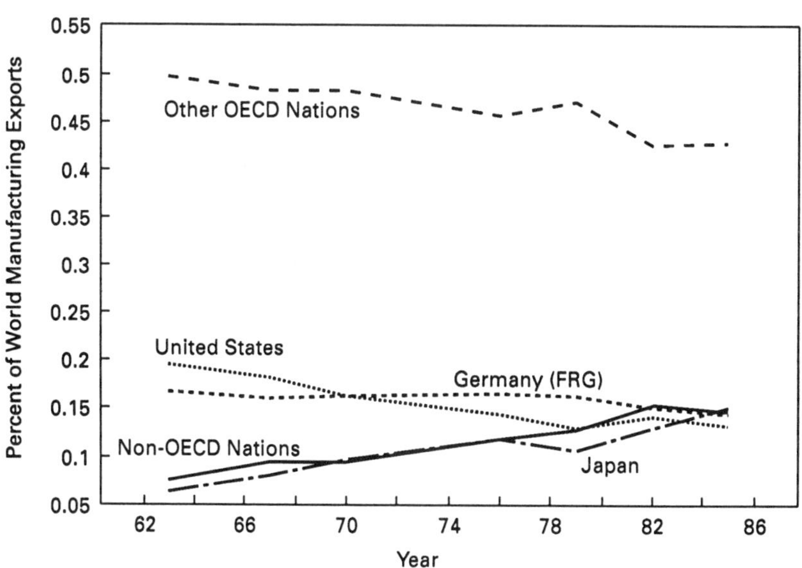

Figure 2.5
World manufacturing export shares by country, 1963–1985 (UN trade data)

ably (13.0% for the United States compared to 11.6% for Germany and 11.2% for Japan). Interestingly, Japan and Germany were exporting almost exactly the same volume in 1985.

Panel A has several other interesting implications. First, the U.S. export share fell from 18% in 1963 to 12% in 1979, but since 1979 its share has been increasing (to 13% in 1985). Second, total OECD exports fell from 77% of total world trade in 1963 to 71% in 1979, but then picked up to almost 80% in 1985. Correspondingly, non-OECD exports gained on the OECD countries from 1963 to 1979, but then declined dramatically in the early and mid-1980s.

Panel C shows the distribution of world manufacturing exports. Japan, as before, showed rapid gains in manufacturing exports, from 6% of the world total in 1963 to 15% in 1985. The United States showed, as before, a sharp decline, from 20% to 13%. The United States made a slight recovery in its share between 1979 and 1982, but by 1985 was back at its 1979 level. Germany, in contrast to its total export share, showed a decline in its share of manufacturing exports, from 17% to 14%. Thus, in 1985 Japan was the world's leading exporter of manufactures, followed by Germany and the United States. Interestingly, the non-OECD countries gained on the OECD between 1963 and 1985, as their share rose from 8% to 15%. However, even by 1985, the total volume of exports of non-OECD nations was approximately equal to that of Japan, Germany, and the United States taken individually.

In relative terms, the only success of the United States was in agricultural exports (panel E), where it held its share of world agricultural exports at 16%. Germany actually showed a rapid gain in agricultural exports, as its share increased from 2% to 5% between 1963 and 1985. Somewhat surprisingly, OECD countries gained on the non-OECD world in agricultural exports, from 58% to almost 70%. Relative to world mineral and energy exports (panel G), the United States showed a precipitous decline, from 10% in 1963 to 5% in 1982.[2] The biggest gains were made by the non-OECD countries, whose share increased from 57% to 67% between 1963 and 1982.

World export shares for Germany, Japan, and the United States are shown for particular commodity groups in table 2.5. Both the levels and trends are quite striking. Successes for the United States, even in relative terms, were quite limited over the period from the early 1960s through the mid-1980s. Perhaps the most successful industry was war munitions, in which the U.S. share of world exports increased from 53% to a staggering

65% between 1963 and 1985. The U.S. export share declined only slightly for tobacco products, from 40% to 37%; and for aircraft, from 59% to 50%,[3] but America still dominated the world export market in these three product groups. The United States also held its own in metal ore and scrap exports, as well as coal and coke exports, while the German export share fell considerably for the latter.

America suffered major declines in its export shares over a broad range of chemical products, with the exception of manufactured fertilizers. The German record was somewhat mixed, with export gains for some chemical lines and losses for others. U.S. exports also showed considerable losses relative to world trade in a whole range of clothing and related manufactures, including leather goods, textile yarn and fabrics, and footwear. Interestingly, Japan's export share suffered similar declines in clothing, footwear, and textile fabrics, while Germany's export share increased in textiles.

The U.S. export share also showed losses in rubber products, paper and paper products, and furniture. Japan's export share showed a gain in rubber products, but a considerable decline in wood products, while Germany's export share showed a large increase in paper products and held its own in the other sectors. The United States also experienced export declines in nonmetal products, both ferrous and nonferrous metals, and metal products. Japan gained in all four sectors except nonmetal products, and particularly in iron and steel, in which its export share increased from 12% to 22% between 1963 and 1985, while Germany lost in all sectors except nonferrous metals.

The most dramatic changes were in machinery and equipment export shares. From 1963 to 1985, the U.S. export share fell from 28% to 21% in nonelectrical machinery, from 24% to 16% in electrical machinery, from 25% to 17% in transport equipment, from 19% to 7% in plumbing, heating, and lighting equipment, and from 21% to 13% in watches, clocks, and related instruments. Particularly sharp declines were sustained in agricultural machinery, from 39% to 18%; metalworking machinery, from 26% to 7%; in telecommunications equipment, from 26% to 11%; and in motor vehicles, from 22% to 13%. On the other hand, the U.S. export share of office machines declined only moderately, from 35% to 30%, as did its share of aircraft, from 59% to 50%, while that of electrical medical equipment actually rose, from 15% to 30%. Germany's export share declined in all of these industries, with the exception of agricultural machinery and aircraft.

In contrast, Japan's export share gained almost across the board in these sectors. In metalworking machinery, its share rose from 2% to 27% of

Table 2.5
Percentage shares of world exports for the United States, Japan, and Germany by commodity group, 1963–85

	United States			Japan			Germany		
Commodity	1963	1976	1985	1963	1976	1985	1963	1976	1985
Tobacco, tobacco products (12)	40	36	37	1	0	0	1	3	7
Metalliferous ores, scrap (28)	12	9	14	0	0	0	2	4	4
Coal, coke, briquettes (32)	33	39	32	0	1	1	41	21	11
Chem. elements, compounds (51)	20	18	16	5	7	6	22	18	16
Coal, petroleum, chemicals (52)	64	10	1	1	1	2	7	4	6
Dyes, tanning, color products (53)	11	7	6	2	5	7	28	31	28
Medicinal products (54)	24	14	17	2	2	2	15	16	15
Perfume, cleaning products (55)	21	13	10	2	2	3	10	15	14
Fertilizers, manufactured (56)	12	19	28	9	5	1	18	8	7
Explosives, pyrotechnic products (57)	16	15	11	4	1	1	18	12	8
Plastic materials, etc. (58)	24	12	11	5	8	8	26	24	21
Chemicals, n.e.c. (59)	40	19	19	1	4	5	17	22	20
Leather, dressed fur, etc. (61)	13	7	7	1	6	4	13	13	11
Rubber manufactures, n.e.c. (62)	20	8	8	9	13	16	14	15	13
Wood, cork mfgs., n.e.c. (63)	7	12	7	13	2	1	7	8	8
Paper, paperboard products (64)	12	12	8	2	3	4	5	10	13
Textile yarn, fabric, etc. (65)	8	7	5	14	12	10	8	14	13
Nonmetal, mineral mfgs., n.e.c. (66)	11	7	6	10	5	7	14	11	10
Iron and steel (67)	9	5	2	12	26	22	19	16	16
Nonferrous metals (68)	9	6	7	1	3	5	6	10	12
Metal manufactures, n.e.c. (69)	17	11	8	8	11	11	22	18	16

Table 2.5 (continued)

	United States			Japan			Germany		
Commodity	1963	1976	1985	1963	1976	1985	1963	1976	1985
Machinery, nonelectrical (71)	28	22	21	2	8	15	23	22	17
Agricultural machinery (712)	39	28	18	0	6	12	11	15	19
Office machines (714)	35	29	30	1	10	16	16	16	9
Metalworking machinery (715)	26	14	7	2	9	27	35	33	21
Electrical machinery (72)	24	17	16	8	17	22	19	17	12
Telecommunications equipment (724)	26	11	11	15	32	34	15	12	8
Electro-medical, X-ray equipment (726)	15	18	30	2	5	17	33	27	19
Transport equipment (73)	25	18	17	6	19	24	22	17	16
Road motor vehicles (732)	22	16	13	3	16	27	29	21	19
Aircraft (734)	59	62	50	0	0	0	3	7	12
Ships and boats (735)	3	3	3	21	40	31	16	9	3
Plumbing, heating, lighting equipment (81)	19	9	7	3	2	3	21	21	15
Furniture (82)	10	5	6	3	2	2	19	23	17
Clothing (84)	5	3	2	12	2	2	8	8	7
Footwear (85)	2	1	1	13	1	0	5	4	4
Instruments, watches, clocks (86)	21	18	13	8	17	27	23	17	13
War firearms, ammunition (95)	53	61	65	0	0	0	0	1	1

Source: United Nations, World Trade Data Tapes. Exports are recorded in current U.S. dollars. World totals are the sum of exports recorded by countries reporting to the United Nations Statistical Office. U.N. trade commodity codes are shown in parentheses. (See the Appendix for details.)

world exports; in telecommunications equipment, from 15% to 34%; in motor vehicles, from 3% to 27%; in ships and boats, from 21% to 31%; and in watches, clocks, and related instruments, from 8% to 27%. Indeed, by 1985, Japan's exports were far exceeding those of the United States in each of these five industries.

High-Technology Industries

Whereas the overall export record of the United States has been rather weak since the early 1960s, it has been less dismal for so-called technology-intensive and high-technology exports. These trends, derived from National Science Foundation data, are shown in table 2.6 (and illustrated in Figure 2.6). Panel A shows world export shares for technology-intensive products for the five major industrialized countries over the 1965–86 period. In this panel technology-intensive products are defined as those produced by industries in which R & D exceeds 2.36% of value added. The U.S. share fell over this period, from 28% to 21%, though its decline was more moderate than for other manufacturing industries. Moreover, its share rose from 22% to 24% between 1979 and 1985, but then fell sharply between 1985 and 1986.

Japan's share increased almost continuously throughout this period, from 7% to 20%, and by 1986 its share was only slightly below that of the United States. Germany's share changed very little over this period (staying mainly between 16% and 17%), while France's share increased slightly, and the United Kingdom's declined.

Export shares for several high-technology and technology-intensive products are shown in panels B and C (see the footnote b to table 2.6 for the definition of high-technology industries). Between 1970 and 1980, the United States experienced declines in export shares in almost every technology-intensive industry, although in almost every case, the declines were relatively moderate. For drugs and medicines the U.S. export share fell from about 17% to 16%; for office and business machines there was almost no change, although its share of world computer exports fell by about 6 percentage points; for electrical machinery and equipment its share declined from 22% to 18%. Bigger losses were sustained in telecommunications equipment and aircraft, as noted above; the U.S. export share fell in electronic components from 40% in 1970 to 28% in 1980; in jet engines from 40% to 32% over the 1970–80 period; and in professional and scientific instruments (panel C) from 29% in 1970 to 15% in 1986.

Japan's export share increased in every sector except drugs, jet engines, aircraft, and industrial inorganic chemicals, in all of which its share was very small in 1970 and remained very small. By the mid-1980s Japan dominated the world export market in radio and televisions, consumer electronics generally, communications equipment, and professional and scientific instruments, while the United States was dominant in aircraft, jet engines, office machines, computers, and agricultural chemicals. Moreover, America was still leading Japan in terms of exports in industrial inorganic chemicals, drugs and medicines, and plastics and synthetics.

2.4 Conclusion

All in all, the record of U.S. industrial output, employment, and exports from the early 1960s to the mid-1980s is mixed. The U.S. share of OECD manufacturing output did decline from 40% in 1961 to 36% in 1975, but then increased to 38% in 1987. These results certainly do not provide much support for the deindustrialization thesis. The United States made particular gains in beverages, tobacco products, wood products, paper and paper products, printing and publishing, plastic products, glass and glass products, and professional goods, including scientific instruments. Its heaviest (relative) losses were in leather and leather products, footwear, and petroleum refinery. During the 1980s, the United States also suffered some heavy losses in office and computing equipment, radios and television, and general machinery. But in these three cases, the losses were preceded by large gains between the early 1960s and the late 1970s, and over the whole 1963–86 period relative gains were made in all three sectors.

Japan's share of total OECD manufacturing output increased from 14% in 1970 to 23% in 1987. Its most spectacular gains were in wearing apparel, leather and leather products, footwear, iron and steel, office and computing equipment, electrical machinery, particularly radios and televisions, and motor vehicles. Germany's manufacturing output share fell, from 14% in 1970 to 11% in 1987.

The result of these changes is that manufacturing output today is distributed among OECD countries more or less in proportion to population. Japan emerged from World War II with a share of OECD industrial output far below the country's share of population. During the following decades, Japan caught up very impressively, but its position among advanced countries today is basically commensurate with its size and does not provide any evidence of Japan becoming a new economic superpower, in the same way that the United States was the dominant economy in the 1950s and

Table 2.6
Export shares of technology-intensive and high-technology products for selected countries, industries, and years, 1965–86

A. *World export shares of technology-intensive products, 1965–86*[a]

	France	Germany	Japan	United Kingdom	United States
1965	7.3	16.9	7.2	12.0	27.5
1967	7.5	16.7	8.5	11.1	28.2
1970	7.1	16.8	10.9	9.8	27.0
1975	8.4	16.8	11.6	9.6	24.5
1976	8.4	17.3	13.7	8.6	23.5
1979	9.3	17.6	13.6	9.9	21.9
1980	8.5	16.3	14.3	10.8	22.9
1982	8.3	15.5	16.2	9.4	24.7
1985	7.9	14.8	19.4	9.2	24.2
1986	7.9	16.0	19.8	9.0	20.9

B. *World export shares of technology-intensive and high-technology products, 1970–80*[b]

	France		Germany		Japan		United States	
	1970	1980	1970	1980	1970	1980	1970	1980
Total technology-intensive products (including high-technology industries)	7.6	9.0	20.4	19.3	9.7	14.5	23.1	19.9
Total high-technology products	7.5	7.9	16.5	16.1	11.6	15.6	28.8	24.4
Drugs and medicinals	9.3	11.6	19.9	17.6	2.7	2.3	17.1	15.8
Business machines and equip.	7.8	7.8	15.1	13.0	8.0	9.9	37.7	37.0
Computers	9.0	7.1	11.2	12.1	11.1	12.3	31.5	25.5
Electrical and electronic machines and equipment	8.1	9.2	19.5	18.7	10.3	18.7	21.6	18.0
Telecommunications equipment	5.5	7.7	15.2	14.6	11.9	23.1	21.9	18.1
Electronic components	8.6	8.8	12.5	14.3	6.3	27.0	39.8	27.6
Consumer electronics	2.3	5.5	14.3	12.0	49.0	53.0	9.3	9.9
Jet engines	5.6	7.8	5.4	5.3	0.1	0.1	40.4	32.0
Aircraft	7.6	9.1	2.9	10.7	0.8	0.4	66.0	53.1
Scientific instruments	7.1	8.1	21.5	19.4	8.7	10.4	29.3	26.8
Technology-intensive, other than high-technology products	7.9	9.7	22.4	20.9	7.5	13.1	20.8	17.7

Table 2.6 (continued)

C. *World export shares of technology-intensive products by type, 1975–86*[c]

	Japan			United States		
	1975	1985	1986	1975	1985	1986
Total technology-intensive products	11.6	19.4	19.8	24.5	24.2	20.9
Aircraft and parts	0.3	0.4	0.6	61.9	50.9	49.7
Industrial inorganic chemicals	6.4	4.2	4.3	18.4	20.7	17.8
Radio and TV receiving equipment	46.3	78.2	69.1	6.5	0.6	0.5
Office and computing machines	9.2	17.7	21.3	31.3	33.1	28.2
Electrical machinery and equipment	8.7	18.4	18.8	21.2	21.9	18.1
Communications equipment	14.9	37.0	38.7	24.4	16.1	14.0
Professional and scientific instruments	15.3	30.0	29.1	19.6	16.9	14.5
Drugs	2.0	2.7	2.7	13.6	18.4	15.9
Plastic materials, synthetics	12.0	9.6	9.2	12.0	13.2	11.6
Engines and turbines	8.7	17.7	19.2	25.9	29.4	23.3
Agricultural chemicals	12.0	3.2	2.8	24.1	30.7	27.0

a. Source: National Science Foundation, *International Science and Technology Data Update 1988,* (NSF 89-307), Washington, D.C., 1988, p. 92. The data reflect information from twenty-four reporting countries on exports to about 200 trading partners. Technology-intensive products are defined as those for which R & D exceeds 2.36% of value added.

b. Source: U.S. Department of Commerce, International Trade Administration, *An Assessment of U.S. Competitiveness in High-Technology Industries,* February, 1983, p. 45. Technology-intensive products are defined as those produced in industries in which spending on R & D is 5% or more of value added and/or ("natural") scientists, engineers, and technicians comprise 5% or more of total industry employment. High-technology products are defined as those produced in industries in which spending on R & D is 10% or more of value added and/or ("natural") scientists, engineers, and technicians comprise 10% or more of total industry employment.

c. Sources: 1975 and 1985—National Science Foundation, *The Science and Technology Resources of Japan: A Comparison with the United States,* (NSF 88-318), Washington, D.C., 1988, p. 38. 1986—National Science Foundation, *International Science and Technology Data Update, 1988* (NSF 89-307), Washington, D.C., 1988, p. 94. The definition of technology-intensive products is the same as for panel A.

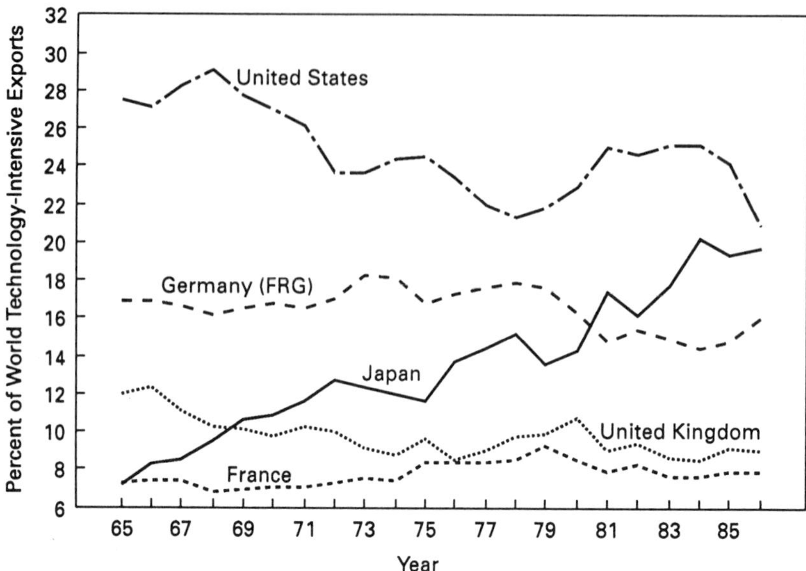

Figure 2.6
World technology-intensive export shares by country, 1965–1986 (National Science Foundation data)

early 1960s. Japan may yet become such a superpower, but its output gains to date represent catching up, not surging ahead.

The U.S. export record since the early 1960s is not as stable as the country's experience with output and employment. U.S. exports as a proportion of world exports declined from 18% in 1963 to 13% in 1986 (and from 20% to 13% for manufactured exports). With the notable exceptions of agricultural products, munitions, fertilizers, and medical equipment, the United States lost export shares in every key industry. Heavy losses occurred in chemicals and in almost all lines of equipment and machinery, including motor vehicles. However, the United States did fare better in technology-intensive and high-technology industries, in which its export share declined only moderately. Moreover, in the mid-1980s America still dominated world export markets in aircraft, jet engines, office machines, computers, and agricultural chemicals.

Offsetting to a significant extent the U.S. loss of export share is the increasing export share of commodities produced by U.S.-owned multinational corporations whose operations are located outside the United States. A recent study by Blomstrom and Lipsey (1989) documents this trend. They found that, whereas the share of world exports produced in the

United States declined from 17% in 1966 to 12% in 1987, the share of world exports produced by U.S.-owned multinational firms remained almost unchanged between 1966 and 1986, at 17%. Thus, the United States has substituted exports from its foreign affiliates located abroad for exports from enterprises located within its geographic boundaries.

One of the striking features of international trade among advanced economies today is the degree of specialization. In many ways the United States, Japan, and Germany are very similar, especially in terms of aggregate characteristics such as per capita gross domestic product (GDP) or per capita industrial output. But the subindustries in which each country exports are quite different. For example, in 1985 the United States accounted for 50% of world aircraft exports, compared to 0% for Japan and 12% for Germany. In iron and steel, on the other hand, the figures were 22% for Japan, 16% for Germany, and 2% for the United States. There are some industries in which all three countries are strong, such as agricultural machinery. But, in general, the export patterns of the three countries are strikingly disparate when examined in a disaggregated manner. This is a theme that we will return to in later chapters: growing convergence at the aggregate level, but strong, perhaps increasing, divergence at the subindustry level. Another important point that will come up again is that the industries in which the United States continues to be a strong exporter are generally those for which the government provides direct or indirect support for technology development.

3 Convergence of Industry Labor Productivity

3.1 The Sources of Aggregate Convergence

What we have established so far is that the aggregate productivity levels of advanced economies have converged on the leader, the United States, over the past few decades. This process has not resulted in a deindustrialization of the United States, as some had feared. The question remains, however, what has been the source of this aggregate convergence? We address this question in both chapters 3 and 4, from different points of view. In this chapter we examine the extent to which labor productivity at the industry level has converged among OECD economies. We also investigate the role of changes in employment mix. In the next chapter we consider the role of technology gains and capital formation in labor productivity growth.

Some industries produce more value added per worker than others, owing to the use of large amounts of capital or skilled labor or of advanced technology. It is possible for countries to have the same labor productivity at the industry level, but nevertheless to have different levels of aggregate productivity because one country's employment mix is shifted toward high-value-added sectors. One of the leading models of international trade, the Heckscher-Ohlin model, predicts that this will be the case among fairly similar countries, such as those in the OECD. Thus aggregate convergence can result from labor productivity converging at the industry level and/or from employment mixes becoming more similar. We address these issues by examining trends in labor productivity in twenty-eight manufacturing industries of thirteen industrial countries over the period 1963–86.[1]

Our main empirical finding is that among these industrial countries there has been convergence of labor productivity levels in virtually every manufacturing industry during the postwar period. Furthermore, throughout this period we find more intercountry variation in productivity at the industry level than at the level of all manufacturing. Productivity convergence is stronger for all manufacturing than within individual industries; this is especially true for heavy industries (like chemicals and steel) and for high-technology industries (like transport equipment and machinery). In 1986 the productivity leader in these industries had an advantage ranging from 25% to 150% over the average of the other countries. It may seem paradoxical that there is stronger convergence at an aggregate level; but this result can be explained by the fact that in 1986 different countries led in different industries.

The second major finding is that variation in the employment mix among industrial countries apparently does not play an important role in explaining cross-country differences in aggregate productivity in all manufacturing—or the convergence of their economies. Convergence in value added per work hour in all manufacturing among these countries has resulted from convergence of productivity levels within individual industries.

3.2 Trade Theory and Labor Productivity

The traditional Heckscher-Ohlin (HO) model of international trade provides a useful framework for analyzing differences in labor productivity among a group of countries that engage in trade.[2] In the simple version of the model there are two factors of production (labor and capital) and two goods, one of which is capital-intensive compared to the other. Trade will take place between two countries if they have different aggregate capital-labor ratios: in particular, the relatively capital-abundant country will export the capital-intensive good. In the process, it is possible that for each industry the capital-labor ratio will be the same in the two economies, with the result that at the industry level labor productivity and wages will be identical as well. Such an equilibrium is characterized by *factor-price equalization.*

What is interesting about this model from the point of view of productivity research is that it points out the possibility that two countries with different aggregate factor endowments can have the same factor intensities and levels of productivity industry by industry. In particular, if factor-price equalization holds among a group of countries, then for each individual industry labor productivity should be identical across such countries.[3] The key to the factor-price equalization result is that countries use the same techniques of production (i.e., capital-labor ratios) at the industry level.

In this model there can still be differences in *aggregate productivity*. Aggregate output in any country h will be the sum of factor earnings:

$$y^h = rK^h + wL^h, \tag{3.1}$$

where y^h is aggregate value added (GDP), K^h and L^h are aggregate quantities of capital and labor, and r and w are the relevant factor prices (which are the same across countries). Aggregate labor productivity is then

$$y^h/L^h = r(K^h/L^h) + w. \tag{3.2}$$

Across countries, aggregate labor productivity will vary (linearly) with the capital-labor ratio.

At the industry level, on the other hand, labor productivity will not vary across countries. This is possible because countries will have different distributions of output and employment across industries. In particular, a capital-abundant country will have more of its labor force and output in the capital-intensive industry. That industry will have relatively more value added per unit of labor input than the labor-intensive sector. Differences in aggregate endowments of nonlabor factors such as capital hence will be reflected in different distributions of employment across industries, not in different techniques of production at the micro level. This model implies that differences in aggregate productivity can then only result from differences in industry mixes.

While the exposition of the HO model with factor-price equalization is easiest in a two-factor, two-sector model, these basic results can hold with many factors and industries.[4] Formally, let v^h be an $n \times 1$ vector of fixed factor supplies for country h. With factor-price equalization there will be an $n \times 1$ factor-price vector, w, that is the same for all countries. GDP or aggregate value added for country h can then be expressed as the sum of factor earnings:

$$y^h = w^T v^h, \tag{3.3}$$

where w^T is the transpose of vector w. Let the first factor in the vector v^h be the aggregate labor supply, L^h. Then aggregate labor productivity can be expressed as

$$y^h/L^h = w_L + \Sigma_{i=2}(w_i v_i^h/L^h), \tag{3.4}$$

where w_L is the wage. In the more general model, one country will have greater aggregate productivity than another if the value of its nonlabor factors (per work hour) is greater. Aggregate labor productivity is also, by definition, a weighted average of labor productivity in individual industries,

$$y^h/L^h = \Sigma_i(a_i^h y_i^h/L_i^h), \tag{3.5}$$

where the weights are employment shares ($a_i^h = L_i^h/L^h$).

The HO model with factor-price equalization predicts that value added per work hour at the industry level is identical across countries, so that high labor productivity at the aggregate level must result from having an employment mix shifted toward high-productivity industries. Industries with high value added per work hour are those that employ much human capital, physical capital, or other nonlabor resources per work hour. It should also be noted that, even with factor-price equalization, exact equality across countries in industry labor productivity would only be observed at a very disaggregated level. Improper aggregation would necessarily introduce some cross-country variation in industry labor productivity. In this case the implication of factor-price equalization can be stated in the following form: cross-country variation in labor productivity at the industry level should be significantly less than variation at the aggregate level, though not necessarily zero.

In earlier work (Dollar, Wolff, and Baumol 1988) we demonstrated that as a *static* observation this prediction of the factor-price equalization hypothesis did not hold very well among thirteen industrial countries in 1980. Differences in labor productivity among these countries at that time were at least as great at the two-digit industry level as at the level of all manufacturing. Nevertheless, the model is a useful framework for analyzing changes in the cross-country variation in labor productivity over time. One interesting question is whether the predictions of the factor-price equalization hypothesis hold better in the 1960s than in the 1980s (or vice versa); and the model does draw attention to the useful distinction between differences in productivity at the industry level versus differences in employment mixes.

3.3 Coverage of the Study

Our examination of the convergence of labor productivity at the industry level covers thirteen industrial countries—the big seven (Canada, France, Germany, Italy, Japan, the United Kingdom, and the United States) plus six smaller economies (Australia, Austria, Denmark, Finland, Norway, and Sweden). Data availability dictated the countries selected and the period of examination; the year 1986 was the most recent for which consistent, cross-country data were available.

To investigate labor productivity at the industry level we use data from the United Nations *Yearbook of Industrial Statistics,* which reports manufacturing output and employment disaggregated into twenty-eight industries. Our output measure is value added, which is reported in current prices, denominated in domestic currency.[5] We used the gross national product (GNP) deflator of each country to convert values of different years into 1983 prices, and then applied purchasing power parity (PPP) exchange rates calculated by the OECD to convert all values into 1983 dollars.[6]

The ideal labor input measure would be hours worked; unfortunately, this was not available at the industry level. So we used number of employees in the industry, adjusted by the average number of hours worked in the country and year in question.[7] Our primary measure of labor productivity then is value added per work hour, denominated in 1983 dollars.[8] If hours worked in the whole economy are not good proxies for hours worked in individual manufacturing industries, then our procedure will introduce some bias (of unknown direction). Hence we also used value added per worker as an alternative measure of labor productivity to ensure that our results are not heavily dependent on this adjustment.

3.4 Convergence in All Manufacturing

For all manufacturing, the United States has maintained a labor productivity lead over the other twelve countries throughout the period under consideration. This can be seen in table 3.1, which presents cross-country indexes of value added per work hour in all manufacturing for 1963, 1970, 1982, and 1986. The U.S. productivity lead, however, has been diminishing. The unweighted average productivity in the other twelve countries was 47% of U.S. productivity in 1963; there was a strong trend toward convergence between 1963 and 1970. By the latter year, the average of the other countries had risen to 58% of U.S. productivity. This convergence of productivity levels can also be seen in the coefficient of variation: this measure of cross-country dispersion declined from .36 in 1963 to .24 in 1970.[9] It is unfortunate that these industry-level data are not available in a consistent format before 1963. It is very likely that the trend between 1963 and 1970 is a continuation of a strong pattern of convergence that began shortly after the end of World War II. Such a development would be consistent with the aggregate data discussed in chapter 1.

The trend toward convergence is much less clear in the period after 1970. There appears to have been some additional convergence during the 1970s, and by 1982 the average productivity in the manufacturing sector of the other industrial countries was 66% of the U.S. level. That figure may be exaggerated, however, by the fact that 1982 was a recession year. There

Table 3.1
Value added per work hour in manufacturing in twelve industrial countries relative to the United States, 1963–86

(index, U.S. = 100)[a]

	1963	1970	1982	1986
United States	100	100	100	100
Canada	77	80	76	93
Germany	54[b]	68	68	66
Japan	26	49	61	65
United Kingdom	52[c]	60	88	54
Sweden	52	68	78	62
Denmark	41	54	59	58
Australia	47	53	56	56[d]
France	53	64	67	56[d]
Italy	45[e]	50	88	55
Finland	34	48	51	51
Austria	37	47	49	51
Norway	46	58	49	51
Coefficient of variation	.36	.24	.23	.24
Unweighted average (excluding U.S.)	47	58	66	60

a. Calculated from aggregate data for all manufacturing.
b. 1965 data.
c. 1968 data.
d. 1985 data.
e. 1967 data.

is evidence that the 1982 recession was more severe in the United States than in other major industrial countries, so that the convergence on the United States may well be overestimated.[10] Between 1982 and 1986 U.S. productivity grew relative to the other countries. In 1986, the average productivity of the twelve industrial countries compared to the United States was 60%, about the same as in 1970. The lack of any strong secular trend between 1970 and today is also reflected in the coefficient of variation, which was virtually the same in 1970 (.24), 1982 (.23), and 1986 (.24).

It is interesting that different countries follow different patterns of convergence. Japan has gained steadily on the United States throughout the period examined, though it must be remembered that it had by far the lowest productivity among industrial countries at the beginning of the period. Many of the countries follow the general pattern of gaining on the United States between 1963 and 1970, and then showing little further progress. Germany, Australia, and France are all examples of this pattern.

Canada is somewhat of an anomaly. It starts out with the productivity level closest to the United States in 1963, but shows little progress between 1963 and 1982. In the 1980s, however, Canada has gained strongly on the U.S., reaching 93% of the U.S. productivity level in 1986. The figures for Italy and the United Kingdom show implausibly large productivity increases between 1970 and 1982, followed by implausibly large decreases between 1982 and 1986. Those anomalies may reflect the manner in which the 1982 recession affected their productivity statistics. Note also that productivity convergence on the United States is strongest for the large economies: the average for Japan, Germany, France, Italy, the United Kingdom, and Canada is 65% of U.S. productivity by 1986. For the six smaller economies, the comparable figure is only 55%.

3.5 Convergence at the Industry Level

In theory, the U.S. productivity advantage in all manufacturing could result from superior productivity in individual manufacturing industries, and/or from an employment mix that, relative to other industrial countries, is shifted toward high-productivity industries. Table 3.2 provides measures of the dispersion in labor productivity among the thirteen countries for twenty-eight manufacturing industries in 1963, 1982, and 1986. Here we are primarily concerned with the beginning and end years of our data set.

It is desirable to impose some order on this large amount of data, so industries have been grouped into four categories. Heavy, medium, and light industries have been identified based on the capital-labor ratio. Since contemporary German data were readily available, the division was made on that basis; the result accords well with our prior beliefs about the relative capital-intensity of different industries. It should be noted that several industries do not fit easily into this tripartite division, and have been placed together under the heading "other industries." The distinctive feature of these industries is that they are very small in terms of employment and/or are closely connected to primary products. Table 3.3 provides unweighted averages of the coefficients in table 3.2 for heavy, medium, and light industries, as well as comparable statistics for all manufacturing.

A number of interesting results emerge from the data in tables 3.2 and 3.3. In 1963 the United States was the productivity leader in virtually every industry, with the only exceptions occurring in small industries like coal products. This is reflected in the average of productivity in the twelve countries relative to the United States. At the industry level the U.S. productivity lead was related to the capital-intensity of the industry, with

Table 3.2
Measures of productivity convergence in twenty-eight manufacturing industries of thirteen industrial countries, 1963–86

	Coefficient of variation			Average of productivity in twelve countries relative to U.S.		
	1963	1982	1986	1963	1982	1986
Heavy industries						
Industrial chemicals	.57	.33	.41	.36	.58	.52
Other chemicals	.49	.43	.44	.37	.45	.44
Iron and steel	.38	.26	.30	.48	.77	.66
Nonferrous metals	.56	.32	.30	.46	.69	.82
Medium industries						
Paper products	.40	.24	.26	.48	.59	.60
Printing	.38	.31	.21	.49	.72	.66
Rubber products	.42	.26	.24	.45	.60	.59
Plastic products	.35	.23	.18	.51	.72	.70
Pottery	.46	.28	.32	.54	.75	.66
Glass products	.38	.26	.28	.43	.69	.65
Nonmetal products, n.e.c.	.36	.23	.21	.53	.80	.74
Metal products, n.e.c.	.39	.25	.22	.46	.69	.66
Machinery	.36	.25	.24	.47	.64	.59
Transport equipment	.46	.30	.39	.42	.54	.50
Light industries						
Textiles	.30	.23	.23	.59	.81	.76
Clothing	.32	.24	.22	.60	.76	.70
Leather products	.26	.30	.22	.63	.79	.79
Footwear	.33	.22	.17	.63	.79	.76
Wood products	.34	.25	.22	.72	.90	.76
Furniture	.37	.27	.14	.50	.82	.78
Electrical goods	.37	.27	.61	.50	.82	.61
Other industries						
Food products	.38	.35	.35	.54	.57	.47
Beverages	.41	.27	.27	.56	.73	.61
Tobacco products	1.06	1.00	1.03	.94	.84	.63
Petroleum refining	.65	.63	.76	.82	.79	1.04
Coal products	.86	.35	.97	1.01	.77	1.00
Professional goods	.42	.33	.30	.43	.51	.48
Manufactures, n.e.c.	.40	.26	.20	.46	.69	.66

Table 3.2 (continued)

	Average of productivity in twelve countries relative to leader	Japanese productivity relative to U.S. productivity		
	1986	1963	1982	1986
Heavy industries				
Industrial chemicals	.51 (Canada)	.24	.69	.84
Other chemicals	.44 (U.S.)	.28	.74	.84
Iron and steel	.61 (Canada)	.30	1.24	1.05
Nonferrous metals	.58 (Canada)	.31	.86	.85
Medium industries				
Paper products	.60 (U.S.)	.27	.52	.60
Printing	.66 (U.S.)	.29	.75	.74
Rubber products	.59 (U.S.)	.24	.59	.65
Plastic products	.70 (U.S.)	.24	.66	.75
Pottery	.55 (Canada)	.21	.53	.56
Glass products	.65 (U.S.)	.38	.96	.99
Nonmetal products, n.e.c.	.63 (Canada)	.24	.68	.70
Metal products, n.e.c.	.63 (Canada)	.24	.61	.73
Machinery	.59 (U.S.)	.27	.67	.73
Transport equipment	.50 (U.S.)	.30	.65	.68
Light industries				
Textiles	.62 (Canada)	.27	.66	.68
Clothing	.70 (U.S.)	.24	.47	.50
Leather products	.62 (France)	.36	.68	.80
Footwear	.75 (Canada)	.32	.73	.87
Wood products	.58 (Canada)	.24	.66	.65
Furniture	.78 (U.S.)	.22	.69	.76
Electrical goods	.61 (U.S.)	.30	.60	.63
Other industries				
Food products	.47 (U.S.)	.20	.41	.43
Beverages	.61 (U.S.)	.23	.64	.70
Tobacco products	.19 (Austria)	.13	.17	.22
Petroleum refining	.33 (France)	.52	1.03	1.03
Coal products	.17 (Germany)	.32	.79	.70
Professional goods	.48 (U.S.)	.22	.40	.46
Manufactures, n.e.c.	.66 (U.S.)	.22	.59	.73

Table 3.3
Average measures of productivity convergence for heavy, medium, and light industries of thirteen industrial countries, 1963–86

	Coefficient of variation			Average of productivity in twelve countries relative to U.S.		
	1963	1982	1986	1963	1982	1986
All manufacturing[a]	.36	.23	.24	.47	.66	.60
Heavy industries[b]	.50	.34	.34	.42	.62	.53
Medium industries[b]	.40	.26	.25	.48	.67	.60
Light industries[b]	.33	.25	.20	.59	.79	.66

a. Calculated from aggregate data for all manufacturing.
b. Unweighted averages of the coefficients presented in table 3.2.

Average measures of productivity convergence for heavy, medium, and light industries of thirteen industrial countries, 1963–86

	Average of productivity in twelve countries relative to leader	Japanese productivity relative to U.S. productivity		
	1986	1963	1982	1986
All manufacturing[a]	.60	.26	.61	.65
Heavy industries[b]	.53	.28	.88	.83
Medium industries[b]	.60	.27	.66	.70
Light industries[b]	.66	.28	.64	.67

a. Calculated from aggregate data for all manufacturing.
b. Unweighted averages of the coefficients presented in table 3.2.

the U.S. advantage noticeably greater in heavy industries than in light industries.

Looking at the coefficients of variation, which measure the dispersion in industry labor productivity across the thirteen countries, we see that in 1963 there was considerably more dispersion in heavy industries (.50) than in all manufacturing (.36). There is less dispersion in medium industries (.40), but still more than in all manufacturing. Light industries (.33) evidence less variation than the whole manufacturing sector.

Japan's experience is unusual and merits special attention. In 1963 Japanese labor productivity in all manufacturing was by far the lowest of the large economies. The German productivity level was about twice that of Japan, while the U.S. advantage was fourfold. Unlike the European economies (plus Canada and Australia), Japan's productivity relative to the United States was no higher in light industries than in heavy industries.

Between 1963 and 1986 the coefficient of variation declined for virtually every industry, indicating that among these countries labor productivity was converging at the industry level. The average of productivity in the twelve countries, relative to the United States, rose in all but three industries (food products, tobacco products, and coal products). The convergence was strongest in the light industries: the other countries on average achieved 66% of U.S. productivity, whereas the comparable figure for all manufacturing was 60%. In heavy and medium industries as well, the other countries made substantial gains relative to the United States. Nevertheless, it remained true in 1986 that there was more variation across countries in labor productivity at the industry level than at the level of all manufacturing. This was particularly the case with heavy and medium industries.[11]

An important change from 1963 is that by 1986 there are quite a few industries in which America is no longer the productivity leader. In fact, the United States is the productivity leader in only about half of the industries (15 out of 28). For that reason tables 3.2 and 3.3 also include a column for 1986 that indicates the average productivity of the twelve follower countries relative to the productivity leader, with the lead country indicated in parentheses. Five different countries hold the lead in at least one industry.

The case of Japan is again interesting. In all manufacturing, Japan's gain relative to the United States over the twenty-four-year period from 1963 to 1986 is quite remarkable, going from 26% of U.S. productivity to 65%. In contrast to the other countries, Japan's gains have been strongest in heavy industries, in which its productivity was 83% of the U.S. level in 1986. In medium and light industries, on the other hand, Japanese productivity gains have been a little less dramatic. In the light industries in particular Japanese productivity tends to lag well behind both the United States and the large European economies.[12]

3.6 Intercountry Variation in Employment Mix

As noted above, intercountry variation in labor productivity in all manufacturing can result from differences in employment mixes, and in this section we explore what role these differences have played and whether that role has changed between 1963 and 1986. In order to do this we conducted two counterfactual experiments. First, we calculated an index of value added per worker in all manufacturing using U.S. employment shares for each country. We decided to use U.S. weights because it seemed likely to us that, compared to other countries in this study, the U.S. employment

Table 3.4
Value added per work hour in manufacturing in twelve industrial countries relative to the United States, 1963–86
(calculated with U.S. employment shares of that year)
(index, U.S. = 100)

	1963	1970	1982	1986
United States	100	100	100	100
Canada	78	80	75	91
Germany	58[a]	64	64	65
Japan	27	52	64	68
United Kingdom	57[b]	60	88	53
Sweden	52	69	75	62
Denmark	42	52	56	56
Australia	46	53	55	56[c]
France	53	64	66	56[c]
Italy	48[d]	49	84	58
Finland	35	48	50	49
Austria	59	47	50	51
Norway	47	60	51	50
Coefficient of variation	.33	.24	.23	.24
Unweighted average (excluding U.S.)	50	58	65	60

a. 1965 data.
b. 1968 data.
c. 1985 data.
d. 1967 data.

mix has been shifted toward high-value-added industries, and we wanted to confirm this.

The indexes that result from this experiment are presented in Table 3.4. They are amazingly similar to the indexes reported in table 3.1, which implicitly use each country's own weights. For example, the index of Germany's relative productivity in manufacturing in the mid-1960s is 54 when German employment weights are used for the calculation. Using U.S. employment weights raises the figure marginally, to 58. In the case of Japan the change is even more minor: relative productivity in 1963 is 27 (U.S. weights), compared to 26 (own weights). The largest difference is that for the United Kingdom: the index with own weights is 52, and rises to 57 with U.S. weights. The situation at the end of the period, 1986, is very similar. In the case of every country except Italy and Japan, the difference between U.S. weights and a country's own weights is no more than two points. For both Italy and Japan, the use of U.S. employment weights raises measured productivity for all manufacturing by three points.

The striking implication of this result is that U.S. manufacturing employment has not, relative to the other countries, been shifted toward high-value-added industries, either at the beginning of this period or at the end. Differences in employment mixes can explain virtually none of the cross-country differences in labor productivity at the level of all manufacturing. Thus the United States had higher aggregate productivity in 1963 not because its output and employment mix was substantially different from other industrial countries, but rather because it had higher labor productivity in every two-digit manufacturing industry.

The second counterfactual experiment involved calculation of an index of value added per worker in all manufacturing, holding each country's employment weights constant through time. For this we used 1982 employment weights; the results are presented in table 3.5, along with indexes calculated with actual employment weights (changing over time). Again, there is strikingly little difference between the constant-weights and actual-weights indexes. In the case of Germany, for example, applying that country's 1982 weights to its mid-1960s productivity levels raises the index of productivity for all manufacturing only a small degree (from 59 to 63). This indicates that between the mid-1960s and the mid-1980s there was a minor adjustment in the German employment mix, in the direction of higher-value-added industries. In the case of Japan, the use of 1982 weights for 1963 productivity levels results in no change in the index of manufacturing productivity. The only exception to this rule is Austria, where the use of 1982 weights results in a large increase in the productivity index for all manufacturing. Except for that one anomaly, all of the countries display only minor changes in the index as a result of the use of contemporary employment weights.

This result implies that in 12 of these 13 economies changes in employment mixes have not played an important role in productivity growth and hence in the convergence of labor productivity at the level of all manufacturing. It should be emphasized that this result does not mean that employment mixes have not changed over time; they almost certainly have. What the results here establish is that the changes cannot be characterized as a shift from low-value-added (presumably labor-intensive) to higher-value-added (capital- and/or technology-intensive) industries.

The final analysis undertaken entailed the construction of an index to measure the degree of difference in industry employment mixes among the thirteen countries in 1963 and 1982. For this purpose we borrowed a metric used for a chi-square goodness-of-fit test. Recalling that a_i^h is industry i's share of manufacturing employment in country h, let a_i^* be the

Table 3.5
Value added per work hour in manufacturing in thirteen industrial countries (index, 1982 = 100)

	1963	1970	1982	1986
United States				
Actual	71	79	100	110
1982 weights	72	79	100	110
Canada				
Actual	72	83	100	135
1982 weights	74	84	100	134
Germany				
Actual	59[a]	78	100	107
1982 weights	63[a]	82	100	107
Japan				
Actual	30	64	100	117
1982 weights	30	63	100	119
United Kingdom				
Actual	46[b]	54	100	68
1982 weights	46[b]	55	100	68
Sweden				
Actual	49	70	100	87
1982 weights	50	73	100	88
Denmark				
Actual	50	72	100	108
1982 weights	52	73	100	109
Australia				
Actual	60	74	100	110[c]
1982 weights	59	77	100	109[c]
France				
Actual	56	77	100	92[c]
1982 weights	55	76	100	93[c]
Italy				
Actual	39[d]	45	100	69
1982 weights	40[d]	45	100	70
Finland				
Actual	48	76	100	110
1982 weights	50	77	100	110
Austria				
Actual	53	75	100	114
1982 weights	85	75	100	114
Norway				
Actual	65	94	100	114
1982 weights	68	98	100	114

a. 1965 data.
b. 1968 data.
c. 1985 data.
d. 1967 data.

unweighted average of the a_i^h of the 13 countries. Then we construct a metric M defined as

$$M = \Sigma_i \Sigma^h (a_i^h - a_i^*)^2. \tag{3.6}$$

This metric measures the extent to which industry employment shares differ among the thirteen countries, with each country given the same weight. If employment mixes are identical in these countries, then $M = 0$; as mixes become increasingly different, M rises. It should be noted that M is not a chi-square statistic, since there is no sampling of observations from the various countries. However, we can compare M for the two years 1963 and 1982 as one gauge of whether there has been convergence in the countries' distribution of manufacturing employment among industries.

Our finding is that between 1963 and 1982 M declines from .094 to .086, indicating that employment mixes have become more similar. There remains the problem of interpreting the magnitude of this change. For that purpose it is useful to divide M by the degrees of freedom [$324 = (13 - 1)$ countries $\times$ $(28 - 1)$ industries] and take the square root to obtain the mean square error. This transformation indicates how much the typical observation deviates from the average for its industry—that is, it is a measure of the average deviation, $(a_i^h - a_i^*)$. In 1963 the mean square error is .017; in 1982 it is .016. It is also useful to express the mean square error relative to the average a_i^*; this procedure yields figures of .48 for 1963 and .45 for 1982. Interpreted in this way, the decrease in M seems rather minor. This result is consistent with the other findings of this study, in particular that changes in employment mixes have not played a significant role in the convergence of aggregate labor productivity.[13]

3.7 Interpretation of the Results

We are left, then, with the conclusion that in 1963 the U.S. lead in labor productivity for all manufacturing was rooted in superior productivity at the industry level. Between 1963 and 1986 labor productivity of the industrial countries covered by this study converged on the U.S. level in virtually every industry, although the degree of convergence differed markedly among industries. This convergence of productivity at the industry level is the proximate source of the convergence in aggregate productivity that has been noted in many studies. Changes in the distribution of employment among industries plays virtually no role in the aggregate convergence.

One of the interesting implications of this last result is that the key to aggregate productivity growth is not a shifting of the nation's employment and output into a few special sectors. Countries like Japan have grown well not because they have captured a small number of high-value-added industries, but rather because their productivity growth has been high in all sectors. What employment shifts have occurred cannot be characterized as a shift from low- to high-value-added activities. In addition to growing well in all industries, successful economies also have a few industries in which their productivity growth is especially high. These high-growth sectors, however, appear to be different in each country, which can explain the greater cross-country dispersion of productivity in individual industries vis-à-vis that of the aggregate.

In interpreting these results, a question that arises naturally is how can one account for the observed intercountry variation in industry labor productivity. Discovery of the source of the productivity differentials should also lead to an explanation of the dimunition of those differentials over time. Two hypotheses, not mutually exclusive, suggest themselves: first, that industry-level capital-labor ratios have converged among the countries in our sample; second, that technological sophistication has converged among the countries.

We know that in 1963 the United States had a much greater aggregate capital-labor ratio than other industrial countries, and probably more human capital per worker as well, though the latter is hard to prove. The HO model predicts that in this situation the U.S. output mix will be shifted toward industries that use physical and human capital intensively, and there is evidence that to some extent this was the case.[14] The factor-price equalization theorem demonstrates that it is possible that the shift in the output mix is of such magnitude that at the industry level the use of capital and other factors per worker is identical among countries, equalizing labor productivity at the industry level. This was clearly not the case among industrial countries in 1963. The United States had a large productivity lead in virtually every industry, and in the heavy industries the U.S. lead was considerably greater than in all manufacturing.

Given our results, it seems likely that in each industry the United States was employing more capital per worker than other countries in 1963. Between 1963 and 1982 the aggregate capital-labor ratios of industrial countries have converged on the U.S. level (as discussed further in chapter 4). The countries with low capital-labor ratios in 1963 have accumulated capital extremely rapidly; this is especially true for Japan, and the importance of capital accumulation as a source of Japanese labor productivity growth has been well documented.[15] This has apparently resulted in the convergence of capital-labor ratios at the industry level, a hypothesis that will be examined formally in the next chapter. This interpretation is consistent with recent empirical studies of the changing U.S. comparative advantage. Bowen (1983, p. 409), for instance, finds that the U.S. position as a capital-abundant country has declined relative to other developed countries, and that "as capital accumulation proceeded in developed countries they were increasingly able to compete with the United States in capital-intensive sectors."

What implication does our work have concerning the relevance of different trade models? Clearly the HO model with factor-price equalization does not help us understand productivity differences among the advanced countries. The important predictions of the model are contravened by the facts. This in itself does not necessarily mean that the more general version of the HO model is not useful. Deardorff (1984) among others demonstrates that the HO model without factor-price equalization implies industry-level productivity differences among countries. These differences, however, will typically have a pattern. Without factor-price equalization, a capital abundant country should be using more capital per worker, and have higher labor productivity, in every industry.[16]

Convergence of industry labor productivity can be reconciled with the HO model if the productivity convergence is driven by convergence of factor endowments. The fact that different countries held productivity leads in different industries in 1986, on the other hand, is not easily reconciled with the HO theory. Such a result is more compatible with the new trade theories based on technological innovation and economies of scale, and is the expected outcome if the technological advance of industrial nations is concentrated in different industries.

Hence another plausible hypothesis that needs to be considered is that our findings concerning industry labor productivity are primarily the result of variation in technology, both among countries and over time. It is possible that there were important technology differences among industrial countries in 1963, and that, in general, these differences have diminished over time, partly as a result of international diffusion of technology. A general convergence of technology levels is not inconsistent with individual countries' developing modest technology leads in different industries, which would account for the fact that today productivity differentials are somewhat larger at the industry level than at the level of all manufacturing.

The next step in our research is to investigate the sources of labor productivity convergence within individual industries. In chapter 4 we document the extent to which the convergence of capital input per worker can account for convergence of output per worker at the industry level. We also estimate total factor productivity at the industry level for the countries in our study, to investigate whether there have been important technology differences among the industrial countries, and whether such differences are diminishing.

Convergence of factor endowments and convergence of technology levels are not mutually exclusive, and in fact both have been occurring. Nevertheless, sorting out the relative importance of each in explaining convergence of labor productivity will enhance our understanding of convergence, and shed additional light on changing comparative advantage among industrial countries.

4 Capital Intensity and TFP Convergence in Manufacturing

4.1 Introduction

As we noted in chapter 1, recent work has demonstrated that OECD countries have become more similar in terms of aggregate characteristics. This growing similarity is evident in the marked convergence of overall labor productivity among industrialized countries in the postwar period, as well as in the convergence of aggregate total factor productivity (TFP) and capital-labor ratios.[1]

In the previous chapter, we began an investigation of how this productivity convergence has manifested itself in particular industries. We addressed two issues in particular: the extent to which shifts in employment from low-value-added to high-value-added activities within manufacturing contributed to aggregate labor productivity convergence; and the extent to which labor productivity convergence has occurred in individual industries.

We found strong evidence of convergence toward the U.S. level in virtually every industry covered by the study. However, differences in employment mix explained almost none of the difference in labor productivity for all manufacturing, and changes in industry employment mix over time accounted for virtually none of the productivity convergence observed in aggregate. We concluded that the convergence of productivity within industries was the proximate cause of the convergence in aggregate labor productivity noted in many studies.

There were three other noteworthy findings in chapter 3. The first was that the degree of catch-up varied considerably among industries—more rapid in so-called light industries, defined as those with low capital-labor ratios, than in heavy industries. A second finding was that, whereas in 1963 the United States led in virtually every industry in terms of labor productivity, by 1986 leadership positions were spread among five different countries. The third was that convergence in industry labor productivity slowed down rather sharply after about 1973.

The previous chapter also left open the question of the source of the intercountry variation in industry labor productivity, as well as the explanation for the changes in these differentials over time. In this chapter, we consider two, not mutually exclusive hypotheses: first, that there are differences in degree of technological sophistication among the countries, although these have narrowed; and, second, that industry-level capital-labor ratios differ, but have converged among industrialized countries.

We find evidence in this chapter of the convergence of TFP levels, meaning homogenization in the level of technological sophistication, both in the aggregate and within industries between 1963 and 1985. However, this process of technological catch-up was much faster in the period before 1972 than after. Moreover, the degree of convergence varied considerably among industries and was particularly strong in the heavy industries, which had much greater dispersion in TFP levels in the early 1960s. As a result, by 1985 the cross-country disparity in TFP levels was very similar among industries.

We also find convergence in capital-labor ratios in both the aggregate and by industry, though this process was also much stronger before 1972 than after. By 1985 the variation in capital intensity among countries was much greater in heavy industries than medium or light, which helps to explain its greater dispersion in labor productivity levels. Differences in aggregate capital intensity were explained almost totally by differences in capital intensity at the industry level (more capital-abundant countries had higher industry capital-labor ratios). Moreover, the convergence of aggregate capital-labor ratios was attributable almost entirely to the convergence of capital intensity within industries, rather than to changes in employment mix.

The results indicate that there were two distinct phases. During the 1963–72 period TFP, capital intensity, and labor productivity all converged rapidly, though most of the catch-up in labor productivity was attributable to the catch-up in TFP. Furthermore, industries and countries that were particularly far behind the leader, the United States, manifested the greatest degree of TFP catch-up, a finding consistent with Gerschenkron's notion that backward countries can benefit from borrowing advanced technology pioneered by the leader. In the 1963–72 period it was also the case that convergence of industry TFP was correlated with convergence of capital-labor ratios. This result may mean that some advanced technology is embodied in machinery so that rapid capital accumulation entails fast

TFP growth. Alternatively, rapid TFP growth brought about by acquiring disembodied technology may make an industry especially profitable and attractive for investment. It is quite plausible that causality runs in both directions, with high investment spurring TFP growth, which in turn attracts more investment. After 1972, convergence slowed in both TFP and labor productivity, and labor productivity catch-up to the United States was achieved primarily through increasing capital intensity. Indeed, several countries surpassed the United States in terms of the capital intensity of production.

Finally, we find that the variation in TFP, capital intensity, and labor productivity was greater at the industry level than in aggregate manufacturing. These results indicate that the countries specialized in different industries, particularly since the mid-1970s. Countries have invested heavily in new technology in different industries, which explains the emergence of countries other than the United States as productivity leaders in some industries. Changes in international comparative advantage thus can be attributed to a combination of worldwide shifts in technology leadership and investment strategies.

The remainder of the chapter is organized into six parts. The first of these (part 2) discusses the measurement of TFP and describes the data sources in use. Part 3 presents comparisons of TFP levels for total manufacturing and for individual industries within manufacturing. Part 4 examines changes in capital intensity both in the aggregate and in individual industries. Part 5 provides a decomposition of the growth of labor productivity into an element attributable to technological change and another attributable to rising capital intensity. Section 4.6 provides further evidence on the relation between labor productivity growth, TFP growth, and the change in capital intensity in a regression framework. The last part offers some concluding remarks and considers several implications of our findings.

4.2 The Measurement of Total Factor Productivity and Data Sources

Because of the nature of the available data, the total factor productivity (TFP) index is measured as the ratio of a sector's value added (Y) to a weighted average of employment (L) and gross capital stock (K):

$$\text{TFP} = Y/[\alpha L + (1 - \alpha)K], \tag{4.1}$$

where α is the wage share. Two different wage shares are used for each industry: (1) individual country averages of the ratio of wages to value added over the full period in each industry; and (2) the mean over all the countries of the individual country wage shares for each industry, which will be called "the international average."[2] The TFP index is normalized so that the U.S. TFP index in 1963 equals 1.0 in each industry. The proper choice between the wage share figures is debatable; hence we report results for the two choices.

We use two different data bases. The first, which we call the Dollar-Wolff data base, is assembled from a variety of sources and includes information on employment, value added, wages, and gross capital stock. The data are available for nine countries: Belgium, Canada, France, Federal Republic of Germany (Germany, for short), Italy, Japan, the Netherlands, the United Kingdom, and the United States. Because of differences in data classification schemes from the various sources, we aggregated the data to twelve industries: ferrous and nonferrous metals (13);[3] nonmetallic minerals and products (15); chemicals (17); (finished) metal products, excluding machinery and transportation (19); machinery (21 and 23); electrical goods (25); transport equipment (28); food, beverages, and tobacco (36); textiles, clothing, footwear, and leather (42); paper and printing (47); rubber and plastic products (49); and other industries (48).

Data on output, employment and labor compensation are taken from the United Nations *Yearbook of Industrial Statistics* for various years. Our output measure is value added, which is reported in current prices, denominated in domestic currency.[4] We use the GNP deflator of each country to convert output values of different years into 1983 prices, and then apply the PPP index calculated by OECD to convert all output values into 1983 U.S. dollars.[5] Our labor input measure is employment.[6] Our capital stock data for the EEC countries come from Eurostat worksheets, for Canada from Statistics Canada worksheets and Statistics Canada (1987), for Japan from the Japan Economic Planning Agency (1988), and for the United States from Musgrave (1986a, 1986b).[7] Only gross capital stock data are available for the nine countries.[8]

The second data source is the OECD International Sectoral Database on Microcomputer Diskette (referred to hereafter simply as the "OECD data base"). This contains data for fourteen countries, including the nine listed above plus Australia, Denmark, Finland, Norway, and Sweden, and for nine manufacturing industries: (1) food, beverages, and tobacco; (2) textiles; (3) wood and wood products; (4) paper, printing, and publishing; (5) chemicals; (6) nonmetal mineral products; (7) basic metal products; (8) machinery and equipment; and (9) other manufactured products. The data set covers the period from 1960 to 1986, although the period of greatest data availability is from 1970 to 1985. The data consist of GDP, already calculated in 1980 U.S. dollar equivalents, total employment, number of employees, compensation of employees, and gross capital stock, already measured in 1980 U.S. dollars. Calculations of productivity were performed using both the number of employees and total employment (the sum of the number of employees and the number of self-employed). Since self-employment is relatively unimportant in manufacturing, the results from the two sets of calculations are almost identical, and we report the results only for the number of employees.

4.3 TFP Comparisons

Table 4.1 shows TFP levels for the whole manufacturing sector for selected years over the period 1963–85. Although the United States has maintained its lead in TFP for the manufacturing sector as a whole, there is strong evidence that other countries have been catching up. Using the Dollar-Wolff data base and own country factor shares, the unweighted average of TFP levels of other countries increased from 61% of the U.S. level in 1963 to 75% in 1982. In fact, every country except Canada gained relative to the United States over the period, with the largest relative gains made by the United Kingdom and Belgium. The coefficient of variation, a measure of intercountry dispersion, declined from 0.24 in 1963 to 0.15 in 1982. The ratio of maximum to minimum TFP levels fell from 2.16 to 1.58 over the same period.

Because of data availability, the sample of countries in the preceding calculation changed over the period. We therefore also show the same set of summary statistics for two constant sample sets of countries (set B and C of panels I and II). The pattern is similar, as are the summary statistics. We also show the same set of results for TFP measures based on international average factor shares (panel II). Here, again, the summary statistics are almost identical.

Most of the convergence occurred by the early 1970s. In 1973, the coefficient of variation in TFP levels was 0.15. The unweighted average of TFP levels of other countries relative to the United States was 0.73, and the ratio of maximum to minimum TFP was 1.63.

Another point of interest is that the dispersion in labor productivity was larger than that of TFP in the early 1960s, but its rate of convergence was

Table 4.1
Total factor productivity (TFP) levels in total manufacturing relative to the United States, 1963–85
(index, U.S. = 100)

I. *Country-specific wage shares*[a]

	Dollar-Wolff data base						OECD data base		
	1963	1967	1970	1973	1979	1982	1970	1979	1985
Australia	—	—	—	—	—	—	81	79	76
Belgium	46	47	61	66	63	66	63	78	81
Canada	68	65	69	72	72	—	81	77	71
Denmark	—	—	—	—	—	—	56	62	59
Finland	—	—	—	—	—	—	61	59	61
France	69	71	84	67	72	80	79	84	75
Germany	—	74	90	78	78	87	84	87	81
Italy	—	47	52	62	60	63	83	85	82
Japan	—	74	92	80	77	88	75	79	86
Netherlands	67	69	85	87	78	69	66	69	68
Norway	—	—	—	—	—	—	77	67	63
Sweden	—	—	—	—	—	—	74	66	65
United Kingdom	56	—	65	74	70	73	66	63	65
United States	100	100	100	100	100	100	100	100	100
A. *Summary statistics based on available data only*									
Coefficient of variation	.24	.23	.20	.15	.14	.15	.15	.15	.15
Maximum/minimum	2.16	2.14	1.92	1.63	1.66	1.58	1.78	1.68	1.70
Unweighted average (excluding U.S.)	61	64	75	73	71	75	73	74	72
Coefficient of variation (TFPU)	.24	.21	.19	.14	.13	.15			
B. *Summary statistics based on data for Belgium, Canada, France, Germany (FRG), Japan, the Netherlands, and the United States*									
Coefficient of variation		.20	.15	.14	.14				
Unweighted average (excluding U.S.)		67	80	75	73				
C. *Summary statistics based on data for Belgium, France, Germany (FGR), Italy, Japan, the Netherlands, and the United States*									
Coefficient of variation		.25	.20	.16	.16	.16			
Unweighted average (excluding U.S.)		63	77	73	71	76			

Table 4.1 (continued)

II. *International average wage shares*

	Dollar-Wolff data base						OECD data base		
	1963	1967	1970	1973	1979	1982	1970	1979	1985
Australia	—	—	—	—	—	—	81	80	78
Belgium	49	48	62	65	60	62	64	76	78
Canada	67	64	67	70	69	—	81	77	71
Denmark	—	—	—	—	—	—	57	62	59
Finland	—	—	—	—	—	—	61	61	63
France	69	71	83	67	71	79	79	85	79
Germany	—	74	90	78	78	87	83	88	84
Italy	—	49	55	65	64	68	84	87	86
Japan	—	68	88	80	79	92	68	82	93
Netherlands	68	69	84	85	76	67	66	68	67
Norway	—	—	—	—	—	—	77	66	62
Sweden	—	—	—	—	—	—	72	62	61
United Kingdom	58	—	65	74	69	70	68	64	64
United States	100	100	100	100	100	100	100	100	100
A. *Summary statistics based on available data only*									
Coefficient of variation	.23	.23	.19	.14	.15	.16	.15	.15	.16
Maximum/minimum	2.05	2.09	1.83	1.54	1.66	1.62	1.75	1.65	1.71
Unweighted average (excluding U.S.)	62	63	74	73	71	75	72	74	73
B. *Summary statistics based on data for Belgium, Canada, France, Germany (FRG), Japan, the Netherlands, and the United States*									
Coefficient of variation		.20	.15	.15	.15				
Unweighted average (excluding U.S.)		66	79	74	72				
C. *Summary statistics based on data for Belgium, France, Germany (FGR), Italy, Japan, the Netherlands, and the United States*									
Coefficient of variation		.24	.19	.16	.16	.17			
Unweighted average (excluding U.S.)		63	77	73	71	76			

a. See the Appendix for details on data availability and the years used to calculate the wage shares in each country.

greater than that of TFP. For the same sample of nine countries in the Dollar-Wolff data base, the coefficient of variation of labor productivity fell from 0.37 in 1963 to 0.15 in 1982, the unweighted average of labor productivity levels relative to the United States increased from 0.52 to 0.73, and the ratio of maximum to minimum labor productivity declined from 2.9 to 1.7. By 1982 the dispersion in labor productivity levels was almost identical to that of TFP.[9]

The same pattern is seen for individual industries, as shown in table 4.2. On the basis of the Dollar-Wolff data base, convergence, as indicated by the decline in the coefficient of variation, occurred in every industry between 1967 and 1979. Moreover, the average TFP level of other countries relative to the United States increased in 9 of the 12 industries in this classification scheme. However, the average dispersion of TFP in manufacturing industries (the unweighted average of the coefficient of variation) was still substantially greater than the degree of dispersion in the total manufacturing sector (0.34 versus 0.23 in 1967, and 0.26 versus 0.15 in 1985).

The industries have again been divided into three groups—heavy, medium, and light—on the basis of the unweighted average of the capital-labor ratios among the relevant group of countries.[10] Convergence was strongest among heavy industries, in which the (unweighted) average coefficient of variation of industries within this group fell by almost half over the 1967–79 period, according to the Dollar-Wolff data, and by 20% between 1970 and 1985, according to the OECD data. The average TFP level of the other countries exceeded that of the United States by 1979, according to the first data set, and reached 87% of the U.S. level by 1985, according to the second.

Among medium and light industries, by the first data set, the average coefficient of variation fell by about a third between 1967 and 1979, and the average productivity of the other countries pulled to about 70% of the U.S. level. According to the OECD data, dispersion remained unchanged among both medium and light industries between 1970 and 1985. By 1985 the dispersion of TFP levels within the three groups of industries was almost equal, whereas it was considerably higher among heavy industries in 1967. This finding is an interesting contrast to our previous chapter, where we found that convergence in labor productivity was strongest among light industries and weakest in heavy industries, and that by 1982 there was considerably more dispersion among heavy industries than among medium or light ones.

The leading country in terms of TFP level is also indicated for each industry in table 4.2. In the Dollar-Wolff data base, the United States led in 10 of the 12 industries in 1967 and 10 in 1979. According to the OECD data, the United States led in 4 of the 9 OECD industries in 1970 and 5 in 1985. In chapter 3 we found that, in terms of labor productivity, the United States led in virtually all of the 28 sampled industries in 1963, but in only 10 of the 28 in 1982. Seven countries, besides the United States, held the lead in at least one industry in 1982. Part of the reason for the difference in results is that the sample of countries used in this chapter is different and the industry classifications are more aggregated than in the previous chapter. However, the major explanation, as we shall see below, is that other countries have not only caught up to but surpassed the United States in terms of capital intensity.

The case of Japan merits special attention. In the Dollar-Wolff data set, its TFP level converged on that of the United States in every industry between 1965 and 1982, and in metals (13) and nonmetallic minerals (15) its TFP surpassed that of the United States (see table 4.2).[11] The catch-up was strongest in the heavy industries, where the ratio of the unweighted average of the TFP levels to that of the United States was 1.05 in 1982; second strongest in the medium industries, where the ratio was 0.88; and weakest in the light industries, where the ratio was 0.83. This is in accord with our earlier findings regarding labor productivity. However, most of the catch-up had been achieved by the early 1970s, and, in both data sets, Japanese technology actually *declined* relative to the United States in several industries over the ensuing decade.

Productivity movements are sensitive to business cycle fluctuations. There is a sizable literature on the proper techniques to use to adjust output and input measures for business cycle changes. Because of data availability, we use capacity utilization indices to adjust our TFP measures. Our new measure is:

$$\text{TFPU} = Y/[\alpha L + (1 - \alpha)uK], \tag{4.1'}$$

where u is the capacity utilization rate. Unfortunately, we do not have data on capacity utilization by individual industry for each of the countries, so that we must rely on the utilization index for the whole manufacturing sector to compute our adjusted TFP index. Data on utilization rates are from OECD, *Main Economic Indicators, 1960–1979*, and Coe and Holtham (1983). Results for the coefficient of variation of utilization corrected total factor productivity (TFPU) are almost identical to unadjusted TFP (see table 4.1).

Table 4.2
Indices of total factor productivity (TFP) convergence by manufacturing industry, 1967–85

	Coefficient of variation			Average TFP relative to U.S. TFP (leader in parentheses)		
I. *Dollar-Wolff data base*[a]	1967	1972	1979	1967	1972	1979
Heavy industries[b]	.45	.38	.24	.70	.90	.84 (Germany)
Ferrous and nonferrous metals	.29	.25	.20	.63	.73	.70 (U.S.)
Chemicals	.47	.28	.23	.45	.60	.63 (U.S.)
Nonmetallic minerals	.58	.61	.30	1.03	1.37	1.20 (Nether.)
Medium industries[b]	.32	.30	.24	.66	.67	.70 (U.S.)
Machinery	.22	.21	.21	.74	.77	.75 (Canada)
Rubber and plastics	.51	.43	.35	.55	.52	.64 (U.S.)
Paper and printing	.28	.31	.18	.65	.71	.73 (U.S.)
Transport equipment	.26	.26	.22	.71	.69	.67 (U.S.)
Light industries[b]	.33	.28	.23	.60	.68	.69 (U.S.)
Metal products	.45	.29	.28	.49	.70	.66 (U.S.)
Other industries	.32	.38	.28	.73	.60	.64 (U.S.)
Textiles	.28	.25	.23	.56	.62	.68 (U.S.)
Electrical goods	.26	.20	.14	.60	.78	.77 (U.S.)
Food, beverages, tobacco	.20	.18	.17	.74	.74	.70 (U.S.)
All manufacturing[b]	.34	.30	.27	.66	.74	.73 (U.S.)
II. *OECD data base*[c]	1970	1979	1985	1970	1979	1985
Heavy industries[b]	.30	.27	.24	.71	.77	.87 (Japan)
Basic metals	.42	.37	.27	.73	.83	1.05 (Japan)
Chemicals	.31	.26	.20	.69	.76	.93 (Germany)
Nonmetallic minerals	.18	.18	.24	.70	.71	.64 (U.S.)
Medium industries[b]	.22	.22	.23	.73	.73	.71 (U.S)
Machinery and equipment	.24	.21	.20	.65	.67	.63 (U.S.)
Paper, printing, publishing	.17	.21	.24	.71	.72	.74 (Italy)
Food, beverages, tobacco	.25	.24	.25	.83	.81	.75 (Italy)
Light industries[b]	.20	.23	.22	.88	.78	.72 (U.S.)
Textiles	.20	.21	.20	.88	.77	.71 (U.S.)
Wood and wood products	.20	.25	.24	.87	.78	.73 (Italy)
Other industries	.38	.28	.47	.65	.63	.42 (U.S.)
All manufacturing[b]	.26	.24	.26	.75	.74	.73 (U.S.)

Table 4.2 (continued)

	Japanese TFP relative to U.S. TFP		
I. *Dollar-Wolff data base*	1965	1972	1982
Heavy industries	.88	.97	1.05
Ferrous and nonferrous metals	.58	.79	1.15
Chemicals	.78	.88	.94
Nonmetallic minerals	—	—	1.07
Medium industries	.84	.90	.88
Machinery	.66	.90	.96
Rubber and plastics	—	—	—
Paper and printing	.85	1.13	.90
Transport equipment	.64	.75	.77
Light industries	.74	.79	.83
Metal products	.70	.94	.91
Other industries	—	.41	.63
Textiles	.57	.74	.81
Electrical goods	.57	.91	.97
Food, beverages, tobacco	.68	.89	.87
II. *OECD data base*	1970	1979	1985
Heavy industries	1.04	1.10	1.16
Base metals	1.14	1.39	1.68
Chemicals	.99	1.05	1.20
Nonmetallic minerals	.65	.67	.61
Medium industries	.70	.69	.67
Machinery and equipment	.44	.58	.71
Paper, printing, publishing	.54	.47	.45
Food, beverages, tobacco	1.13	1.09	.85
Light industries			
Textiles	.54	.43	.48
Wood and wood products			
Other industries	.76	.67	.59

TFP calculations are based on country-specific wage shares.
a. Missing data are as follows: Ferrous and nonferrous metals (the Netherlands; the United Kingdom in 1967); chemicals (the Netherlands in 1967, 1979; the United Kingdom in 1967, 1972); nonmetallic minerals (Japan in 1967, 1972; the United Kingdom in 1967); machinery (Belgium; the Netherlands; the United Kingdom in 1967); rubber and plastics (Japan; the Netherlands; the United Kingdom in 1967); paper and printing (the United Kingdom in 1967, 1972); transport equipment (Belgium; the United Kingdom in 1967); metal products (Belgium; the Netherlands in 1972; the United Kingdom in 1967, 1972); other industries (the United Kingdom in 1967); textiles (the United Kingdom in 1967, 1972); electrical goods (Belgium; the United Kingdom in 1967); and food, beverages, tobacco (the United Kingdom in 1967).
b. Unweighted average of industries within group.
c. Missing data are as follows: Australia and Finland (all years and industries); and the Netherlands (all industries, 1985). Wood and wood products includes only Canada, Denmark, Germany, Italy, Norway, Sweden, and the United States.

4.4 Capital Intensity in the Aggregate and by Industry

As we noted in the introduction, recent studies have documented a convergence in aggregate, economy-wide capital-labor ratios among industrialized countries over the postwar period. We next look at the extent to which the convergence in aggregate capital-labor ratios has been translated into a convergence in capital-labor ratios in individual industries. Because the summary statistics are very sensitive to the sample of countries chosen, we show results only for constant sample sets of countries (see table 4.3). The choice of countries is based on data availability. For each industry, we choose the set of countries that has employment and capital stock data for the maximum number of years.

There is strong evidence of convergence in capital intensity among the group of nine countries in the Dollar-Wolff data base. The coefficient of variation fell from 0.36 to 0.20, while the ratio of maximum to minimum capital-labor ratio fell from 3.4 to 1.8. For the whole manufacturing sector, the (unweighted) average capital-labor ratio among countries other than the United States increased from three-fourths of the U.S. level in 1965 to almost perfect equality by 1983. Catch-up in capital intensity was much stronger than in TFP (in 1985 the average TFP of other countries was only 72% that of the United States). Every country gained on the United States in terms of capital intensity over the 1963–83 period, and countries with lower initial capital endowments gained more (the correlation coefficient between the 1965 capital-labor ratio and the annual rate of growth of the capital-labor ratio over the 1965–83 period was −0.85 among the nine countries). The aggregate capital-labor ratio of Japan, in particular, increased from 40% of the U.S. level in 1965 to 83% in 1983.[12] Aggregate capital stock data indicate that Canada was first in 1963 and the United States second.[13] In 1983 Canada still ranked first, the Netherlands was second, Italy was third, and the United States was fourth, with Belgium a close fifth.

As in the case of TFP, most of the convergence was achieved by the mid-1970s. In 1974 the coefficient of variation for total manufacturing (based on the aggregate data) was 0.23, and the unweighted average capital-labor ratio among other countries had climbed to 91% that of the United States. The OECD data confirm this result. The dispersion of capital-labor ratios among the fourteen countries in this sample reached a minimum in 1975, and then remained relatively unchanged over the next ten years. In 1985 the leading country in terms of capital intensity was the

Table 4.3
Measures of convergence in capital-labor ratios by industry, 1965–85

	Average capital-labor ratio relative to U.S.				Coefficient of variation of capital-labor ratios			
I. *Dollar-Wolff data base*[a]	1965	1972	1979	1983	1965	1972	1979	1983
Heavy industries[b]	.59	.66	.76	.68	.47	.37	.36	.36
Ferrous and nonferrous metals	.83	.72	.92	.72	.43	.45	.43	.37
Chemicals	.62	.83[e]	.83	.85	.40	.25[e]	.34	.35
Nonmetallic minerals	.34[d]	.43	.52	.47[g]	.57[d]	.41	.30	.35[g]
Medium industries[b]	.74	.83	.95	.99	.39	.28	.22	.25
Machinery	.47	.67[e]	.83	.70	.40	.19[e]	.13	.20
Rubber and plastics	.90	.97	1.05	1.25	.17	.13	.15	.21
Paper and printing	.83	.94[e]	1.05	1.12	.71	.59[e]	.40	.39
Transport equipment	.78	.75	.87	.88	.29	.21	.18	.18
Light industries[b]	.85	1.07	1.21	1.26	.35	.44	.31	.33
Metal products	.69	.94[e]	.98	.93	.49	.51[e]	.43	.37
Other industries	1.08	1.44	1.40	1.60	.29	.50	.29	.29
Textiles	1.15	1.42[f]	1.62	1.80	.23	.27[f]	.38	.47
Electrical goods	.82	.76	.89	.84	.31	.36	.27	.26
Food, beverages, tobacco	.82	.95	1.05	1.03	.35	.30	.26	.24
All manufacturing[b]	.75	.88	1.00	1.00	.39	.36	.29	.30
II. *OECD data base*[c]		1970	1979	1985		1970	1979	1985
Heavy industries[b]		.88	1.04	1.02		.50	.45	.46
Basic metals		.60	.68	.56		.49	.42	.42
Chemicals		.86	1.02	.97		.21	.27	.28
Nonmetallic minerals		1.19	1.42	1.54		.82	.67	.69
Medium industries[b]		1.10	1.26	1.26		.36	.31	.29
Machinery and equipment		1.05	1.25	1.13		.33	.26	.21
Paper, printing, publishing		1.19	1.37	1.56		.53	.45	.46
Food, beverages, tobacco		1.06	1.17	1.10		.24	.22	.22
Light industries[b]		1.44	1.64	1.79		.29	.32	.31
Textiles		1.37	1.73	1.72		.25	.35	.26
Wood and wood products		1.52	1.55	1.86		.35	.30	.38
Other industries		1.12	1.23	1.24		.56	.50	.59
All manufacturing[b]		1.11	1.27	1.30		.41	.38	.39

a. Missing data are as follows: Ferrous and nonferrous metals (the Netherlands and Italy); chemicals (the Netherlands and Italy); nonmetallic minerals (Canada and Japan); machinery (includes only Canada, France, Germany, Japan, the United Kingdom, the United States); rubber and plastics (includes only Belgium, Canada, France, Germany, the United Kingdom, the United States); paper and printing (Italy); transport equipment (Belgium and Italy); metal products (Belgium and Italy); other industries (Italy); textiles (Italy); electrical goods (Belgium and Italy); food, beverages, and tobacco (Italy); total manufacturing (Italy).

b. Unweighted average of industries within group.

c. Missing data are as follows: Australia and Finland (all years and industries); and the Netherlands (all industries, 1985). Wood and wood products includes only Canada, Denmark, Germany, Italy, Norway, and the United States.

d. 1967.

e. 1973.

f. 1974.

g. 1982.

Netherlands, followed by Canada, Sweden, Belgium, and Norway. The United States ranked eighth out of fourteen.

The same pattern is also seen for individual industries. Between 1965 and 1983, according to the Dollar-Wolff data, the (unweighted) average capital-labor ratio in the eight countries relative to the United States increased in 11 of the 12 industries; the coefficient of variation fell in 9 of the 12 industries and remained the same in one; and the ratio of maximum to minimum capital-labor ratio fell in 9 of the 12 and in 2 remained almost unchanged. By 1983 the other countries were, on average, considerably ahead of the United States in capital intensity in the light industries,[14] at virtual parity with the United States in the medium industries; but still rather far behind the United States in the heavy industries. The disparity in capital-labor ratios was greatest among heavy industries and smallest among medium industries.[15]

As with TFP, the dispersion of capital-labor ratios is more marked in individual industries than in the aggregate. This result emerges from a comparison between the unweighted average coefficient of variation among the various industries with that of the aggregate data: 0.30 versus 0.20 in 1983 on the basis of the Dollar-Wolff data and 0.39 versus 0.20 in 1985 on the basis of the OECD data. This finding is somewhat surprising. In a comparison between a developed and developing country, one generally finds capital-labor ratios more similar in industries than in the aggregate. A recent study of South Korea and West Germany, for instance, found that differences in capital-labor ratios were modest at the industry level, though Germany had a far higher aggregate ratio (Dollar 1991). The reason for this is that, compared to South Korea, Germany's employment mix is shifted toward capital-intensive industries. This pattern is predicted by the Heckscher-Ohlin model of international trade. Given the capital abundance of the United States in the early postwar period, we expected to find a similar relationship between the United States at that time and the other OECD countries: greater dispersion of capital-labor ratios in the aggregate than within industries. However, such was not the case.

We can address this issue more formally. Define:

s_i^h country h's employment in industry i as a proportion of country h's total employment;

κ_i^h ratio of country h's capital-labor ratio to U.S. capital-labor ratio in industry i,

where we have standardized the industry capital-labor ratios in each country by expressing them as ratios to the U.S. levels. Then:

$$\kappa^h = \Sigma_i s_i^h \kappa_i^h, \tag{4.2}$$

where κ^h is country h's capital-labor ratio in all manufacturing. The international average employment shares by industry and the international average capital intensity of an industry are calculated as weighted averages:

$$\bar{s}_i = \Sigma_h L_i^h / [\Sigma_h \Sigma_i L_i^h] \tag{4.3}$$

and

$$\bar{\kappa}_i = \Sigma_h r_i^h \kappa_i^h, \tag{4.4}$$

where $r_i^h \equiv L_i^h / \Sigma_i L_i^h$. In both cases, define the international average aggregate capital-labor ratio as:

$$\bar{k} = \Sigma_i \bar{s}_i \bar{\kappa}_i. \tag{4.5}$$

Then the deviation of a country's aggregate capital labor ratio from the international average capital-labor ratio is given by:

$$\text{DEV}(\kappa^h) \equiv \kappa^h - \bar{\kappa} = \Sigma_i s_i^h \,\text{DEV}(\kappa_i^h) + \Sigma_i \bar{\kappa}_i \,\text{DEV}(s_i^h). \tag{4.6}$$

where $\text{DEV}(\kappa_i^h) \equiv \kappa_i^h - \bar{\kappa}_i$ and indicates the deviation of industry i's capital-labor ratio in country h from the international average for industry i, and $\text{DEV}(s_i^h) \equiv s_i^h - \bar{s}_i$ and indicates the difference between industry i's employment share in country h from the international average for industry i. The first term on the right-hand side of (4.6) reflects the relative capital intensities of the industries within a country. The second terms reflects the allocation of labor among industries of different capital intensities.

The results of these calculations, shown in panel A of table 4.4, indicate that differences in capital intensity by industry explain almost all of the differences in aggregate capital-labor ratios. This held true for every country except Italy and Japan and for each of three years—1972, 1979, and 1985. Countries with high aggregate capital-labor ratios tend to have higher than average capital-labor ratios in most industries, and conversely.[16]

Another interesting issue is the extent to which convergence in the overall capital-labor ratio among countries has resulted from the convergence of industry employment mix. We can address this issue in a fashion similar to the preceding calculation. From (4.2),

$$\Delta\kappa^h = \Sigma_i s_i^h (\Delta\kappa_i^h) + \Sigma_i (\Delta s_i^h) \kappa_i^h \tag{4.7}$$

where Δ indicates change over time (for example, $\Delta\kappa^h \equiv \kappa_t^h - \kappa_{t-1}^h$). From panel B of table 4.4, we see that almost all the change in aggregate coun-

Table 4.4
Decomposition of country capital-labor ratios into industry-level employment and capital-labor effects

A. *Decomposition of the deviation of country's capital-labor ratio from the international average*[a]

	1972			1979			1985		
	DEV(κ^h)	DEVκ_i^h	DEVs_i^h	DEV(κ^h)	DEVκ_i^h	DEVs_i^h	DEV(κ^h)	DEVκ_i^h	DEVs_i^h
Belgium	5.2	5.4	−0.3	21.6	24.4	−2.8	28.5	32.4	−3.9
Canada	50.3	61.2	−10.9	40.2	37.3	2.8	44.4	42.0	2.4
Denmark	−1.8	−5.7	3.9	9.2	6.7	2.5	−7.1	−9.5	2.4
France	9.9	12.5	−2.6	17.3	20.4	−3.1	23.8	28.4	−4.6
Germany	−8.9	−8.1	−0.8	−11.1	−10.5	−0.6	−15.7	−13.8	−1.8
Italy	20.0	13.4	6.6	9.4	4.4	5.0	8.7	2.1	6.6
Japan	−20.7	−16.6	−4.1	−5.1	−1.8	−3.4	−1.0	2.5	−3.4
Netherlands	35.3	36.9	−1.6	50.4	53.9	−3.5	44.5	49.0	−4.5
Norway	7.0	4.7	2.3	17.4	16.1	1.3	27.7	26.6	1.1
Sweden	54.9	54.2	0.7	65.1	64.5	0.6	59.7	58.7	1.1
United Kingdom	−17.5	−14.2	−3.2	−21.0	−16.6	−4.4	−12.9	−8.4	−4.5
United States	5.6	3.1	2.5	−3.3	−5.4	2.1	−1.8	−4.9	3.1
Average[b]	11.6	12.2	−0.6	15.8	16.1	−0.3	16.6	17.1	−0.5

B. *Decomposition of the change over time in country's capital-labor ratio*[c]

	1972–79			1979–85			1972–85		
	$\Delta\kappa^h$	$\Delta\kappa_i^h$	Δs_i^h	$\Delta\kappa^h$	$\Delta\kappa_i^h$	Δs_i^h	$\Delta\kappa^h$	$\Delta\kappa_i^h$	Δs_i^h
Belgium	22.5	25.3	−2.9	5.4	5.4	0.0	28.1	30.7	−2.6
Canada	26.8	−1.2	28.0	1.9	2.7	−0.8	28.6	1.5	27.1
Denmark	18.7	19.9	−1.2	−17.8	−17.8	−0.0	0.8	2.1	−1.3
France	15.1	16.2	−1.2	5.3	5.1	0.3	20.5	21.3	−0.8
Germany	4.6	6.6	−2.1	−7.8	−6.0	−1.8	−3.3	0.6	−4.0
Italy	−2.2	−1.8	−0.4	−2.5	−2.1	−0.4	−4.4	−3.9	−0.4

Japan	22.8	24.5	−1.6	1.8	2.7	−0.9	23.9	27.2	−3.3
Netherlands	18.1	24.0	−5.9	−12.3	−9.5	−2.9	7.0	14.6	−7.6
Norway	19.7	19.3	0.4	8.2	8.8	−0.6	28.3	28.1	0.2
Sweden	19.4	19.1	0.3	−7.4	−6.8	−0.5	12.9	12.3	0.6
United Kingdom	3.7	5.4	−1.7	7.4	6.6	0.7	10.9	12.0	−1.1
Average[b]	15.4	14.3	1.1	−1.6	−1.0	−0.6	13.9	13.3	0.6

C. *Addendum: Change in country employment distribution* $[\Sigma_i |s_i^h - \bar{s}_i|]$.

	1972	1979	1985
Belgium	.38	.35	.39
Canada	.33	.33	.30
Denmark	.35	.33	.26
France	.28	.26	.30
Germany	.19	.21	.25
Italy	.38	.36	.42
Japan	.40	.39	.40
Netherlands	.33	.40	.46
Norway	.40	.38	.39
Sweden	.29	.29	.27
United Kingdom	.12	.13	.16
United States	.15	.17	.19
Average[b]	.30	.30	.32

Results are based on the OECD data base. For the Netherlands, 1983 is used instead of 1985.

a. The decomposition is based on equation 4.6.

b. Unweighted average.

c. This decomposition is based on equation 4.7. The United States is excluded from this panel, because its capital-labor ratio is used as the base value.

try capital-labor ratios over the 1972–85 period can be attributed to the change in industry capital-labor ratios rather than to changes in employment mixes among industries. This was the case for each country, with the exception of Canada, and for each of the time periods considered—1972–79 and 1979–85.[17] In fact, results from panel C indicate that there was virtually no greater similarity among countries in their employment mixes in 1985 than in 1972.

Finally, it should be noted that in the 1980s, the dispersion of capital-labor ratios in all manufacturing, as measured by the coefficient of variation, was greater than that of TFP levels. This was also true for each of the three industry groups and for the great majority of individual industries. This suggests that technology transfer is relatively easy among industrialized countries and, as a result, the state of technology is becoming very similar among these nations, but that national investment rates, as well as investment rates in particular industries, still display relatively great differences among countries.

4.5 Decomposition of Labor Productivity Growth

We established in the previous chapter that convergence of aggregate labor productivity among industrial countries has resulted from convergence of labor productivity within industries. We next investigate the sources of this labor productivity convergence within individual industries. As shown above, between the early 1960s and the mid-1980s, both TFP and capital-labor ratios have converged toward the U.S. level, although most of this occurred by the early 1970s. The next issue we address is the extent to which the convergence in labor productivity within industries was attributable to the convergence in TFP and to what extent it was a result of the catch-up in capital deepening.

We use a standard growth accounting framework. Formally, assume that for each industry i and country h there is a Cobb-Douglas value-added production function:

$$\text{Ln}\, Y_i^h = \zeta_i^h + \alpha_i \,\text{Ln}\, L_i^h + (1 - \alpha_i)\, \text{Ln}\, K_i^h. \tag{4.8}$$

The parameter ζ_i^h is country-specific and indicates country h's technology level in industry i. The output elasticity of labor in industry i, α_i, is assumed to be the same among countries. If factors are paid their marginal products, then the output elasticity is equal to labor's distributive share. In our study, we will take the cross-country (unweighted) average of labor's share in industry i as our estimate of α_i.

We will use two measures of TFP growth. The first is crude TFP growth, defined as the time derivative of equation 4.1. The second measure of TFP growth is the Divisia index, defined as

$$\rho_i^h = \hat{Y}_i^h - \alpha_i \hat{L}_i^h - (1 - \alpha_i)\hat{K}_i^h, \tag{4.9}$$

where a hat ($\hat{}$) denotes the time derivative or relative rate of change. Consistent with this measure of TFP growth is a second method of calculating TFP level, often referred to as the translog index of TFP:

$$\text{Ln}\,\text{TFP}_i^h = \text{Ln}\,Y_i^h - \alpha_i\,\text{Ln}\,L_i^h - (1 - \alpha_i)\,\text{Ln}\,K_i^h. \tag{4.10}$$

Comparison of equation 4.10 with equation 4.8 reveals that this measure of TFP is implicitly based on a Cobb-Douglas form for the production function.

We can now formally decompose the convergence of labor productivity growth into a component attributable to technology convergence and a part attributable to convergence in capital-labor ratios. Let the United States be the benchmark country, and define:

π_i^h ratio of country *h*'s labor productivity to U.S. labor productivity in industry *i*;

τ_i^h ratio of country *h*'s technology level to U.S. technology level in industry *i*;

and, as before,

κ_i^h ratio of country *h*'s capital-labor ratio to U.S. capital-labor ratio in industry *i*.

Equations 4.8 and 4.10 then imply that

$$\text{Ln}\,\pi_i^h = \text{Ln}\,\tau_i^h + (1 - \alpha_i)\,\text{Ln}\,\kappa_i^h. \tag{4.11}$$

Differentiating this with respect to time yields

$$\hat{\pi}_i^h = \hat{\tau}_i^h + (1 - \alpha_i)\hat{\kappa}_i^h. \tag{4.12}$$

Hence, the convergence of country *h*'s labor productivity in industry *i* on the U.S. level can be decomposed into the convergence of technology and the convergence of capital-labor ratios.

Results for equation 4.12 are shown in table 4.5 for the translog index of TFP.[18] During the period 1963–72, most of the catch-up in labor productivity is attributed to the catch-up in technological capabilities. Though there is some variability among countries, the unweighted cross-country

Table 4.5
Decomposition of labor productivity convergence into a technology and capital-intensity component, 1963–72 and 1970–85
(annual rates of growth in percent)

	1963–72			1970–85		
	LPROD ($\hat{\pi}_i^h$)	TFP ($\hat{t}_i^h$)	K/L [$(1-\alpha_i)\hat{\kappa}_i^h$]	LPROD ($\hat{\pi}_i^h$)	TFP ($\hat{t}_i^h$)	K/L [$(1-\alpha_i)\hat{\kappa}_i^h$]
A. *Total manufacturing by country*						
Australia	—	—	—	−0.03	−0.23	0.20
Belgium	—	—	—	2.41	1.62	0.78
Canada	0.61	0.50	0.11	−0.53	−0.55	0.02
Denmark	—	—	—	0.09	−0.01	0.10
Finland	—	—	—	0.42	0.36	0.06
France	0.51	−0.30	0.81	0.55	0.12	0.42
Germany	2.23	1.38	0.85	0.00	−0.15	0.15
Italy	0.29	1.87	−1.58	0.17	0.24	−0.06
Japan	6.82	3.20	3.62	2.74	1.77	0.97
Netherlands	—	—	—	1.70	0.99	0.71
Norway	—	—	—	−0.85	−1.32	0.46
Sweden	—	—	—	−0.53	−0.78	0.25
United Kingdom	2.11	1.49	0.61	−0.05	−0.61	0.55
B. *Unweighted industry average across countries*[a]						
All manufacturing	2.09	1.36	0.74	0.47	0.11	0.35
Heavy industry	2.90	2.43	0.47	1.93	1.62	0.31
Basic metals	3.42	3.87	−0.46	2.78	2.95	−0.17
Chemicals	4.32	2.72	1.60	2.22	1.86	0.36
Minerals	4.71	1.77	2.94	0.53	−0.17	0.71
Medium industry	0.64	0.82	−0.18	0.07	−0.27	0.34
Machinery	0.86	−0.53	1.39	0.08	−0.15	0.23
Rubber, plastics	0.70	1.09	−0.39	—	—	—
Paper, printing	1.62	0.81	0.82	0.88	0.32	0.56
Transport equipment	1.87	2.37	−0.49	—	—	—
Food, beverages, tobacco	1.70	0.27	1.43	−0.49	−0.80	0.31
Light industry	1.71	1.43	0.28	−0.40	−0.79	0.39
Metal products	3.48	2.38	1.10			
Textiles	1.34	0.28	1.06	−0.01	−0.57	0.56
Electrical goods	2.06	3.65	−1.59			
Wood products				−0.29	−0.69	0.40
Other industry	0.28	−1.26	1.53	−2.00	−2.52	0.52

The decomposition is based on equation 4.12. The translog index of TFP growth is used. Calculations for 1963–72 are based on the Dollar-Wolff data base and those for 1970–85 are based on the OECD data base. International average wage shares are used. Periods are as indicated in the table, with the following exceptions: for Germany, Italy, Japan, and the Netherlands, 1965–72 is used in place of 1963–72; for the United Kingdom, 1963–73 is used in place of 1963–72; and for the Netherlands, 1970–83 is used in place of 1970–85. See the Appendix for additional details on data availability.

a. Unweighted average among countries with available data in each industry or industry group.

average indicates that about two-thirds of labor productivity convergence was attributable to technology transfer and the remaining third to increasing capital intensity. Japan's results are interesting. They indicate that a little over half of their labor productivity convergence came from increasing capital intensity. There are also differences among individual industries. However, for the aggregate heavy, medium, and light industries, the preponderance of the catch-up was achieved from convergence in technology.

In contrast, between 1970 and 1985 labor productivity catch-up toward the United States was achieved primarily through increasing capital intensity (three-fourths on the basis of the unweighted cross-country average). Though there were both country and industry differences, this result held for 8 of the 13 countries and for 7 of the 9 industries. Japan was, again, an exception, since about two-thirds of its labor productivity convergence to the United States was achieved through technology catch-up. The heavy industries, particularly basic (ferrous and nonferrous) metals and chemicals, were another exception, for which about four-fifths of the labor productivity convergence was attributable to technology transfer.

Our calculations thus far beg the question of whether there is any connection between technology catch-up and the rate of capital accumulation in a country. To address this issue, we now turn to regression analysis.

4.6 Regression Analysis

In this section we use a regression framework to test two hypotheses concerning technology convergence. The first can be labeled the "catch-up hypothesis," which states simply that industries and countries that lagged farthest behind the United States in technological sophistication in the 1960s had the most opportunities to imitate and purchase advanced technology, and hence should exhibit the fastest rate of technology convergence. Taking each industry in each country as an observation, this hypothesis implies that the rate of growth of τ_i^h between the mid-1960s and the mid-1980s is inversely correlated with the level of τ_i^h at the beginning of the period. Our approach provides a large number of observations to test this hypothesis.

A second hypothesis is that there are positive interactions between capital accumulation and technological advance. In particular, it is likely that substantial capital accumulation is necessary to put new inventions into practice and to effect their widespread employment. This association is often referred to as the "embodiment effect," since it implies that at least some technological innovation is embodied in capital. It is also consistent with the "vintage effect," which states that new capital is more productive than old capital per (constant) dollar of expenditure. If the capital stock data do not correct for vintage effects, then this hypothesis suggests that the rate of growth of τ_i^h will be positively correlated with the rate of growth of κ_i^h. Again, we can treat each industry in each country as an observation to test this hypothesis.

Both hypotheses can be tested using the following regression specification:

$$\hat{\tau}_{it}^h = b_0 + b_1 \tau_{it}^h + b_2 \hat{\kappa}_{it_h}^h + \Sigma c_h \,\text{CNTYDUM}_i^h + \Sigma d_i \,\text{INDDUM}_i + \varepsilon_t^h, \tag{4.13}$$

where τ_{it}^h is country h's (translog) TFP relative to the United States at the start of each period, CNTYDUM^h is a dummy variable for each country h (except the United States), INDDUM$_i$ is an industry dummy variable (excluding the other industry category), and ε is a stochastic error term. Country and industry dummy variables are included to control for country-specific effects, such as the degree of trade openness, culture, and government policy; and industry-specific effects, such as market structure and diffusion patterns for new technology. Both two-year and three-year averages are used for the growth variables to reduce random noise. The regression is performed on both the Dollar-Wolff data base and the OECD data base. For the former, we introduce an additional dummy variable, D6372, defined as unity on or before 1972 and zero thereafter, which interacts with κ_i^h to control for period effects. The United States is excluded from this regression equation, since the value of the dependent variable is always unity.

The results, shown in table 4.6, confirm the catch-up hypothesis, showing a highly significant inverse relation between the rate of TFP convergence by industry and country and its initial TFP level, relative to the United States. The results on the vintage hypothesis are interesting. The term κ_i^h has a negative and significant coefficient for the regressions performed on the OECD data base over the period 1970–85; the term also has a negative coefficient in the Dollar-Wolff data base, but the interactive term κ_i^h. D6372 is positive and highly significant. These results suggest the likelihood that the embodiment effect was important during the 1963–72 period, when productivity convergence was very strong among OECD countries, but inoperative between the mid-1970s and the mid-1980s. Indeed, the negative sign of the coefficient suggests that adjustment costs associated with the introduction of new capital equipment may actually

Table 4.6
Regression of relative productivity growth ($\hat{\tau}_{it}^h$) on relative productivity level and growth in relative capital intensity

Dependent variable	Independent Variables: Constant	τ_{it}^h	$\hat{\kappa}_{it}^h$	$\hat{\kappa}_{it}^h \cdot$ D6372	R^2	Adj. R^2	Std. err. of reg.	Sample size
A. *OECD data base,* 1970–85								
Two-year averages								
$\hat{\tau}_{it}^h$	0.0097	−0.057**	−0.227**		0.18	0.15	0.055	643
	(0.4)	(4.6)	(5.7)					
Three-year averages								
$\hat{\tau}_{it}^h$	0.0006	−0.042**	−0.194**		0.25	0.21	0.039	457
	(1.0)	(4.0)	(4.9)					
B. *Dollar-Wolff data base,* 1963–83								
Two-year averages								
$\hat{\tau}_{it}^h$	0.054**	−0.048**	−0.673**	0.490**	0.21	0.18	0.065	694
	(4.2)	(5.8)	(9.9)	(6.3)				
Three-year averages								
$\hat{\tau}_{it}^h$	0.066**	−0.061**	−0.646**	0.455**	0.30	0.26	0.047	460
	(5.6)	(7.8)	(8.4)	(6.1)				

T-ratios are shown in parentheses below the coefficient estimates. Country and industry dummy variables are included in the specification (results not shown). The observations are based on two- or three-year averages, as indicated. Key:

τ_i^h ratio of country *h*'s technology level to U.S. technology level in industry *i* at the beginning of the period.

$\hat{\tau}_{it}^h$ annual rate of growth of τ_i^h.

$\hat{\kappa}_i^h$ annual rate of change of ratio of country *h*'s capital-labor ratio to U.S. capital-labor ratio in industry *i*.

D6273: dummy variable, defined as one for 1963–72 and zero thereafter.

** significant at the 1% level.

inhibit productivity growth once an industry has reached the technological frontier.[19]

4.7 Concluding Remarks

The U.S. aggregate labor productivity advantage in the early 1960s was rooted in superior labor productivity in virtually all industries. The United States had higher TFP values than other OECD countries in each industry, and also employed more capital per worker in each industry. It is interesting that the U.S. capital abundance at that time was reflected almost totally in the use of more capital per worker in industries. U.S. capital abundance did not lead to employment of a larger share of its work force in capital-intensive industries. Indeed, there was no significant difference between the U.S. employment mix and those of other developed countries in relation to the capital- or labor-intensity of production.

Between the early 1960s and the mid-1970s labor productivity levels of other OECD countries converged on the United States in every manufacturing industry. Convergence of TFP was the primary source of this development, with convergence of capital-labor ratios playing a secondary role. In addition, there is evidence that countries and industries that lagged particularly far behind in terms of technological capability experienced the most rapid TFP convergence. This finding is consistent with Gerschenkron's (1952) notion of the advantage of relative backwardness. The countries and industries that were particularly far behind had the greatest capacity to gain from technology transfer, and proceeded to grow most rapidly.

In the period 1963–72 there was also a positive correlation between TFP convergence and convergence of capital intensity. This result can be interpreted in two ways: advanced technology is embodied in machines and hence rapid capital accumulation occasions rapid TFP growth; or high TFP growth, through acquisition of disembodied technology, improves the profitability of an industry, hence attracts new investment. These issues of causality are difficult to sort out, but we think it is likely that the causality runs in both directions.

By the mid-1970s TFP levels of industrial countries were fairly similar, though the United States continued to hold a lead in most industries. There has been no further convergence of TFP since the mid-1970s. Convergence of labor productivity within industries has continued, though at a slower rate than before, and in the recent period has resulted almost entirely from capital accumulation. By the late 1980s differences in capital-labor ratios among OECD countries were minor. What labor productivity lead the

United States still has today results from the modest technology lead that it retains in most industries.

The nature of the international economy has changed significantly between the 1960s and today. In the former period, the United States had labor and total factor productivity advantages in all manufacturing industries. What appears to be the situation today is that different countries are developing modest labor and total factor productivity leads in different industries. With this kind of international specialization, dispersion of productivity measures is greater within industries than in the aggregate. These results accord with the notion that the industrial countries today are nearly equal technological rivals.

5 The Experience of Nonmanufacturing Sectors

In previous chapters we have argued that there are a number of different reasons to expect convergence in productivity levels among countries for sectors of the economy that produce tradable commodities. The evidence presented in the last two chapters verifies this to be the case among the industrialized economies for individual manufacturing industries, particularly during the 1960s, and for total manufacturing during the 1960s, 1970s, and early 1980s. Moreover, chapter 4 provided evidence that differences in capital-labor ratios for both total manufacturing and for individual manufacturing industries had narrowed. The results also showed that the variation in productivity levels and capital intensity was greater for individual industries than for all manufacturing—a finding that supported our argument of country specialization in different industries since the mid-1970s.

In this chapter we consider whether the same patterns hold for other sectors of the economy. The advantages-of-backwardness thesis, which underlies most convergence models, suggests that backward nations, or backward sectors in advanced nations, have at their disposal the advanced technology of the leading countries. This availability, coupled with suitable investment and the impetus for lowering costs, could lead to the deployment of leading-edge technology. However, the rate of catch-up of sectors not engaged in trade would presumably be less, since they are immune from the international competition. Moreover, the role of the multinational corporations (MNCs) as carriers of world technology would appear to play a lesser role, since their activities have been principally concentrated in the manufacturing industries.

This chapter replicates the analysis of the two preceding chapters for all sectors of the economy among our sample of OECD countries. It also considers productivity trends for the total economy. Have labor productivity levels converged in these sectors and in the total economy? Have technology (TFP) levels and capital-labor ratios converged? What explains the intercountry dispersion in productivity levels among nonmanufacturing sectors? How much of the catch-up in labor productivity at the sectoral level is due to declining dispersion in technology levels and how much to convergence in capital intensity? How much of the convergence in economy-wide productivity levels is due to catch-up in productivity at the sectoral level and how much to changing industrial mixes?

Our results for the total economy are quite similar to those for the aggregate manufacturing sector. We find convergence among OECD countries of labor productivity levels, technology levels, and capital-labor ratios for both the total economy and for individual sectors as well. However, the similarity of and the degree of convergence in technology, capital intensity, and labor productivity levels was greater for the total economy than at the individual sectoral level. These results confirm our ongoing thesis that countries have specialized in both new technology and investment in different sectors, which explains the greater convergence of productivity at the aggregate level than the sectoral level.

We also find that the manufacturing sector, which is the most open with regard to trade and investment, has shown the least variation in productivity levels among all the sectors of the economy for the industrialized countries. Dispersion in productivity levels was particularly high in sectors that are insulated from international trade—such as utilities and community, social, and personal services. Resource-based sectors, such as agriculture and mining, also displayed medium to high levels of intercountry dispersion. The results support the argument that international trade plays a crucial role in the convergence process.

This chapter is organized into five parts. Section 5.1 presents results on labor productivity movements by country and industry over the 1970–85 period. Section 5.2 examines changes in capital intensity at both the aggregate and individual industry level. Section 5.3 presents comparisons of TFP levels for the total economy and for individual sectors. In Section 5.4 the growth in labor productivity on the sectoral level is decomposed into one component attributable to technological change and another attributable to rising capital intensity. In addition, the effect of employment shifts on overall productivity catch-up is assessed. Concluding remarks are made in the last section.

5.1 Labor Productivity on the Sectoral Level

We use data on output, employment, capital stock, and labor compensation taken from the OECD data base for fourteen OECD countries and ten major sectors: (1) agriculture; (2) mining and quarrying; (3) manufacturing; (4) electricity, gas, and water utilities; (5) construction; (6) wholesale and retail trade, restaurants, and hotels; (7) transportation, storage, and communication; (8) finance, insurance, and real estate; (9) community, social, and personal services; and (10) producers of government services. The first five of these sectors are grouped together as "goods" industries, and the latter five as "service" industries.

The data set provides relatively complete data for the period from 1970 to 1985, and the analysis concentrates on these years. The data consist of GDP, calculated in 1980 U.S. dollar equivalents; total number of employees; total employment (the sum of employees and self-employed); compensation of employees; and gross capital stock, measured in 1980 U.S. dollars.

Differences between total number of employees and total employment are small for most sectors (see table 5.A1). However, agriculture includes a large number of small, owner-operated farms. In all countries, except the United Kingdom, paid employees constituted less than half the agricultural work force in 1979. The 1979 proportion ranged from 11% in Belgium to 57% in the United Kingdom.

The construction trades also have a large number of independent contractors. The ratio of total employees to total employment in 1979 ranged from 66% in Australia to 94% in Finland. Owner-operated stores, hotels, and restaurants are also common in many countries. The employee proportion of total employment in 1979 ranged from 43% in Italy to 91% in Finland. Personal services are also provided by a large number of self-employed workers. The corresponding ratio ranged from 69% in Italy to 89% in Norway.

It is of interest that Japan had the lowest proportion of employees in total employment of any of the countries: 72% for the whole economy. Even excluding agriculture, Japan had the lowest ratio, at 81%. The corresponding ratio for the United States was 92% and that for the United Kingdom was 93%. These differences suggest that comparative productivity measures can be sensitive to the choice of employment statistics. We feel that the total employment statistics provide a better gauge of actual productivity levels, since figures based on the number of employees are sensitive to the relative share of self-employment in the total work force. Our calculations were all performed using total employment.

Labor productivity levels for the total economy showed convergence from 1970 through the early 1980s (see table 5.1). The coefficient of variation fell from 0.22 in 1970 to 0.14 in 1983; the ratio of maximum to minimum productivity levels fell from 2.1 to 1.4; the average labor produc-

Table 5.1
Labor productivity levels in the total economy, 1970–85
(index, U.S. = 100)

	1970	1975	1979	1983	1985
Australia	84	89	92	97	96
Belgium	—	—	—	—	—
Canada	91	93	94	94	95
Denmark	62	66	70	73	73
Finland	54	60	68	73	74
France	—	—	—	—	—
Germany	72	79	90	95	95
Italy	—	—	—	—	—
Japan	48	57	66	74	78
Netherlands	—	—	—	—	—
Norway	69	82	95	103	105
Sweden	74	78	79	82	82
United Kingdom	—	63	67	72	72
United States	100	100	100	100	100
All industries					
Coefficient of variation	.22	.18	.16	.14	.14
Maximum/minimum	2.08	1.75	1.52	1.42	1.46
Average/U.S.	.69	.74	.80	.85	.85
Average/leader	.69	.74	.80	.82	.81
Leader	U.S.	—	—	—	Norway
All industries except mining and quarrying					
Coefficient of variation	.18	.15	.14	.12	.11
Maximum/minimum	1.99	1.70	1.52	1.45	1.44
Average/U.S.	.71	.77	.82	.86	.86
Average/leader	.71	.77	.82	.85	.86
Leader	U.S.	—	—	—	U.S.
All industries except agriculture and mining and quarrying					
Coefficient of variation	.15	.14	.12	.11	.11
Maximum/minimum	1.72	1.58	1.53	1.45	1.45
Average/U.S.	.74	.78	.83	.87	.87
Average/leader	.74	.78	.83	.87	.87
Leader	U.S.	—	—	—	U.S.

Results are based on the OECD data base.

tivity level relative to the United States increased from 0.69 to 0.85; and that relative to the leading country rose from 0.69 to 0.82. From 1983 to 1985, there is no evidence of continued convergence.

The United States led in overall labor productivity from 1970 to 1982, at which point it was overtaken by Norway. All the countries in the sample gained on the United States between 1970 and 1985. In 1985, the United States ranked second, 5% behind Norway. Australia trailed the United States by 4%; Canada and Germany, by 5%.[1]

We also show computations for the total economy with the exclusion of two resource-based sectors, agriculture and mining and quarrying. Productivity in both these sectors is heavily dependent on the resource base. Agriculture depends on the amount and quality of arable land available, weather, and the like; mining and quarrying (which includes petroleum and natural gas extraction), depends on the availability of particular resources, such as coal, iron ore, and copper. When these two sectors are excluded, the dispersion of productivity levels becomes smaller, but the results still show convergence in average labor productivity levels. By 1985, the coefficient of variation had fallen to 0.11.[2]

Table 5.2 displays labor productivity statistics for individual sectors: 7 of the 10 sectors show a declining dispersion of country labor productivity levels between 1970 and 1985; 1, utilities (electricity, gas, and water), shows no change; and 2, mining and quarrying and finance, insurance, and real estate, show a rising dispersion. The figure for mining and quarrying rather heavily reflects the very high labor productivity levels for Norway (from oil deposits) and the Netherlands (natural gas deposits). Once these two countries are excluded, the coefficient of variation shows a decline. Moreover, average labor productivity relative to the leading country increased in 7 of the 10 sectors (and in 9 of the 10, once Norway and the Netherlands are excluded from mining and the Netherlands from utilities). Thus, there was generally convergence in labor productivity on the level of individual sectors as well as for the total economy.

There were very large differences, however, in the degree of productivity dispersion among sectors. As expected, the smallest intercountry variation was found in manufacturing (this was true for all years). Indeed, the coefficient of variation in manufacturing was very close to that for the overall economy, shown in the last line. Low dispersion was also found for the trade, restaurant, and hotel sector, as well as for transportation and communications. Agriculture; construction; finance, insurance, and real estate; and government services all show moderate levels of intercountry dispersion. The degree of dispersion was highest in mining and quarrying (even with the exclusion of Norway and the Netherlands), and second highest in utilities.

On balance, there appear to be two reasons for cases in which intercountry differences in labor productivity are low: first, if products are heavily involved in international trade (manufacturing) and, second, if technology is easily transferable (manufacturing; construction; trade, restaurants, and hotels; transportation and communication; finance, insurance, and real estate; and government services). Dispersion appears to be high where production is resource-based (mining and quarrying and utilities). The moderate level of dispersion in agriculture is somewhat of a surprise, since production is heavily resource-based and the sector is protected in most OECD countries. The high level of productivity variation found in the community, social, and personal service sector may be attributable to the unique attributes of the personal service component of this sector in many countries.

Also of interest is the fact that the overall (aggregate) statistics show lower dispersion than the corresponding unweighted averages. In 1985 the coefficient of variation for all industries was 0.14, whereas the unweighted average of the ten sectors was 0.39. This result is consistent with our argument about country specialization. Interestingly, the same result holds for the goods industries as a group and for the service industries as a group.

Leadership by industry is also indicated in table 5.2. In 1970 the United States had the highest labor productivity in 5 of the 10 sectors: agriculture; manufacturing; construction; trade, restaurants, and hotels; and transportation and communications. The Netherlands led in mining and quarrying and utilities, Germany in finance, insurance, and real estate, Italy in community, social, and personal services, and Australia in government services. By 1985 the United States was highest in only two sectors—manufacturing and transportation and communications. Five other countries (not including Japan) led in the other sectors. Thus, as among individual manufacturing industries (chapter 3), leadership in the nonmanufacturing sectors was becoming more dispersed.

We have singled out Japan and Germany for more detailed comparison with the United States (the second panel of table 5.2). In 1970 Japan's productivity trailed the United States in all ten sectors. Between 1970 and 1985 Japan gained on the United States in every sector, and by 1985 its productivity exceeded that of the United States in three sectors—utilities; finance, insurance, and real estate; and government services. Interestingly, in manufacturing, Japan's relative productivity increased from 50% to only 79%, still considerably behind that of the United States. Moreover, in 1985

Japanese productivity was still very far behind the United States in several sectors—agriculture (24%), mining and quarrying (36%), transportation and communications (57%), and construction (63%). On average, Japanese productivity in 1985 was much closer to that of the United States in the service sectors than in the goods sectors.

Over the same period, German productivity gained on the United States in every sector except manufacturing, where it remained unchanged in relative terms. Germany led the United States in two sectors in 1970—finance, insurance, and real estate; and community, social, and personal services—a lead which increased over the fifteen-year period. In 1985 German productivity in the service industries was higher than that of the United States, whereas in the goods industries it was lower. Indeed, German productivity in agriculture was only 44% that of the United States; in mining and quarrying only 22%, and in utilities 59%.

5.2 Total Factor Productivity in the Economy

Labor productivity differences among countries are attributable to two influences: differences in technology and differences in the capital-labor ratio (capital intensity). We first consider total factor productivity for the whole economy and for individual sectors. As in the previous chapter, we measure TFP by:

$$\text{TFP} = Y / [\alpha L + (1 - \alpha)K], \tag{5.1}$$

where Y is a sector's value added, L is the labor input (which we measure here by total employment), K is the gross capital stock (in 1980 U.S. dollars), and α is the wage share. As before, the TFP index is normalized so that the U.S. TFP index in 1970 equals 1.0 in each industry.

Two different wage shares are used for each industry: (1) country-specific averages of the ratio of wages to value added over the full period in each industry; and (2) the mean over all the countries of the country-specific wage shares for each industry, hereafter known as the "international average." The proper choice of wage share is debatable; and we report results for the two choices. For country wage shares, two further measures are developed. The first, or "unadjusted wage share," is defined as the ratio of employee compensation to GDP. The second, or "adjusted wage share," also includes an imputation for the labor-income portion of self-employment income (which is normally included in property income) in the numerator of the ratio (see the Appendix for further details).

Table 5.2
Indices of labor productivity convergence by sector, 1970–85

	Coefficient of variation				Average productivity relative to leader (in parentheses)	
	1970	1975	1979	1985	1970	1985
Goods industries						
Agriculture	.41	.37	.32	.31	.54 (U.S.)	.69 (Austral.)
Mining and quarrying						
a) All countries	1.06	1.90	1.62	1.18	.20 (Nether.)	.17 (Nether.)
b) Excl. Norway and the Netherlands	.92	.76	.57	.81		
Manufacturing	.19	.17	.15	.15	.68 (U.S.)	.73 (U.S.)
Electricity, gas, water	.65	.81	.72	.65	.29 (Nether.)	.26 (Nether.)
Construction	.27	.19	.17	.24	.55 (U.S.)	.59 (Canada)
Service industries						
Trade, restaurants, and hotels	.20	.19	.17	.16	.77 (U.S.)	.80 (Nether.)
Transportation and communications	.26	.22	.22	.19	.60 (U.S.)	.65 (U.S.)
Finance, insurance, and real estate	.18	.19	.23	.28	.65 (Germany)	.52 (Germany)
Community, social, and personal services	.53	.53	.52	.50	.34 (Italy)	.46 (Italy)
Government services	.24	.22	.22	.21	.62 (Austral.)	.69 (Nether.)
Unweighted averages						
Goods industries	.51	.68	.60	.51	.45	.49
Service industries	.28	.27	.27	.27	.60	.62
All industries	.39	.47	.43	.39	.52	.56
Overall statistics						
All goods industries	.33	.28	.25	.24	.59 (U.S.)	.72 (Nether.)
All service industries	.14	.13	.12	.11	.80 (U.S.)	.91 (Belgium)
All industries	.22	.18	.16	.14	.69 (U.S.)	.81 (Norway)

Table 5.3 documents the convergence in TFP levels for the overall economy among OECD countries. The coefficient of variation of TFP calculated on the basis of the international average-wage share declined from 0.16 to 0.10 between 1970 and 1985; the ratio of maximum to minimum TFP from 1.7 to 1.4. Average TFP relative to the United States increased from 0.81 to 0.91; and that relative to the leader from 0.77 to 0.90. Similar results are obtained on the basis of each country's own unadjusted and adjusted wage shares and on the basis of total number of employees. Thus, by all indicators, there was considerable convergence in TFP levels among these countries. Moreover, the dispersion in TFP among these countries was consistently smaller than that of labor productivity levels. In 1985 the co-

Table 5.2 (continued)

	Japanese productivity relative to U.S. level				German productivity relative to U.S. level			
	(index, U.S. = 100)							
	1970	1975	1979	1985	1970	1975	1979	1985
Goods industries								
Agriculture	22	28	28	24	33	40	48	44
Mining and quarrying	11	20	31	36	16	18	25	22
Manufacturing	50	56	68	79	73	74	80	73
Electricity, gas, water	95	81	98	107	52	53	71	59
Construction	49	59	67	63	50	67	82	92
Service industries								
Trade, restaurants, hotels	43	54	69	80	73	75	83	85
Transport and communication	50	51	46	57	60	54	63	73
Finance, insurance, real estate	84	106	128	161	132	144	181	220
Community, social, personal	89	84	84	90	194	212	235	245
Government services	98	104	114	129	95	98	99	100
Overall statistics								
Goods industries	36	43	52	58	56	62	72	68
Service industries	62	70	77	89	91	95	105	114
All industries	48	57	66	78	72	79	90	95

Results are based on the OECD data base. Missing data are as follows: mining and quarrying (Belgium, France, and Italy; the United Kingdom in 1970–72); finance, insurance, and real estate (Italy and the Netherlands); goods industries (Belgium, France, and Italy; the United Kingdom in 1970–72); service industries (Italy and the Netherlands); and total economy (Belgium, France, Italy, and the Netherlands; the United Kingdom in 1970–72).

efficient of variation in TFP was 0.10, compared to 0.14 for labor productivity. We have encountered a similar result in chapter 4 in the analysis of TFP for manufacturing industries.

Canada had the highest overall TFP level in 1970, a lead it maintained until the early 1980s, when it was surpassed by Norway. In 1970 the United States ranked second, while in 1985 it was tied with Canada, slightly behind Australia and Norway, and was followed fairly closely by Japan and Germany.

Results shown in table 5.4 indicate a rather mixed pattern of convergence on the industry level. Over the 1970–85 period the intercountry coefficient of variation in industry TFP declined substantially in only 3 of the 10 sectors, declined slightly in 5, and increased slightly in two. Average TFP relative to the leading country gained in 7 sectors and retreated in 3. Thus, unlike labor productivity, there was no clear pattern of convergence in TFP on the sectoral level. As we shall see below, most of the catch-up in sectoral labor productivity levels over the 1970–85 period can be attributed to capital investment.

Table 5.3
Total factor productivity (TFP) levels in the total economy, 1970–85
(index, U.S. = 100)

	International average unadjusted wage share				Country's own unadjusted wage share			
	1970	1975	1979	1985	1970	1975	1979	1985
Australia	96	99	97	101	97	100	98	100
Belgium	—	—	—	—	—	—	—	—
Canada	105	106	102	100	104	106	102	100
Denmark	72	74	76	80	71	74	76	80
Finland	61	66	69	74	62	66	69	74
France	—	—	—	—	—	—	—	—
Germany	84	88	94	95	84	88	94	95
Italy	—	—	—	—	—	—	—	—
Japan	70	80	86	96	77	85	90	99
Netherlands	—	—	—	—	—	—	—	—
Norway	77	87	94	101	77	87	94	100
Sweden	83	86	83	85	80	85	83	86
United Kingdom	—	81	82	87	—	78	80	86
United States	100	100	100	100	100	100	100	100
Coefficient of variation	.16	.13	.12	.10	.16	.13	.12	.10
Maximum/minimum	1.70	1.60	1.48	1.37	1.69	1.60	1.48	1.37
Average/U.S.	.81	.85	.87	.91	.82	.86	.87	.91
Average/leader	.77	.80	.85	.90	.78	.80	.85	.91
Leader	Canada	—	—	Norway	Canada	—	—	Australia
Using country's own adjusted wage shares								
Coefficient of variation					.19	.15	.13	.10
Maximum/minimum					1.74	1.60	1.46	1.36
Average/U.S.					.77	.82	.85	.90
Average/leader					.76	.79	.85	.88
Leader					Canada	—	—	Norway

Results are based on the OECD data base.

Table 5.4
Indices of total factor productivity (TFP) convergence by sector, 1970–85

	Coefficient of variation				Average TFP relative to leader (in parentheses)	
	1970	1975	1979	1985	1970	1985
Goods industries						
Agriculture	.26	.25	.26	.29	.65 (Belgium)	.60 (Austral.)
Mining and quarrying	1.13	1.06	.90	.69	.16 (Nether.)	.32 (Nether.)
Manufacturing	.16	.14	.15	.15	.71 (U.S.)	.70 (U.S.)
Electricity, gas, water	.73	.78	.67	.61	.27 (Nether.)	.29 (Nether.)
Construction	.25	.21	.20	.24	.62 (U.S.)	.66 (Canada)
Service industries						
Trade, restaurants, and hotels	.19	.17	.15	.15	.72 (U.S.)	.77 (U.S.)
Transportation and communications	.24	.18	.18	.16	.67 (Belgium)	.74 (U.S.)
Finance, insurance, and real estate	.22	.23	.21	.20	.71 (Canada)	.75 (Japan)
Community, social, and personal services	.41	.39	.40	.42	.56 (Italy)	.53 (Denmark)
Government services	.21	.20	.19	.18	.69 (Nether.)	.68 (Nether.)
Total economy	.16	.13	.12	.10	.78 (Canada)	.91 (Austral.)
Unweighted averages	.38	.36	.33	.31		

Results are based on the OECD data base. Computations are performed with the country's own unadjusted wage share and total employment.

Sectoral differences in the intercountry dispersion of TFP levels are quite similar to those based on labor productivity. Manufacturing had the least dispersion. Trade, restaurants, and hotels; transportation and communications; and government services also had low coefficients of variation in TFP levels. Moderate levels of dispersion were found for agriculture; construction; and finance, insurance, and real estate. Mining and quarrying; utilities; and community, social, and personal services had the most variation, with mining and quarrying the highest. Also, as with labor productivity, the dispersion in TFP on the sectoral level was consistently greater than the dispersion of TFP for the overall economy. In 1985 the coefficient of variation for the overall economy was 0.10, compared to an unweighted average for the sectors of 0.31.

Technology leadership positions were also similar to those based on labor productivity. In 1970, the United States led in 3 sectors—manufacturing; construction; and trade, restaurants, and hotels—Belgium led in 2, the Netherlands in 3, and Canada and Italy each in 1. In 1985, the U.S. was ahead in 3 sectors—manufacturing; trade, restaurants, and hotels; and transportation and communication—the Netherlands in 3; and Australia, Canada, Japan, and Denmark each in 1. As with labor productivity, different countries were enjoying technology advantages in different industries.

5.3 Capital Intensity

Previous work (Bowen 1983; Wolff 1991, for example) has documented convergence in overall capital intensity among industrialized countries, and we report similar findings here for the period between 1970 and 1985 (table 5.5). The coefficient of variation in aggregate capital-labor ratios fell from 0.26 to 0.18 and the ratio of the highest to lowest capital-labor ratio declined from 4.1 to 1.9. The (unweighted) average capital intensity of all

Table 5.5
Capital-labor ratios in total economy, 1970–85
(index, U.S. = 100)

	1970	1975	1979	1983	1985
Australia	72	77	87	89	89
Belgium	—	—	—	—	—
Canada	70	72	82	89	91
Denmark	67	73	81	80	80
Finland	70	79	96	95	102
France	—	—	—	—	—
Germany	67	78	89	95	99
Italy	—	—	—	—	—
Japan	24	36	47	53	58
Netherlands	73	84	97	103	107
Norway	76	85	102	106	109
Sweden	75	78	88	89	92
United Kingdom	48	51	57	60	61
United States	100	100	100	100	100
All industries					
Coefficient of variation	.26	.22	.20	.19	.18
Maximum/minimum	4.10	2.80	2.18	2.01	1.87
Average/U.S.	.64	.71	.82	.86	.89
Average/leader	.64	.71	.81	.80	.80
Leader	U.S.	—	—	—	Norway
All industries except agriculture and mining and quarrying					
Coefficient of variation	.24	.21	.18	.17	.17
Maximum/minimum	3.54	2.55	2.03	1.89	1.85
Average/U.S.	.66	.72	.83	.87	.90
Average/leader	.66	.72	.81	.82	.82
Leader	U.S.	—	—	—	Netherlands

Results are based on the OECD data base. Capital is measured in 1980 U.S. dollars and labor by total employment.

countries increased from 64% of the U.S. level to 89%, while the ratio relative to the most capital-intensive country rose from 64% to 80%. Similar results are obtained when agriculture and mining and quarrying are excluded from the country statistics (and on the basis of the ratio of capital to the total number of employees).

Though the United States led in terms of capital intensity in 1970, it was surpassed by Norway in the late 1970s. By 1985, it ranked only fourth, behind Norway, the Netherlands, and Finland, with Germany a very close fifth. Indeed, in 1985 Norway was foremost in the world not only in terms of capital intensity, but also in labor productivity and TFP. In contrast, the United States ranked second in terms of labor productivity, third in TFP, and fourth in its overall capital-labor ratio.

Results on the industry level are shown in table 5.6. Over the 1970–85 period the intercountry dispersion in capital-labor ratios fell in 7 of the 10 sectors, although in 3 the declines were very modest, and increased slightly in the other 3. Average capital intensity narrowed in every sector relative to the United States (result not shown), and in 8 of the 10 sectors relative to the country with the highest capital-labor ratio.

A comparison of tables 5.2, 5.4, and 5.6 reveals two interesting patterns. The first is an apparent anomaly. On the one hand, the dispersion in capital intensity among these countries was consistently greater than that of labor productivity and TFP levels. In 1985, for example, the coefficient of variation in aggregate capital intensity was 0.18, compared to 0.14 for overall labor productivity and 0.10 for overall TFP. This is generally true on the sectoral level as well. On the other hand, there was very little change in the dispersion of TFP levels on the sectoral level between 1970 and 1985, whereas the variation of both sectoral labor productivity levels and sectoral capital-labor ratios continued to decline. The reason is that by the early 1970s, intercountry differences in technology among the major sectors of the economy (as among individual manufacturing industries) had reached their narrowest point. During the ensuing decade, convergence in sectoral labor productivity levels resulted almost exclusively from continuing convergence in the capital intensity of production. (This was also our finding for individual manufacturing industries.) The results of the next section will provide further confirmation of this finding.

The second pattern displayed in tables 5.2, 5.4, and 5.6 is that, like labor productivity and TFP levels, the dispersion in capital intensity on the sectoral level was consistently higher than that for the overall economy in all sectors. In 1985 the coefficient of variation for the overall economy was 0.18, compared to an unweighted average of 0.44. Moreover, by 1985, industry leadership in terms of capital intensity was spread among 6 differ-

Table 5.6
Measures of convergence in capital-labor ratios by sector, 1970–85

	Coefficient of variation				Average capital-labor ratio relative to leader (in parentheses)	
	1970	1975	1979	1985	1970	1985
Goods industries						
Agriculture	.40	.31	.27	.24	.59 (U.K.)	.67 (Norway)
Mining and quarrying	.71	.94	.93	.74	.38 (U.S.)	.40 (Norway)
Manufacturing	.24	.20	.21	.21	.65 (Canada)	.74 (Nether.)
Electricity, gas, water	.42	.37	.35	.33	.45 (Sweden)	.53 (Sweden)
Construction	.37	.38	.41	.39	.61 (Denmark)	.50 (Norway)
Service industries						
Trade, restaurants, and hotels	.29	.28	.29	.28	.59 (Finland)	.68 (Finland)
Transportation and communications	.47	.47	.42	.33	.40 (Norway)	.51 (Nether.)
Finance, insurance, and real estate	.48	.46	.48	.51	.37 (Germany)	.34 (Germany)
Community, social, and personal services	.70	.66	.65	.62	.34 (U.K.)	.41 (Germany)
Government services	.77	.70	.77	.73	.23 (Austral.)	.28 (Austral.)
Total economy	.26	.22	.20	.18	.64 (U.S.)	.80 (Norway)
Unweighted averages	.49	.48	.48	.44		

ent countries (also, 6 for labor productivity and 6 for TFP). These results all indicate the continuing specialization of OECD countries in particular industries during the 1970s and 1980s.

A comparison of Japan, Germany, and the United States in terms of capital intensity highlights these sectoral differences. As shown in the second part of table 5.6, Japan was considerably behind the U.S. in 1970 for both the overall economy and for each of the ten sectors. Between 1970 and 1985 Japan made considerable gains on the United States in every sector. By 1985 its capital intensity was 80% of the U.S. level in manufacturing and actually exceeded the U.S. level in two sectors—finance, insurance, and real estate and government services. However, Japan was still far behind the United States in agriculture (56%), in mining and quarrying (15%), and transportation and communication (20%). On average, Japanese capital intensity in 1985 was closer to that of the United States in the service sectors (67%) than the goods sectors (56%).

Over the same period, the capital-labor ratio in Germany gained on the United States in every sector except government services, where it declined very slightly. Germany led the United States in 3 sectors in 1970

Table 5.6 (continued)

	Japanese capital-labor ratio relative to U.S. level				German capital-labor ratio relative to U.S. level			
	(index, U.S. = 100)							
	1970	1975	1979	1985	1970	1975	1979	1985
Goods industries								
Agriculture	18	30	37	56	54	65	73	80
Mining and quarrying	6	12	16	15	12	19	25	24
Manufacturing	50	64	78	80	71	75	82	76
Electricity, gas, water	38	45	57	75	67	69	77	86
Construction	28	39	55	99	72	80	89	113
Service industries								
Trade, restaurants, hotels	41	60	76	87	133	138	149	140
Transportation and communication	10	13	16	20	58	64	75	80
Finance, insurance, real estate	57	79	105	135	224	243	299	362
Community, social, personal	18	28	33	55	241	272	326	397
Government services	55	75	97	132	70	68	70	69
Overall statistics								
Goods industries	27	37	48	56	54	61	69	69
Service industries	30	42	53	67	97	105	118	131
All industries	24	36	47	58	67	78	89	99

Results are based on the OECD data base. Capital is measured in 1980 U.S. dollars, and labor by total employment. Missing data are as follows: Mining and quarrying (Belgium, France, and Italy); finance, insurance, and real estate (Italy); and total economy (Belgium, France, and Italy).

and 4 sectors in 1985—construction; trade, restaurants, and hotels; finance, insurance, and real estate; and community, social, and personal services. By 1985 German capital intensity in the service industries was considerably higher than that of the United States; in the goods industries it was lower, particularly mining and quarrying (24%); and overall, Germany was on a par with the United States.

5.4 Decompositions of Labor Productivity Growth

As we did for the individual manufacturing industries in the previous chapter, we now investigate the sources of labor productivity convergence within the major sectors of the economy. We have already found in this chapter that there has been convergence in labor productivity levels within almost all sectors between 1970 and 1985. Moreover, there was also convergence in capital-labor ratios in almost all sectors, but relatively little convergence in TFP. Here, we formally analyze the extent to which the convergence in labor productivity on the sectoral level was due to the convergence in technology levels and the extent it was due to the catch-up in capital intensity.

As in chapter 4, we employ the Divisia index to measure TFP growth:

$$\rho_i^h = \hat{Y}_i^h - \alpha\hat{L}_i^h - (1 - \alpha)\hat{K}_i^h, \tag{5.2}$$

where a hat ($\hat{}$) denotes the time derivative or relative rate of change. In our decomposition of productivity growth in manufacturing industries, we used the United States as the benchmark country because it was the clear leader. Thus, we measured changes in productivity levels as their percentage of the U.S. figures. However, in the case of nonmanufacturing sectors, productivity leadership was highly dispersed, and there were leadership changes over time in most sectors. As a result, we performed our decomposition here using actual growth rates of productivity and capital intensity.

From (5.2), we can formally decompose the growth of labor productivity into a component attributed to technological (TFP) progress and a component ascribable to the growth in the capital-labor ratio:

$$\hat{\Pi}_i^h = \rho_i^h + (1 - \alpha_i)\hat{k}_i^h, \tag{5.3}$$

where Π_i^h is the rate of growth of labor productivity of sector i in country h, ρ_i^h the corresponding (Divisia) growth rate of TFP, $\hat{k}_i^h$ the growth rate of the capital-labor ratio, and α_i the average wage share in industry i.[3]

Results for individual sectors are shown in table 5.7. It is first of interest to look at actual rates of productivity growth by sector (the left-hand panel). Over the 1970–85 period average labor productivity growth was highest in mining and quarrying (5.0% per year), followed by agriculture (4.1%), manufacturing (3.4%), utilities (3.2%), transportation and communication (2.4%), and trade, restaurants, and hotels (1.7%). It fell below 1.0% in the other sectors. In contrast, TFP growth was highest in manufacturing (2.0% per year), followed by mining and quarrying (1.6%), utilities (1.2%), and transportation and communications (1.3%). It was quite low (less than 1.0% per year) in the other sectors.

As suggested in section 5.3, capital accumulation was the more important contributor to labor productivity growth on the sectoral level in most sectors. On average, across all sectors, it accounted for three-fourths of the growth in labor productivity, while technological advance contributed the remaining fourth.[4] This preeminence of capital formation was especially strong in agriculture; construction; and community, social, and personal

Table 5.7
Decomposition of labor productivity growth by industry into capital intensity and technology component, 1970–85

	Annual growth rates (percent)			Percent contribution to labor productivity growth	
	LPROD ($\hat{\Pi}_i^h$)	TFP (ρ_i^h)	K/L ($\hat{k}_i^h$)	TFP (ρ_i^h)	K/L $[(1-\alpha_i)\hat{k}_i^h]$
Goods industries					
Agriculture	4.14	−0.50	5.77	−12.1	112.1
Mining and quarrying	5.01	1.63	5.86	32.6	67.4
Manufacturing	3.43	2.01	4.26	58.7	41.3
Electricity, gas, water	3.20	1.15	2.99	35.9	64.1
Construction	0.95	−0.44	4.15	−45.9	145.9
Service industries					
Trade, restaurants, hotels	1.67	0.26	3.25	15.5	84.5
Transportation and communication	2.38	1.30	3.19	54.9	45.1
Finance, insurance, real estate	0.78	0.28	0.70	36.5	63.5
Community, social personal	0.88	−0.19	2.47	−21.6	121.6
Government services	0.18	0.12	0.92	67.7	32.3
Unweighted average	2.26	0.56	3.36	24.8	75.2

Results are based on the OECD data base. The rate of TFP growth is defined by equation 5.2. The contribution of TFP growth to labor productivity growth is defined as the ratio: $\hat{\pi}_i^h/\rho_i^h$; the contribution of capital-labor growth to labor productivity growth is defined as the ratio: $(1-\alpha_i)\hat{k}_i^h$-ρ_i^h (see equation 5.3). Percentage contributions are based on the unweighted averages for each sector. All computations are performed with the international unadjusted wage share and total employment. Missing data are as follows: Mining and quarrying (Belgium, France, Italy, and the United Kingdom); and finance, insurance, and real estate (Italy and the Netherlands).

services, all of which recorded negative TFP growth. Capital accumulation also made the major contribution to labor productivity growth in mining and quarrying; utilities; trade, restaurants, and hotels; and finance, insurance, and real estate. However, in manufacturing, transportation and communications; and government services, technological advance played the more important role (although for the last of these there was hardly any productivity growth).

Shifts in Employment Shares

In chapter 3, we investigated the role of employment shifts on overall labor productivity within total manufacturing. We found that changes in the distribution of employment among individual manufacturing industries played almost no role in overall growth of manufacturing labor productivity within OECD countries. Here, we repeat the analysis for shifts in employment shares among the major sectors of the economy on labor productivity growth for the total economy.

Define:

Π_i^h labor productivity level of sector i in country h;

Π^h labor productivity level of country h.

Then:

$$\Pi^h = \Sigma_i s_i^h \cdot \Pi_i^h, \tag{5.4}$$

where $s_i^h = L_i^h / L^h$, the share of sector i's employment in the total employment of country h. As in chapter 3, we recompute what overall labor productivity would have been in country h if sectoral employment shares had remained unchanged over time.

It is first of interest to look at the trends in employment shares over the 1970–85 period (table 5.8). These are shown for both the United States and as an unweighted average of the countries in the sample. Although the employment shares differed in magnitude between the United States and other OECD countries, the trends were quite similar. The biggest decline was in manufacturing, whose employment share fell by 5.5 percentage points in the United States and also by 5.5 percentage points for the OECD countries as a whole. We had commented on this finding earlier, in chapter 2, where we argued that all OECD countries had experienced relative losses of employment in manufacturing. Indeed, the so-called deindustrialization of America received no support from a comparison of U.S. manufacturing employment with the total for OECD—that is, the relative fall in the share of manufacturing employment in the United States was below the average for the OECD. The other major decline among OECD countries was recorded in agriculture, whose employment share fell by 4.1 percentage points (the U.S. share was already very low in 1970).

The biggest increase in the United States was in finance, insurance, and real estate, whose share rose by 4.7 percentage points, while it increased by 2.5 percentage points on average for OECD countries. The largest increase among OECD countries was for government services, whose share increased by 5.2 percentage points, while it declined in the United States by 2.2 points. All told, the percentage of the labor force engaged in services increased by 6.5 points in the United States and 10.7 points in OECD countries generally.

Table 5.8
Distribution of total employment among major sectors in OECD countries, 1970 and 1985 (percent)

	United States		International average shares	
	1970	1985	1970	1985
Goods industries	33.9	27.5	47.9	37.2
Agriculture	4.6	3.2	10.7	6.6
Mining and quarrying	0.7	0.8	0.9	0.8
Manufacturing	22.7	17.2	27.2	21.7
Electricity, gas, water	0.8	0.8	1.0	1.1
Construction	5.1	5.5	8.1	7.0
Service industries	66.0	72.5	52.2	62.9
Trade, restaurants, hotels	21.2	23.8	17.3	18.1
Transportation and communication	4.6	4.1	6.9	6.7
Finance, insurance, real estate	8.2	12.9	5.2	7.7
Community, social, personal	13.7	15.6	8.6	11.0
Government services	18.3	16.1	14.2	19.4
Total	100.0	100.0	100.0	100.0

Results are based on the OECD data base.

Has employment tended to shift to sectors with high value added per worker and away from sectors with low productivity? Table 5.9 displays the effects of changes in employment shares on overall labor productivity growth, showing first the actual productivity levels by year for each country, and then what productivity levels would have been if the employment shares had remained unchanged at their 1970 composition. If employment had shifted toward high-productivity sectors over the 1970–85 period, then productivity levels computed for later years with 1970 weights should be *lower* than actual levels.[5]

The important result is that for almost all countries changes in employment shares had little impact on actual productivity movements. That is to say, there is no evidence that employment shares in OECD countries had generally shifted to sectors with higher value added per worker over the 1970–85 period. The exceptions were Norway, Japan, and the United Kingdom, though even for them the effects were modest. For Norway, overall productivity in 1985 would have been 10% lower than its actual level if employment shares had remained unchanged from their 1970 levels; for Japan, it would have been 6% lower. For the United Kingdom, on the other hand, productivity would have been 4% *higher*.

Table 5.9
Labor productivity in total economy with employment weights standardized by year, 1970–85
(index, actual 1985 labor productivity = 100)

	1970	1975	1979	1985
Australia				
Actual	79	86	91	100
1970 weights	79	87	92	100
Canada				
Actual	85	91	94	100
1970 weights	85	91	93	101
Denmark				
Actual	77	84	91	100
1970 weights	77	82	89	99
Finland				
Actual	64	75	87	100
1970 weights	64	71	83	95
Germany				
Actual	67	77	90	100
1970 weights	67	75	87	96
Japan				
Actual	55	68	81	100
1970 weights	55	65	77	94
Norway				
Actual	59	72	86	100
1970 weights	59	71	82	90
Sweden				
Actual	80	89	92	100
1970 weights	80	88	92	102
United Kingdom				
Actual	—	82	88	100
1970 weights	—	82	89	104
United States				
Actual	89	93	95	100
1970 weights	89	92	93	100

Results are based on the OECD data base. All computations are performed with total employment. Overall labor productivity in year t with employment share weights of year y is given by equation 5.4. 1970 employment weights are based on own country employment shares in that year.

5.5 Conclusion

Our most notable result in this chapter is that the major findings reported in chapters 3 and 4 with regard to the productivity performance of individual manufacturing industries carry over almost wholly intact when the analysis is extended to all sectors of the economy. Labor productivity levels among OECD countries for the total economy showed convergence from 1970 to 1985. Moreover, the intercountry variation in labor productivity on the individual sectoral level declined as well. Capital-labor ratios also showed declining dispersion for the total economy and individual sectors, but there was no clear pattern of convergence in TFP on the sectoral level. On average, three-fourths of the convergence of labor productivity levels on the sectoral level was attributable to declining differences in capital intensity and one-fourth to declining technology differences. Shifts in sectoral employment shares within a country played no role in either the growth of country-wide productivity or the convergence of productivity levels among countries.

As in our analysis of individual manufacturing industries, we consistently found evidence of greater dispersion in labor productivity levels, TFP levels, and capital-labor ratios within sectors than for the total economy. Moreover, sectoral leadership in terms of technology, capital intensity, and labor productivity was dispersed among a large number of countries (unlike manufacturing, the United States did not dominate all sectors of the economy in 1970). These results are all consistent with our basic thesis that countries are specializing in different industries and that in those industries each is developing modest leads in both technology and labor productivity.

There was also a close correspondence on the sectoral level between leadership position (and relative rankings) in terms of labor productivity and that based on TFP. This suggests that leadership in labor productivity on the sectoral level is largely related to preeminence in technology. This was true for individual manufacturing industries as well.

We also found that intercountry differences in both labor productivity and TFP on the sectoral level were lowest for manufacturing; trade, restaurant, and hotel sector; and transportation and communications; and highest for mining and quarrying and utilities. As expected, the degree of sectoral productivity dispersion was related to three influences: the extent to which a sector's products were traded internationally, the apparent ease of technology transfer, and an industry's dependence on specific resources.

Appendix Table 5A.1
Ratio of total number of employees to total employment by sector and country, 1979

	Australia	Belgium	Canada	Denmark	Finland	France	Germany
Goods industries							
Agriculture	.333	.106	.381	.228	.214	.206	.165
Mining and quarrying	.963	—	.994	.909	1.000	—	1.000
Manufacturing	.953	.932	.988	.941	.976	.951	.952
Electricity, gas, water	.944	.997	1.000	1.000	1.000	.995	1.000
Construction	.656	.844	.834	.793	.936	.827	.903
Service industries							
Trade, restaurants, hotels	.915	.619	.901	.783	.913	.754	.769
Transport and communication	.877	.937	.950	.884	.871	.955	.933
Finance, insurance, real estate	.830	.837	.930	.894	.962	.906	.999
Community, social, personal	.775	.776	.726	.711	.800	.836	.777
Government services	1.000	1.000	1.000	1.000	1.000	1.000	1.000
Total economy							
All industries	.829	—	.897	.842	.845	—	.866
All except agriculture	.862	.853	.927	.898	.948	.896	.909

Goods industries							
Agriculture	.384	.141	.254	.134	.360	.447	.571
Mining and quarrying	—	.953	—	.968	.982	.975	1.000
Manufacturing	.869	.862	.949	.966	.977	.982	.981
Electricity, gas, water	.978	.982	1.000	1.000	1.000	.983	1.000
Construction	.838	.797	.891	.813	.855	.778	.779
Service industries							
Trade, restaurants, hotels	.429	.738	.828	.881	.901	.898	.862
Transport and communication	.751	.933	.358	.907	.905	.934	.944
Finance, insurance, real estate	—	.875	.923	.882	.938	.874	.916
Community, social, personal	.689	.691	1.000	.894	.814	.881	.851
Government services	1.000	1.000	1.000	1.000	1.000	1.000	1.000
Total economy							
All industries	—	.720	—	.863	.913	.906	.925
All except agriculture	—	.813	.904	.929	.946	.924	.934

Results are based on the OECD data base.

6 Factor-Price Convergence in the Manufacturing Industries and Determinants of Industry Investment

6.1 Introduction

In this chapter, we return to the issue of competitiveness in tradables—in particular, manufacturing. As we argued in chapter 1, a country can compete in international markets either through low wages or through leading-edge technology (and high wages). Our definition of competitiveness refers to the latter. In this chapter, we extend this notion to include *profitability*. An industry or country is considered competitive if it can compete internationally with both high wages and high profitability.

In this regard, our major focus in this chapter is on examining whether there are systematic differences in both industry wages and industry profit rates among OECD countries and whether they have narrowed over time. We also present measures of *unit costs*, defined as a weighted average of both labor and capital costs. If factor prices (wage rates and profit rates) are equal among countries, then differences in unit costs will stem predominantly from relative levels of TFP.[1] Comparative advantage is based almost directly on unit costs, and in the next chapter we shall provide evidence of the linkage between technological advantage and trade patterns.

We also consider a related issue, the determinants of industry capital accumulation. In chapter 4 we found evidence of a strong interaction effect between capital accumulation and technological change among manufacturing industries during the 1960s and early 1970s. This result is consistent with the so-called embodiment effect—that is, the embodiment of advanced technology in new capital equipment. However, we suggested that causation can also run the other way, with expected technological gains acting as an inducement to capital investment. Here, we examine the latter relation, through a regression of capital investment on TFP growth. We also consider the effects of industry profitability on capital accumulation.

We do find strong evidence of real-wage convergence within manufacturing industries among countries over the period from 1963 to 1983. Interestingly, the results show little tendency toward equalization of wage rates *among industries* within countries, a result consistent with efficiency wage models. Moreover, there is little persuasive evidence that there has been a trend toward the equalization of profit rates across countries within total manufacturing, although there has been a (weak) tendency within individual manufacturing industries. There has also been no tendency for differences in profitability to narrow among industries within countries. However, the correlation between TFP and unit costs in total manufacturing has increased over time, and by the early 1980s unit cost differences were more strongly related to differences in TFP than to differences in real wages. We also find that (lagged) TFP growth was a significant determinant of industry investment. Industry profitability also had a significant effect on investment.

Section 6.2 provides a description of the data and the measurement concepts used in the chapter. Section 6.3 presents the basic evidence on convergence of real wages among countries, and section 6.4 reports industry trends in profitability and unit costs. Section 6.5 presents regression results on the determinants of capital accumulation, both by industry and country. Concluding remarks are made in the last section.

6.2 Data Sources and Concepts

We use the Dollar-Wolff data base for the data analysis in this chapter. Data on output and employment are from the United Nations *Yearbook of Industrial Statistics*, which are reported for twenty-eight manufacturing industries. Our output measure is value added, which is reported in current prices, denominated in domestic currency. Value added is reported net of indirect business taxes, so that it is comparable among countries. We used the GNP deflator of each country to convert output values of different years into 1983 prices, and then applied the PPP index calculated by OECD to convert all output values into 1983 U.S. dollars. Our labor input measure is employment; our capital input measure is gross capital stock.[2]

Total employee compensation is also provided by industry for each country. This is defined as wages and salaries plus fringe benefits including contributions to social insurance (both employee and employer). The real-wage series was constructed by first converting employee compensation of different years into 1983 prices using the household consumption expenditure deflator and then applying the OECD PPP index to convert all values into 1983 U.S. dollars. Real wages were then calculated by dividing total employee compensation in 1983 U.S. dollars by industry, country, and year by the corresponding figure on total employment. No adjustment was made for differences in hours worked or the number of part-time employees.[3]

Gross profits in current prices and domestic currency are defined as value added less employee compensation, both of which are also in current prices and domestic currency. Gross profits include retained earnings, dividends paid out, net interest paid, as well as depreciation. Gross profits are valued before corporate income taxes, but after indirect business taxes. The gross profit rate is the accounting rate of return defined as the ratio of gross profits in current prices and domestic currency to gross capital stock in current prices and domestic currency. Our results on convergence in profit rates will thus be biased insofar as net profits and depreciation are subject to differences in corporate income tax treatment, both among industries and among countries.

Data for computing profit rates, real wage rates, and TFP indices were available for the 1963–83 period for eight countries: Belgium, Canada, Germany, Italy, Japan, the Netherlands, the United Kingdom, and the United States. We used the same twelve manufacturing industries for the analysis as in chapter 4.[4]

6.3 Evidence on Real Wage Convergence

Before examining the results, it is perhaps helpful to consider the theoretical foundations for the hypothesis that wage rates will be equalized among countries. There are two competing models for average wage rates that deserve consideration. The first is the Heckscher-Ohlin model, discussed in chapter 3, which predicts factor price equalization among countries under certain conditions. The second derives from a standard neoclassical model, in which the real wage is equal to the marginal product of labor. This is most easily illustrated where the aggregate production function in country h is of Cobb-Douglas form:

$$Y_t = e^{gt} L_t^{\alpha} K_t^{(1-\alpha)}, \tag{6.1}$$

where Y_t is output at time t, L_t the labor input, K_t capital input, g is the rate of Hicks-neutral technological progress, and the country superscript h has been suppressed for expository convenience. Then, the wage w is given by:

$$w = \partial Y / \partial L = \alpha e^{gt} L^{(\alpha-1)} K^{(1-\alpha)} \tag{6.2}$$

And the wage for country superscript h is given by:

$$w^h = \alpha^h (Y/L)^h \tag{6.3}$$

Insofar as the labor share, α^h, tends to be relatively equal among countries,[5] the real wage will be directly correlated with the average labor productivity of the country. Since aggregate labor productivity levels have converged over time among our sample of countries, we should expect to find, as from the Heckscher-Ohlin model, a trend toward equalization of average wage rates in our sample.

Models of *industry* wage differences among countries are harder to come by. Most standard models of wage determination assume as a basic tenet that real wages will be equalized among industries within a country. Thus, insofar as *average* real wages converge across countries, so should industry wages. Of course, this is subject to many caveats, such as difference in the degree of concentration, unionization, and skill levels (or human capital) among industries. Moreover, recent studies of efficiency-wage differentials have established persistent interindustry real-wage differences in the United States, even after controlling for differences in industry skill levels or human capital (see, for example, Kreuger and Summers 1987; or Dickens and Katz 1987). Thus, insofar as industry wage differentials exist and have different structures across countries, we may expect to find smaller convergence of industry wages than average manufacturing wages.

As shown in table 6.1, the evidence for convergence of real wages in total manufacturing among countries is compelling. All four indices of dispersion indicate very strong equalization in average real wages among countries.[6] The coefficient of variation dropped from 0.40 to 0.16 between 1963 and 1983, the ratio of maximum to minimum declined from 4.1 to 1.5, and the unweighted average mean employee compensation increased from 54% to 83% of the U.S. level.[7] Interestingly, according to these data, the United States had the highest real wages in manufacturing until 1977, when it was overtaken by Canada. Also, by 1982 the Netherlands had almost reached parity with the United States.

Results by industry, shown in table 6.2, are just as strong. The coefficient of variation of real wages among countries fell in every industry over the 1963–82 period, while the unweighted average real wage relative to the leader increased in each industry. It is interesting that there was very little difference in both relative levels of wage dispersion and the degree of convergence in wages among the three large groupings of industries, heavy, medium, and light. Also, a comparison of the wage dispersion indices from the unweighted average among all manufacturing industries

Table 6.1
Mean employee compensation for total manufacturing sector by country for selected years, 1963–83
(index, U.S. = 100)

	1963	1967	1970	1972	1979	1982	1983
Belgium	47	53	61	66	75	82	—
Canada	84	86	96	98	102	102	103
Germany	—	54	60	67	85	88	87
Italy	—	—	28	58	74	75	—
Japan	24	33	44	49	65	71	72
Netherlands	61	69	83	85	98	99	—
United Kingdom	54	50	63	59	67	69	70
United States	100	100	100	100	100	100	100

A. *Summary statistics based on countries with available data*

	1963	1967	1970	1972	1979	1982	1983
Coefficient of variation	.40	.33	.35	.24	.17	.15	.16
Maximum/minimum	4.12	3.01	3.63	2.04	1.57	1.47	1.46
Unweighted average relative to U.S.	.54	.58	.62	.69	.81	.84	.83
Unweighted average relative to leader	.54	.58	.62	.69	.79	.82	.80

B. *Summary statistics based on Belgium, Canada, Germany, Japan, the Netherlands, the United Kingdom, and the United States*

	1965	1967	1970	1972	1979	1982
Coefficient of variation	.36	.33	.27	.24	.17	.14
Unweighted average relative to leader	.55	.58	.68	.71	.80	.84

C. *Summary statistics based on Belgium, Canada, Japan, the Netherlands, and the United States*

	1963	1967	1970	1972	1979	1982
Coefficient of variation	.40	.35	.27	.25	.19	.16
Unweighted average relative to leader	.54	.58	.69	.71	.79	.83

See Appendix for years and industries included for calculating mean employee compensation in each country.

Table 6.2
Indices of dispersion of mean employee compensation across countries by manufacturing industry for selected years, 1963–82

		Coefficient of variation				Unweighted average in seven countries relative to leader			
	NACE	1963	1972	1979	1982	1963	1972	1979	1982
Heavy industries									
Ferrous and nonferrous metals	13	.44	.28	.21	.19	.52	.63	.68	.73
Chemicals	17	.44	.22	.13	.14	.51	.70	.80	.79
Nonmetallic minerals	15	.49	.36	.28	.29	.48	.52	.56	.54
Medium industries									
Machinery	21/23	.44	.28	.17	.19	.53	.63	.76	.71
Rubber and plastics	49	.48	.26	.13	.13	.49	.66	.81	.77
Paper and printing	47	.40	.25	.14	.10	.62	.67	.77	.81
Transport equipment	28	.41	.28	.21	.20	.55	.62	.69	.70
Light industries									
Metal products	19	.54	.32	.23	.20	.46	.61	.70	.76
Other industries	48	.45	.29	.20	.16	.62	.65	.71	.80
Textiles	42	.37	.24	.22	.21	.63	.70	.65	.64
Electrical goods	25	.43	.29	.21	.19	.53	.68	.72	.72
Food, beverages, tobacco	36	.44	.28	.20	.17	.53	.70	.75	.78
Unweighted averages[a]									
All manufacturing		.44	.28	.19	.18	.54	.65	.72	.73
Heavy industry		.46	.29	.21	.21	.50	.62	.68	.69
Medium industry		.43	.27	.16	.16	.55	.65	.75	.75
Light industry		.44	.28	.21	.19	.56	.67	.71	.74
Weighted averages[b]									
All manufacturing		.40	.24	.17	.15	.54	.69	.79	.82
Heavy industry		.46	.28	.19	.18	.53	.64	.74	.74
Medium industry		.43	.28	.18	.17	.55	.65	.77	.77
Light industry		.41	.26	.17	.13	.56	.68	.75	.84

Missing data are as follows: Industries 13, 17, 49, and heavy industry (the Netherlands; Germany and Italy in 1963); Industries 15, 47, 48, 42, 36, and all manufacturing (Germany and Italy in 1963); Industries 21, 23 and medium industry (Belgium, Germany, Italy, and the Netherlands in 1963; Belgium and the Netherlands in 1972–82); and industries 28, 19, 25, and light industry (Belgium; Germany and Italy in 1963).

a. Unweighted average of corresponding statistics in each industry group.

b. Statistics based on aggregate employee compensation in 1983 U.S. dollars and aggregate employment for industries in each industry group.

Table 6.3
Indices of dispersion of mean employee compensation across industries by country for selected years, 1963–83

	1963	1967	1970	1972	1979	1982	1983
A. *Coefficient of variation*[a]							
Belgium	.19	.21	.19	.20	.22	.22	—
Canada	.17	.16	.16	.17	.16	.21	.22
Germany	.12[c]	.12	.32	.12	.13	.13	.13
Italy	—	.17[d]	.18	.17	.12	.11	—
Japan	.23	.20	.20	.19	.20	.21	.22
Netherlands	.26	.27	.21	.22	.20	.20	—
United Kingdom	.23	.25	.24	.13	.13	.14	.14
United States	.17	.16	.16	.16	.20	.19	.20
B. *Unweighted average relative to leading industry*[b]							
Belgium	.75	.67	.72	.71	.71	.68	—
Canada	.74	.74	.71	.71	.69	.65	.61
Germany	.80[c]	.79	.77	.81	.80	.79	.79
Italy	—	.77[d]	.72	.74	.80	.80	—
Japan	.67	.67	.69	.72	.72	.71	.70
Netherlands	.68	.66	.75	.76	.79	.79	—
United Kingdom	.56	.55	.55	.83	.82	.80	.81
United States	.77	.81	.81	.78	.73	.76	.73

a. Defined as the coefficient of variation of industry wage rates for industries within each country with the requisite data. Industries for which data are not available are as follows: Belgium: 19, 21–23, 25, and 28; the Netherlands: 13, 17, 21–23, and 49.
b. Defined as the ratio of the unweighted average of industry mean employee compensation among all industries except that with the highest mean employee compensation to the highest industry mean employee compensation. Only industries with the rquisite data are included. See footnote a for the list of industries that are excluded for each country.
c. 1965.
d. 1968.

with that for aggregate manufacturing shows very little difference. Thus, the convergence of real wages on the individual manufacturing industry level was just as strong as that for total manufacturing. This stands in sharp contrast to the comparable findings on the convergence of labor productivity levels (chapter 3) and TFP levels (chapter 4) in manufacturing industries. Another interesting contrast is that the rate of convergence in real wages was just as rapid after the early 1970s as before. In comparison, the convergence of industry labor productivity and TFP levels essentially ceased by the early 1970s.

However, evidence on real-wage convergence among industries within country is quite mixed (see table 6.3). Over the 1963–83 period, industry wages moved closer together in Italy, the Netherlands, and the United

Kingdom, whereas they diverged in Canada and the United States. In the other three countries there was no clear trend. These results, combined with those of the previous table, suggest that the structure of industry wage differentials are quite similar among countries (at least, those in this sample).[8] They also imply that barriers against wage equalization are stronger between industries than among countries.

6.4 Trends in Industry Profitability and Unit Costs

Most economic theories, both classical and neoclassical, assume a tendency for equalization in profit rates both among industries within a country and among countries over time.[9] Indeed, in the Heckscher-Ohlin model, a key assumption is that factor prices, both profit rates and wage rates, will be equal both among industries and among countries.

There are, of course, several caveats. First, it is necessary to distinguish between the accounting rate of return, on the one hand, and the real cost of capital, the internal rate of return, and the rental rate of capital, on the other. Most theories predict a tendency toward equalization for one of the latter three measures of the rate of return; none, as far as we are aware, predicts equalization in the accounting rate of return. Since we, as in most other studies, use the accounting rate of return, convergence in this measure of profitability is more problematic from a theoretical point of view.

Second, the convergence of profit rates within country is subject to many qualifications, since industry concentration and various sources of economic rent (such as proprietary technologies) will deter complete equalization.[10] Indeed, Mueller (1986) has found persistent interindustry differences in profit rates in the United States. Third, the convergence of profit rates among countries is subject to other qualifications, such as differences in the tax treatment of profits and depreciation and the degree of country risk.

Table 6.4 shows gross profit rates for the whole manufacturing sector for selected years over the 1963–83 period. The profit rates, at first glance, appear quite high, ranging for the most part between 20% and 40%. However, it should be recalled that the profits are before tax and depreciation and include all forms of property (nonwage) income. Moreover, the denominator includes only fixed capital.

It is of interest to look next at the movement of the rate of profit over the period. In all eight countries, with the exception of the United Kingdom, a clear downward trend is evident for the rate of profit over the twenty-year period. However, the direction of change was not uniform.

Table 6.4
Gross profit rates for whole manufacturing sector by country for selected years, 1963–83 (percent)

	1963	1967	1970	1972	1979	1982	1983
Belgium	25.9	22.3	27.7	—	25.5	16.9	—
Canada	23.3	22.5	20.4	21.9	24.9	—	17.6
Germany	—	48.3	53.0	46.2	35.8	29.1	—
Italy	—	—	36.2	26.3	28.5	23.9	—
Japan	—	62.6	65.6	56.7	43.1	38.3	38.9
Netherlands	33.3	35.4	39.4	—	31.8	18.3	—
United Kingdom	25.8	—	27.2	—	29.7	24.7	26.7
United States	47.4	50.4	44.0	45.4	43.3	35.1	38.1

A. *Summary statistics based on countries with available data*

	1963	1967	1970	1972	1979	1982	1983
Unweighted mean	31.1	40.3	39.2	39.3	32.8	26.6	30.3
Coefficient of variation	.28	.37	.36	.33	.21	.28	.29
Maximum/minimum	2.03	2.81	3.21	2.59	1.74	2.27	2.21
Unweighted average relative to leader	.57	.57	.54	.62	.72	.64	.71

B. *Summary statistics based on Belgium, Germany, Italy, Japan, the Netherlands, the United Kingdom, and the United States*

	1970	1974	1979	1982
Coefficient of variation	.31	.20	.19	.28
Unweighted average relative to leader	.58	.70	.75	.64

C. *Summary statistics based on Belgium, Canada, Germany, Japan, the Netherlands, and the United States*

	1965	1967	1970	1972	1979	1982
Coefficient of variation	.32	.37	.36	.22	.22	.28
Unweighted average relative to leader	.67	.57	.56	.71	.74	.66

See Appendix for years and industries included for calculating gross profit rates in each country.

For most countries, the rate of profit in manufacturing rose between the early 1960s and the early 1970s and then declined. The unweighted average (shown in panel A) increased from 31% in 1963 to 39% in 1972, and then fell to 30% in 1983. There was also a sizable drop between 1979 and 1982, very likely a consequence of the worldwide recession of 1981–82.

Four measures of intercountry dispersion are presented in panel A. The first, the coefficient of variation, increased from 0.28 in 1963 to 0.36 in 1970, declined to 0.21 in 1979, and then rose to 0.29 in 1983. Over the whole period there is no discernible trend in this index. The second is the ratio of the maximum rate of profit to its minimum value in the sample. This measure of dispersion has a similar pattern, increasing between 1963 and 1970, declining between 1970 and 1979, and then rising in the early 1980s. If anything, there is a slight upward trend in this index of dispersion over the full twenty years. The third is the ratio of the unweighted mean gross profit rate among all countries (excluding the one with the highest profit rate) to that of the leader. Japan had the highest profit rate in manufacturing in all years except 1963 and 1976–79, when the United States led.[11] This index has a somewhat similar pattern to the other two, declining from 1963 to 1970, rising until 1979, and then declining slightly to 1983, though the overall trend shows declining dispersion over the twenty-year period.[12]

For individual industries the pattern is mixed, as shown in table 6.5. Convergence of gross profit rates among countries, as evidenced by the decline in the coefficient of variation and the increase in the unweighted average relative to the leader, occurred in six industries: chemicals; machinery; rubber and plastics; paper and printing; transport equipment; and metal products. There is clear evidence of divergence of gross profit rates in two industries: the "other industries" category and food, beverages, and tobacco. In the other four industries, no clear trends are discernible, or the behavior of the two indices is contradictory. Results for the unweighted average among all manufacturing industries (last row) show that, on average, there was a moderate tendency toward profit rate equalization among individual manufacturing industries.

Table 6.6 shows another slice of the profit-rate convergence issue. The data provide indices of dispersion of profit rates among individual industries within each country. In Belgium, Germany, Italy, and the United States, profit rates became more unequal among the twelve manufacturing industries over the 1963–83 period. In Japan, the Netherlands, and the United Kingdom, industry profit rates moved closer together over the twenty-year period. For Canada, the two indices show inconsistent trends.

Table 6.5
Indices of profit rate dispersion across countries by manufacturing industry for selected years, 1963–82

		Coefficient of variation				Unweighted average in seven countries relative to leader			
	NACE	1963	1972	1979	1982	1963	1972	1979	1982
Heavy industries									
Ferrous and nonferrous metals	13	.57	.50	.42	.61	.41	.39	.53	.43
Chemicals	17	.48	.43	.37	.33	.41	.54	.58	.59
Nonmetallic minerals	15	.46	.88	1.12	.49	.50	.26	.16	.39
Medium industries									
Machinery	21/23	.30	.33	.29	.25	.60	.52	.61	.65
Rubber and plastics	49	.86	.68	.60	.76	.29	.38	.54	.42
Paper and printing	47	.58	.62	.28	.30	.51	.34	.64	.66
Transport equipment	28	.42	.37	.30	.24	.46	.59	.71	.70
Light industries									
Metal products	19	.79	.58	.32	.27	.40	.37	.64	.67
Other industries	48	.18	.39	.23	.30	.76	.56	.67	.61
Textiles	42	.36	.41	.40	.45	.48	.55	.57	.51
Electrical goods	25	.31	.37	.27	.29	.54	.46	.61	.57
Food, beverages, tobacco	36	.20	.33	.29	.42	.70	.54	.61	.60
All manufacturing[a]		.28	.33	.21	.28	.57	.62	.72	.64
Unweighted average[b]		.46	.49	.41	.39	.51	.46	.57	.57

Missing data are as follows: Industry 13 (the Netherlands; Germany, Italy, and Japan in 1963; Canada in 1982); industry 17 (the Netherlands; Germany, Italy, and Japan in 1963; the United Kingdom in 1972; Canada in 1982); industry 15 (Germany, Italy, and Japan in 1963; Japan in 1972; Canada in 1982); industries 21 and 23 (Belgium and the Netherlands; Germany, Italy, and Japan in 1963; Canada in 1982); industry 49 (Japan and the Netherlands; Germany, Italy, and Japan in 1963; Canada in 1982); industries 47 and 42 (Germany, Italy, and Japan in 1963; the United Kingdom in 1972; Canada in 1982); industries 28 and 25 (Belgium; Germany, Italy, and Japan in 1963; Canada in 1982); industry 19 (Belgium; Germany, Italy, and Japan in 1963; the Netherlands and the United Kingdom in 1972; Canada in 1982); industries 48 and 36 (Germany, Italy, and Japan in 1963; Canada in 1982); and all manufacturing (Germany, Italy, and Japan in 1963; Belgium, the Netherlands, and the United Kingdom in 1972; Canada in 1982).

a. Statistics based on aggregate gross profits and aggregate capital stock for the total economy.

b. Unweighted average of corresponding statistics for each industry.

Table 6.6
Indices of dispersion of industry profit rates within country for selected years, 1963–83

	1963	1967	1970	1972	1979	1982	1983
A. *Coefficient of variation*[a]							
Belgium	.74	.82	.70	.75	.86	.93	—
Canada	.48	.53	.56	.52	.51	—	.55
Germany	.44[c]	.46	.42	.50	.48	.47	—
Italy	—	.27[d]	.30	.31	.31	.37	—
Japan	.40[c]	.38	.43	.43	.29	.34	.36
Netherlands	.60	.55	.57	.81[e]	.27[f]	.22	—
United Kingdom	.45	.47[d]	.49	.36[e]	.38	.36	.33
United States	.33	.31	.36	.36	.28	.39	.39
B. *Unweighted average relative to leading industry*[b]							
Belgium	.39	.33	.36	.34	.29	.29	—
Canada	.44	.42	.43	.37	.42	—	.56
Germany	.60[c]	.57	.53	.45	.41	.45	—
Italy	—	.53[d]	.47	.55	.50	.46	—
Japan	.36[c]	.37	.35	.36	.47	.42	.41
Netherlands	.29	.32	.18	.13[e]	.36[f]	.40	—
United Kingdom	.46	.40[d]	.41	.45[e]	.53	.59	.61
United States	.59	.70	.51	.49	.53	.51	.51

a. Defined as the coefficient of variation of industry profit rates for industries within each country with the requisite data. Industries for which data are not available are as follows: Belgium: 19, 21–23, 25, and 28; Japan: 15 and 49; and the Netherlands: 13, 17, 21–23, and 49.
b. Defined as the ratio of the unweighted average of industry profit rates among all industries except that with the highest profit rate to the highest industry profit rate. Only industries with the requisite data are included (see footnote a).
c. 1965.
d. 1968.
e. 1973.
f. 1980.

In sum, there is no persuasive evidence showing a trend towards convergence in gross profit rates within total manufacturing among the eight countries in the sample over the 1963–83 period. The evidence does indicate convergence during the 1970s but a pattern of dispersion during the 1960s and early 1980s. However, there is some evidence of profit rate equalization within individual industries (on the basis of the unweighted averages among countries), though the trend is relatively weak. With regard to profit rate equalization among different industries within the same country, the evidence is mixed. In 4 of the 8 countries industry profit rates became less equal over the twenty-year period, and in three they became more equal.

Table 6.7
Unit costs for total manufacturing sector by country for selected years, 1963–83 (index, U.S. = 100)

	1963	1968	1972	1979	1982
Belgium	123	126	126	125	137
Canada	113	118	122	128	135
Germany	—	81	92	119	120
Italy	—	—	94	95	93
Japan	71	69	77	90	88
Netherlands	108	109	103	111	132
United Kingdom	118	117	113	114	112
United States	100	100	100	100	100
Coefficient of variation	.16	.19	.15	.12	.16
Correlation with					
Wages (ω)	0.35	0.38	—	0.24	0.44
TFP level[a]	0.06	−0.21	—	−0.47	−0.62

a. The 1982 correlation coefficient between unit costs and TFP levels excludes Canada.

Unit-Cost Differences

Unit costs, UC, are defined as

$$UC = [\omega L + rK] / Y, \tag{6.3}$$

where, as before, L is total employment, K is gross capital stock, and Y is real value added; and ω is current wages (in U.S. dollar equivalents) and r is the rate of profit.[13] We are interested first in whether unit-cost differences have narrowed over time among countries. Unit costs depend on both factor prices and the level of productivity. Higher wages and profits will increase the unit cost but higher productivity will lower it.[14] Thus, insofar as average wages in a country vary with its average productivity level, we should expect to see much less dispersion in unit labor costs than in either productivity levels or wage levels.

Results from panel A of table 6.7, for total manufacturing, generally confirm that this pattern prevailed. The dispersion in unit costs, as measured by the coefficient of variation, was uniformly less than the corresponding measure for real wages (table 6.1) and TFP levels (table 4.1), except for 1982, when the three measures were almost the same. Differences in unit costs were much less than those of real wages or TFP levels during the 1960s (with coefficients of variation in 1963 of 0.16, 0.40, and 0.23, respectively), but the gap closed very quickly during the 1970s. This is to be expected, because wages tend to rise in conjunction with overall productivity levels. Correspondingly, there is almost no trend in the dispersion of unit costs between 1963 and 1982—a result of the convergence in both real wages and productivity levels over the period.

It is also of interest to examine comparative unit costs among the countries in the sample. The United States was among the lower-cost countries throughout the period (second lowest in 1963, fourth lowest in 1972, and third lowest in the other years). Japan maintained its position as the lowest-cost producer throughout these years, despite the rapid increase of real wages in the country (second only to Italy). Germany, on the other hand, shifted from a low-cost producer during the 1960s to a middle-cost one by the early 1980s.

We next look at the determinants of unit cost differences at the aggregate level among countries. As noted above, there are two dominant factors: relative wage differences among counties and differences in productivity (TFP) levels. We use a correlation coefficient to measure the importance of each of the factors. Difference in wage costs was the dominant factor in explaining the variation in unit costs in the early 1960s. It remained important throughout the period under consideration (the correlation coefficient varied between 0.24 and 0.44). On the other hand, differences in TFP levels explained none of the differences in unit costs in the early 1960s; however, their importance increased through the period, and by 1982 differences in TFP levels were more important than the variation of wages in explaining unit cost differences among countries.[15] Indeed, this is true despite the fact that productivity levels and real wages converged to the *same* degree by the early 1980s. This suggests that by the 1980s trade patterns depended more on technological advantage than on wage differences between countries, a result that we will confirm in the next chapter.[16]

6.5 Determinants of Industry Investment

Before examining the factors that influence capital formation both among industries and among countries, it is of interest to consider first basic statistics on the rate of capital accumulation by country (table 6.8). There is considerable dispersion among nations. Over the 1963–82 period the annual average rate of capital growth in total manufacturing ranged from a low of 2.9% in the United Kingdom to 8.8% in Japan, with the United States slightly below average at 4.0%.

However, there are marked differences between the 1963–72 and 1972–82 periods. Capital growth was much stronger in the first, averaging 6.1%

Table 6.8
Average capital stock growth for total manufacturing by country, 1963–82 (percent per annum)

	1963–82	1963–72	1972–82
Belgium[a]	4.5	6.3	3.1
Canada[b]	4.4	5.2	3.6
Germany	3.9	5.8	2.1
Italy	3.2	4.1	2.5
Japan[c]	8.8	12.9	5.8
Netherlands[d]	4.7	6.8	3.2
United Kingdom[e]	2.9	3.5	2.2
United States	4.0	4.4	3.7
Mean	4.5	6.1	3.3
Coefficient of variation	0.37	0.45	0.34

a. For Belgium, 1971 is used instead of 1972.
b. For Canada, 1983 is used instead of 1982.
c. For Japan, 1965 is used instead of 1963.
d. For the Netherlands, 1971 is used instead of 1972 for total manufacturing and 1973 is used instead of 1972 for industry 19.
e. For the United Kingdom, 1973 is used instead of 1972 for industries 17, 19, 42, and 47.

per year, than in the second, at 3.3% per year. The rate of capital accumulation fell in every country. This is consistent with the finding of Boyer and Petit (1981) of a sharp break in productivity, output, and employment growth in 1973 among EEC countries. Moreover, on the basis of the coefficient of variation, there was less dispersion in capital growth in the 1972–82 period.

Table 6.9 shows the rate of growth of the capital stock by industry averaged across countries. Here, too, there is considerable variation in capital growth rates among industries. For the 1963–82 period, they range from a low of 1.8% per year in textiles to 5.7% in electrical goods. As for total manufacturing, the capital stock growth rate declined between the 1963–72 and 1972–82 subperiods in every industry. The coefficient of variation for capital growth rates is also shown by industry. Whereas the coefficient of variation fell for total manufacturing between the two subperiods, the pattern is quite mixed by industry. For 4 of the 12 industries, there was a clear decline in the coefficient of variation, for 5 there was a substantial increase, and for the remaining 2 the change was very small.

In sum, the results indicate that aggregate rates of capital accumulation within total manufacturing were showing some convergence among the eight countries in our sample over the 1962–83 period. Moreover, for some industries, rates of capital accumulation were becoming more equal

Table 6.9
Average capital stock growth by industry, 1963–83
(percent per annum)

	NACE	Unweighted average among countries			Coefficient of variation among countries		
		1963–72	1972–82	1963–82	1963–72	1972–82	1963–82
Heavy industries							
Ferrous and nonferrous metals	13	6.2	2.3	4.1	.52	.51	.47
Chemicals	17[a]	7.0	3.8	5.3	.38	.43	.30
Nonmetallic minerals	15	5.6	2.9	4.2	.28	.33	.20
Medium industries							
Machinery	21/23	6.8	4.8	5.7	.55	.36	.43
Rubber and plastics	49	6.1	3.2	4.6	.46	.44	.42
Paper and printing	47[a]	5.7	3.7	4.7	.39	.76	.53
Transport equipment	28	6.3	4.1	5.1	.64	.39	.51
Light industries							
Metal products	19[b]	7.0	3.7	5.2	.73	.52	.61
Other industries	48	6.2	2.4	4.1	.55	1.07	.30
Textiles	42[a]	3.4	0.5	1.8	.57	2.37	.71
Electrical goods	25	6.7	4.8	5.7	.33	.34	.31
Food, beverages, tobacco	36	5.2	3.1	4.1	.56	.46	.48
All manufacturing[c]		6.1	3.3	4.5	.45	.34	.37

Missing data are as follows: Industry 13, 17 (Netherlands); Industry 21, 23 (Belgium, Netherlands); Industry 49 (Japan, Netherlands); Industry 28, 19, 25 (Belgium).

a. 1973 is used instead of 1972 for the United Kingdom.

b. 1973 is used instead of 1972 for the Netherlands and the United Kingdom.

c. 1971 is used instead of 1972 for Belgium and the Netherlands; 1983 is used instead of 1982 for Canada; 1965 is used instead of 1963 for Japan; and 1973 is used instead of 1972 for the United Kingdom.

among countries, whereas for other industries they were becoming less equal.

The basic data reveal no easily discernible pattern for capital accumulation by industry or country. Below, we engage in a regression analysis that relates the rate of capital growth by industry and country to a corresponding set of variables. In section 6.1 we have already argued that capital formation should be positively affected by the expected rate of productivity (TFP) growth. We measure this effect in two ways: first by the lagged rate of TFP growth; and second by the initial TFP level of the industry. The first of these is used under the assumption that expected technological advance is directly related to previous gains.[17] The rationale for the second measurement approach is that potential technological gains may be greater in a low-productivity industry than in a more advanced one (the "advantages of backwardness" effect).

Two other influences should also prove important. The first of these is profitability. Many economic theories assume that profit rates will tend to be equalized (both among firms in an industry and among industries in a country) and that the equilibrating mechanism is the flow of capital to the industries and countries with relatively high profit rates. Although we have not found strong evidence of profit-rate equalization, we may still expect to find that high profits are an inducement to capital investment. We use the lagged value of the profit rate in the regression analysis under the assumptions that current investment is a response to expected profitability and that the latter is directly related to past profit rates.

The second of these other variables is the real-wage level. The argument comes originally from Marx (1967), who stated in volume 1 of *Capital* that high wages may act as an inducement for labor-saving capital investment. In other words, high wages should create pressure for new investment and should be positively associated with capital growth. We also use the lagged value of the wage rate in the regressions, for reasons similar to those for the use of lagged profits.

In our regression analysis, the dependent variable is

CAPGRTH_{it}^{h} the rate of growth of the capital stock in industry i of country h in year t.

The independent variables are

$\text{TFPGRTH}_{i,t-1}^{h}$ the rate of growth of total factor productivity, based on the Tornqvist-Divisia index (equation 4.9), in industry i of country h in year $t - 1$.[18]

RELTFP^h_{it}	the TFP level of industry i in country h relative to that of industry i in the United States in year t.
$\text{PROFRATE}^h_{i,t-1}$	the gross profit rate in industry i of country h in year $t-1$.
$\text{WAGERATE}^h_{i,t-1}$	mean employee compensation in 1983 U.S. dollars in industry i of country h in year $t-1$.
DUM_{65-72}	dummy variable equal to 1 for the 1965–72 period and zero otherwise.

Moreover, in some specifications, we add dummy variables for 7 of the 8 countries (excluding the United States) and for 11 of the 12 industries (excluding industry 48) to capture country-specific and industry-specific effects. Because of missing data problems and substantial year-to-year fluctuations in capital growth rates and industry profit rates, we actually use two-year and three-year averages for CAPGRTH, PROFRATE, WAGERATE, and TFPGRTH. The sample covers eight countries and twelve industries. The two-year average variables cover nine time periods (from 1965 to 1983), and the three-year average variables cover six time periods (1965 to 1983). Lags are in terms of periods (for the two-year average variables, the lag is two years).

The regression results are shown in table 6.10. The most important finding is that capital investment is significantly related to expected technological gains, as measured by lagged TFP growth and the relative TFP level of the industry. The coefficient of the former is positive and highly significant; the coefficient of the latter has the expected negative sign and is significant at the 1% level when two-year averages are used, and at the 5% level with three-year average values. Also, as predicted, the lagged profit rate is a positive and highly significant determinant of the rate of capital accumulation.

The coefficient of the lagged wage rate variable is positive and statistically significant in the two forms without industry dummy variables, but becomes insignificant when they are included in the regression specification. This is consistent with our finding in section 6.3 of persistent industry wage differentials (so that much of the variation in industry wage rates is captured by the industry dummy variables). Together, the results lend support to the argument that, ceteris paribus, high wages provide an inducement for investment to offset the high costs of labor. The dummy variable for the 1965–72 period is positive and highly significant. The magnitude of the coefficient indicates that, ceteris paribus, the rate of capi-

Table 6.10
Regressions of rate of growth of capital stock on total factor productivity (TFP), profit rate, and real wage rate

	Dependent variable: $CAPGRTH^h_{it}$			
Independent variables	Two-year average values			Three-year averages
Constant	0.0142**	−0.0081	0.0198	0.0219
	(2.77)	(0.84)	(1.70)	(1.59)
$TFPGRTH^h_{i,t-1}$	0.1203**	0.1097**	0.1156**	0.1305**
	(6.16)	(5.99)	(6.28)	(4.46)
$RELTFP^h_{it}$	−0.0326**	−0.0231**	−0.0324**	−0.0176*
	(5.36)	(3.98)	(4.41)	(2.32)
$PROFRATE^h_{i,t-1}$	0.0781**	0.0576**	0.0733**	0.0466**
	(8.93)	(6.56)	(6.48)	(4.31)
$WAGERATE^h_{i,t-1}$ (US$10,000)	0.0068*	0.0146**	−0.0071	−0.0078
	(2.22)	(3.53)	(1.40)	(1.31)
DUM_{65-72}	0.0267**	0.0307**	0.0205**	0.0227**
	(9.15)	(10.1)	(6.40)	(6.72)
COUNTRY DUMMIES	excluded	included	included	included
Ind. DUMMIES	excluded	excluded	included	included
R^2	0.275	0.383	0.466	0.492
$\bar{R}^2$	0.269	0.371	0.445	0.461
Std. error	0.033	0.030	0.028	0.026
Sample size	637	637	637	406

Results are based on two-year averages for CAPGRTH, PROFRATE, WAGERATE, and TFPGRTH (three-year averages in the last column). The sample covers the time period from 1965 to 1982, eight countries, and twelve industries. Lags are in terms of periods (for the two-year average variables, the lag is two years). Eestimated coefficients are shown next to the respective independent variable and the absolute value of the *t*-statistic is shown in parentheses.
*Significant at the .05 level (two-tailed test).
**Significant at the .01 level (two-tailed test).

tal growth was 2 to 3 percentage points higher during the 1965–72 period than in the ensuing years.

A comparison of columns 1 and 2 of the table indicate that there is a considerable increase in both the R^2 and the adjusted-R^2 statistics, as well as a corresponding reduction of the standard error of the regression, when country dummy variables are included in the equation. All seven of the country dummy variables have positive coefficients, indicating that each of them had a higher rate of capital growth than the United States after the other factors are controlled for. The estimated coefficient is highest for

Japan, at 0.045, and next highest for Belgium, at 0.012. These are the only two countries for which the dummy variable is statistically significant.

In the third column, industry dummy variables are included. There is, again, a sharp increase in both the R^2 and the adjusted-R^2 statistics, and a corresponding decline in the standard error of the regression. All eleven of the industry dummy coefficients, with the exception of industry 42, are positive and statistically significant, indicating higher rates of capital growth than other manufacturing (industry 48). The highest coefficients, in descending order, are found for chemicals (0.033), ferrous and nonferrous metals (0.031), rubber and plastics (0.032), and transport equipment (0.031).

There are also some interesting changes in the coefficients of the country dummy variables when industry dummy variables are included. The dummy variable for Japan is cut in half, to 0.022, though its significance level remains unchanged, at the one percent level. The coefficients of Belgium, Germany, Italy, and the United Kingdom are now all negative, and those of Germany and Italy are statistically significant at the 5% level. The results indicate that much of the difference in country rates of capital accumulation is due, ceteris paribus, to differences in industry composition. In particular, once industry effects and other differences are controlled for, the United States no longer had the lowest rate of capital accumulation but was, instead, in the middle of the pack.[19]

6.6 Conclusion

The convergence in real wage rates among industrial countries has been well documented (see, for example, Hooper and Larin 1989; or Mokhtari and Rassekh 1989), and we find a similar result. Convergence in real wages was very strong for total manufacturing and equally strong for individual manufacturing industries. However, we find little convergence of wages among industries. Moreover, the results indicate considerable variation in profit rates both among countries and industries and over time. The results show some tendency toward convergence within industry among countries, but no tendency toward profit rate equalization for total manufacturing.

Differences in unit costs did not exhibit any tendency to diminish over the period between 1963 and 1982, because of the strong correlation between average real wages and the average productivity level within a country. Thus, high productivity levels within an industry were largely offset by high wages, and conversely. During the 1960s unit cost differences between countries were dominated by real wage differences, but by 1982 the variation in TFP levels was the dominant factor. This result is consistent with the finding that we will report in chapter 7 that export patterns in the 1980s depended primarily on technological advantage. Japan remained the lowest-cost producer throughout the period from 1963 to 1982, despite the second highest rate of growth of real wages. This fact may help to explain the country's sizable manufacturing exports, despite its failure to achieve technological superiority in a large number of manufacturing industries.

We find a very strong and statistically significant relation between an industry's expected technological gains, as measured by its past TFP growth and its degree of technological backwardness, and its rate of capital growth. This finding is consistent with that reported in chapter 4 of strong complementarities between technological advance and capital formation. It also reinforces our belief that the relation runs both ways, with new technology embodied in new investment and with TFP growth acting as a stimulus to new capital formation. We find that capital has flowed to industries with high profit rates. There is some evidence that high wages act as an inducement for investment, presumably in labor-saving technology.

The results indicate that once other effects are controlled for, the rate of capital growth was 2 to 3 percentage points higher during the 1965–72 period than during 1972–82. This is consistent with the basic data which show a pronounced slowdown in capital accumulation during the latter period. They also indicate industry-specific effects on capital accumulation. Interestingly, without effects of industry differences in the investment behavior among industries, the United States had the lowest rate of capital accumulation of the eight countries, after adjustment for other factors. However, once such industry differences are taken into account, U.S. investment performance appears much stronger, with only Japan and Canada having statistically significant higher rates of capital formation. This implies that part of the lower overall capital buildup of the United States in manufacturing can be attributed to industrial composition.

7 Productivity Growth and the Changing Pattern of Trade

It has been established in previous chapters that industrial economies have become more similar in the postwar period. This is indicated by a convergence of several economy-wide measures, such as GDP per worker, the overall capital-labor ratio, aggregate TFP, and average real wages. In chapters 3, 4, and 6 we have shown that there is a similar convergence of labor productivity, capital intensity, and TFP, as well as of real wages, at the industry level within the manufacturing sectors of developed countries.

It is interesting, however, that, except for real wages, convergence at the industry level is generally not as strong as that in more aggregated indices. For instance, value added per work hour in all manufacturing has converged very strongly among OECD countries. But there has been less convergence at the industry level, and in fact aggregate convergence is to some extent attributable to the modest labor productivity leads that different countries acquire in different industries. The results for TFP are similar. Different countries have tended to gain on and, in several cases, surpass the United States in different industries, so that again convergence in aggregate TFP is stronger than convergence at the industry level. Furthermore, convergence in TFP at the industry level appears to have come to a halt about the mid-1970s.

In this chapter we investigate what has been happening to trade patterns of industrial countries in the period 1970–86. Our choice of time period was dictated by data availability. We confine ourselves to the same nine countries and twelve manufacturing industries that we examined in chapters 4 and 6 (on the basis of the Dollar-Wolff data base), and address two basic questions. First, has there been a convergence of trade patterns (particularly, export composition) for these industrial countries? Second, as suggested in chapter 6, is there any clear relationship between TFP growth at the industry level and changing comparative advantage?

7.1 Trade Patterns and Productivity Growth: An Analytical Framework

Before proceeding to the empirical analysis, it is useful to reiterate briefly some of the themes that emerged in chapter 3. In general, trade theory does not provide any clear predictions about the relationship between productivity and trade patterns in a world with many countries and many goods. The one exception to this statement is the Heckscher-Ohlin (HO) model with factor-price equalization. That model makes very sharp predictions about cross-country patterns in labor and total factor productivity at the industry level; namely, that productivity should be the same in all countries. The results presented in chapter 3, however, demonstrate clearly that this unambiguous prediction is not borne out at all in data for developed countries in the postwar period. In general there is more variation in both labor and total factor productivity at the industry level than at aggregate levels, which conflicts with the predictions of the factor-price equalization construct.

Other trade models, such as the HO model without factor-price equalization or the Ricardo-Viner (specific-factors) model, generally do not yield clear, testable implications about productivity or other pertinent variables. Nevertheless, they do provide a framework within which we can explore a number of general propositions. As noted, there has been a marked convergence of labor productivity, capital-labor ratios, and TFP in the aggregate for developed economies in the postwar period. There has been a similar convergence at the industry level, although it is weaker for capital intensity than for labor productivity or TFP. An HO type of model suggests that convergence in aggregate capital-labor ratios should be accompanied by a convergence in the trade patterns of these countries. On the other hand, our research on convergence of aggregate TFP suggests that this convergence may be the result of different countries' developing relatively high levels of TFP in different industries. In that case, there may be a growing *divergence* of trade patterns as different countries increasingly concentrate production and exports in different industries. In the next section we investigate these ideas by examining the changing trade patterns among nine developed countries over the period 1970–86, and by assessing in particular whether there is any trend toward convergence or divergence.

In section 7.3 we ask the specific question, Is changing comparative advantage related to the growth of TFP at the industry level? For simplicity, we focus this analysis on the United States and Japan. The theoretical justification for this examination is the idea that growth of TFP may be capturing an increase in some industry-specific factor, which should lead to a shift in production and exports toward that industry. Actually, it is growth of TFP in one country relative to other countries that is important here. If TFP in a particular industry is growing rapidly throughout the world, then this should have no effect on any one country's comparative advantage. On the other hand, if in that industry one country's TFP is growing rapidly relative to other countries, then we would expect that country's industry to become increasingly competitive and to expand its share of the world market.

It should also be noted that our findings on convergence of factor prices at the industry level, reported in chapter 6, greatly strengthen the notion that TFP growth should be an important determinant of changing comparative advantage. We showed that, from the early 1960s to the mid-1980s, there was a strong tendency toward convergence of real wages and a relatively weak one for the return to capital for individual industries in developed countries. That result implies that among OECD countries differences in the cost of labor (and, to some extent, capital) were not important determinants of differences in unit costs by the 1980s. Given the similarity in factor prices, trends in relative TFP then become crucial determinants of cost competitiveness. In particular, increased relative TFP in a particular industry and country should translate into increased competitiveness and exports.[1]

7.2 Convergence of Trade Patterns?

In this section we investigate whether trade patterns of developed countries have tended toward convergence over the last two decades. The countries included and the industry classification employed are the same as in chapter 4; they were evaluated on the basis of the Dollar-Wolff data base and selected on the basis of data availability. In particular, comparable cross-country data on capital stock at the industry level were only available for manufacturing disaggregated into twelve industries and for nine countries: Belgium, Canada, France, Germany, Italy, Japan, the Netherlands, the United Kingdom, and the United States.

Trade data in a much more disaggregated form are available on computer tape from the OECD, but unfortunately only begin in 1970 (and run until 1986). We aggregated the trade data to conform to the twelve-industry classification. In examining changes in trade patterns, we use Balassa's revealed comparative advantage (RCA) measure (Balassa 1965). For industry i and country j this measure is

$$\mathrm{RCA}_{ij} = [X_{ij} / \Sigma_j X_{ij}] / [(\Sigma_j X_{ij}) / (\Sigma_i \Sigma_j X_{ij})], \tag{7.1}$$

where X_{ij} is country j's exports of good i.

The aggregation over j covers the nine countries in our study, and the aggregation over i covers the twelve manufacturing industries. Hence this measure takes as its benchmark (denominator) country j's share of total manufacturing exports for these nine countries. The numerator is country j's share of product i exports for the nine countries. An RCA above or below 1 indicates that country j's share of the group's product i exports is higher or lower than its share of total manufactured exports. By construction, some RCAs for a country will be greater than 1, while others will be less than 1 (unless the country has exactly the same share of every export market). This index indicates in which product lines a country's exports are concentrated, which is taken as a measure of revealed comparative advantage.

There is no ideal measure of comparative advantage. Net exports are often employed; however, net exports change as a result not just of alterations in the pattern of trade, but also of fluctuations in the overall trade balance, which is basically a macroeconomic phenomenon and not indicative of comparative advantage. Hence we prefer the Balassa RCA measure, even though it focuses only on exports.

We calculated RCAs for the nine countries and twelve industries and investigated what happened to the cross-country dispersion in these measures. Table 7.1 shows the coefficient of variation among countries for each industry in 1970, 1976, 1982, and 1986. Industries are grouped on the basis of the capital-labor ratio, as in chapter 4. There is no clear trend over this period: between 1970 and 1986 dispersion increased in 6 industries and decreased in 6 industries. Furthermore, there is no important difference between heavy and light industries. Among major heavy industries, for instance, variation in RCAs declined in basic metals, but increased in chemicals. In the medium industries, dispersion increased in transport equipment, but decreased in machinery. In the two main light industries, textiles and electrical goods, the coefficient of variation went up.

This result is somewhat surprising in light of the evidence that aggregate measures of factor endowments (such as aggregate capital-labor ratio or TFP for the whole economy) have become more similar for these developed economies. On the other hand, the result is consistent with our finding that dispersion of TFP at the industry level remains high, and that there has been no strong trend toward cross-country convergence of industry-level TFP since the mid-1970s. It appears that countries are developing

Table 7.1
Coefficients of variation in revealed comparative advantage (RCA) measures for nine developed countries and twelve industries, 1970–86

	Coefficient of variation across nine countries			
	1970	1976	1982	1986
Heavy industries				
Basic metals	.55	.48	.39	.41
Chemicals	.28	.31	.33	.37
Nonmetallic minerals	.58	.74	.70	.65
Medium industries				
Machinery	.44	.41	.39	.35
Rubber and plastics	.44	.36	.33	.30
Paper and printing	1.10	1.27	1.12	.95
Transport equipment	.39	.40	.44	.50
Light industries				
Metal products	.18	.20	.23	.25
Other industries	.21	.23	.23	.19
Textiles	.55	.58	.69	.79
Electrical goods	.40	.43	.51	.55
Food, beverages, tobacco	.74	.67	.63	.67

Source: Trade data are from OECD tape.

specializations in different industries; in this way, convergence of aggregate TFP can be consistent with continuing divergence of industry-level TFP and a continuing high dispersion in export patterns.

To examine this latter idea table 7.2 lists for each country in 1982 the two industries with the highest RCAs and the two industries with the lowest.[2] Inspection of this table indicates that these countries' exports are concentrated in different industries. In the column indicating the highest two RCA measures, every industry appears at least once, and no industry appears more than twice. By construction, if the RCA for industry i is high in one country, it has to be low somewhere else. But there is no algebraic constraint on two or three countries having similar RCAs; and it is quite surprising that there are no such similarities. Also, the absolute size of the RCAs is of interest; small differences in trade patterns would be indicated by RCAs that deviate little from 1. In table 7.2, however, there are quite a few in the 2–5 range, indicating very substantial specialization.

The smaller economies, in particular, appear to be highly specialized in their exports. Canada, for instance, has an extremely high RCA of 5.1 in paper and printing. Belgium has RCAs close to 2 in two heavy industries, nonmetallic minerals and basic metals. The Netherlands has RCAs above 2 in nonmetallic minerals and in food, beverages, and tobacco. The high

Table 7.2
Revealed comparative advantage (RCA) in manufacturing industries of nine developed countries, 1982

	Highest two RCAs	Lowest two RCAs
United States	Machinery 1.49	Basic metals .39
	Paper and printing 1.12	Textiles .47
Japan	Electrical goods 1.96	Food, beverages, tobacco .13
	Basic metals 1.60	Paper and printing .26
Canada	Paper and printing 5.10	Textiles .25
	Transport equipment 1.64	Electrical goods .47
Belgium	Nonmetallic minerals 1.88	Machinery .38
	Basic metals 1.75	Electrical goods .47
France	Food, beverages, tobacco 1.70	Other industries .74
	Rubber and plastics 1.54	Machinery .76
Germany	Metal products 1.15	Nonmetallic minerals .64
	Transport equipment 1.13	Food, beverages, tobacco .79
Italy	Textiles 2.99	Transport equipment .48
	Rubber and plastics 1.61	Paper and printing .57
Netherlands	Nonmetallic minerals 3.25	Transport equipment .27
	Food, beverages, tobacco 2.86	Machinery .46
United Kingdom	Chemicals 1.23	Basic metals .80
	Other industries 1.16	Transport equipment .81

degree of specialization for the relatively small economies suggests that economies of scale may be important, either in direct production, or more likely, in development of the specific capabilities such as knowledge and skilled labor needed to produce particular manufactures.

A related question of interest is whether trade patterns for the two largest market economies, the United States and Japan, have become more similar. Our results on productivity convergence indicate that Japan's convergence on the United States has been particularly rapid. Table 7.3 lists the RCA measures for the United States and Japan in 1970 and 1982. Exporting patterns of these two countries could hardly have been more different in 1970: the United States is revealed to have had comparative advantage in 7 industries, and in 5 of these Japan had a comparative disadvantage. The main U.S. advantage was in machinery and in transport equipment. Similarly, in 4 of the 5 industries in which the United States was at a disadvantage, Japan had comparative advantage. Japan's main export industries were basic metals, rubber and plastics, textiles, and electrical goods. All four were industries in which the United States had comparative disadvantage in 1970. The rank correlation between U.S. RCAs and Japanese RCAs in 1970 is $-.60$.

Table 7.3
Revealed comparative advantages (RCAs), 1970 and 1982, and relative total factor productivity (TFP), 1965 and 1982, for the United States and Japan

	1970			1982		
	U.S. RCAs	Japanese RCAs	Japanese relative TFP[a]	U.S. RCAs	Japanese RCAs	Japanese relative TFP
Heavy industries						
Basic metals	.58	1.47	.58	.39	1.60	1.15
Chemicals	1.13	.73	.78	1.10	.48	.94
Nonmetallic minerals	.67	.52	—	.73	.30	1.07
Medium industries						
Machinery	1.38	.59	.66	1.49	.88	.96
Rubber and plastics	.59	1.55	—	.60	.89	—
Paper and printing	1.13	.33	.85	1.12	.26	.90
Transport equipment	1.19	1.03	.64	.99	1.46	.77
Light industries						
Metal products	1.03	.90	.70	.87	.83	.91
Other industries	1.02	1.18	—	1.08	1.05	.63
Textiles	.32	1.50	.57	.47	.75	.81
Electrical goods	.97	1.84	.57	1.11	1.96	.97
Food, beverages, tobacco	1.11	.41	.68	.99	.13	.87
Rank correlation between U.S. and Japanese RCAs		−.60			−.10	

a. 1965 data.

The main changes in U.S. revealed comparative advantages between 1970 and 1982 are declines in the RCAs for basic metals (from .58 to .39), transport equipment (1.19 to .99), and metal products (1.03 to 87); and increases in those for machinery (1.38 to 1.49), electrical goods (.97 to 1.11), and textiles (.32 to .47). In the case of Japan, the changes are very large. Major increases in Japan's revealed comparative advantages are registered for machinery (.59 to .88), transport equipment (1.03 to 1.46), basic metals (1.47 to 1.60), and electrical goods (1.84 to 1.96). Two of Japan's major exporting industries in 1970—textiles and rubber and plastics—experienced large declines in the RCA measure and were at a revealed disadvantage in 1982.

As a result of these changes, the differences between U.S. and Japanese trade patterns were less extreme in 1982. The rank correlation between U.S. RCAs and Japanese RCAs increased to −.10. Hence there has been some tendency for U.S. and Japanese trade patterns to become less dissimilar, particularly as a result of Japan's shift out of textiles and rubber and plastics. However, there is still no positive correlation between the countries' RCAs, and there are reasons to doubt that such a correlation will emerge in the future. The countries appear to be going in opposite directions in a number of major industries—for instance, basic metals, nonmetalic minerals, and transport equipment.

7.3 Changes in Comparative Advantage and Relative Productivity Growth

The last question that we want to address in this chapter is whether changes in comparative advantage can be linked to productivity growth at the industry level. This is not an easy question to formalize, in that the productivity growth of a particular industry in a particular country should be considered relative to the same industry in other countries and to other industries within the same country. In order words, rapid TFP growth may have no effect on comparative advantage if it is occurring in the same industry in every country. At the same time, rapid TFP growth in every industry of one country should also have little effect on comparative advantage, since it would not enhance the competitiveness of any industry relative to other industries in the economy. Consequently, we approach this question in a simple and ad hoc way, asking whether changes in U.S. and Japanese revealed comparative advantages exhibit any clear relationship to changes in Japanese TFP relative to U.S. TFP at the industry level.

Before doing this, we first consider whether or not *levels* of RCAs in these two countries can be related to *levels* of relative TFP. We make the comparisons for 1970 and 1982. As suggested in chapter 6, we should expect to find a much stronger relation between the two in the latter year, since by the early 1980s unit cost differences between countries were dominated by differences in TFP levels. Our results generally confirm this.

Table 7.3 lists Japanese TFP relative to U.S. TFP at the beginning (1965) and end (1982) of the period covered by our examination of TFP convergence in chapter 4.[3] Also listed in the table are the RCA measures for Japan and the United States in 1970 (the earliest year of our trade data) and in 1982, as discussed above. In 1970 Japan clearly displayed no tendency to export in the industries where we measured its relative TFP to be high. Its relative TFP, for instance, was low in textiles, electrical goods, and basic metals, all of which were major export industries. Relative TFP, on the other hand, was high in chemicals and in paper and printing, industries in which Japanese RCAs were low. In general, the industries that had high RCAs in 1970 were light industries, notably electrical goods, textiles, and other industries. (The latter includes luggage, toys, sporting goods, and some other labor-intensive sectors.) Japan's other major manufactured exports were basic metals, which is one of the most capital-intensive activities, and rubber and plastics, a medium industry by our classification.

The situation had changed by 1982. Relative TFP was high in a number of Japan's major exporting industries. In basic metals, Japan's TFP had surpassed the U.S. level by 1982. In electrical goods, another major export industry, Japan's TFP was roughly on a par with the U.S. level. Relative TFP was below average, on the other hand, in textiles and in food, beverages, and tobacco, industries with low RCAs in 1982. The major anomaly was transport equipment, in which Japan had a relatively low relative TFP in 1982 but which was nevertheless a major export industry. This result may reflect the fact that the United States still had very high TFP in this sector based primarily on its aircraft production, whereas Japan had become competitive in a different subindustry, namely motor vehicles.

We turn now to the question of whether changes in Japan's measures of comparative advantage are linked to its TFP growth relative to the United States.[4] Table 7.4 lists the percent changes in industry RCAs between 1970 and 1982, ranking the industries in descending order. The table also lists the changes in Japan's industry-level TFP relative to the United States between 1965 and 1982.[5]

Table 7.4
Percent changes in Japan's revealed comparative advantages (RCAs) and relative total factor productivity (TFP), 1970–80 and 1965–82

	Percent change in RCA, 1970–82	Percent change in TFP relative to the United States, 1965–82
Industries with increasing comparative advantage		
Machinery	49.0	45.5
Transport equipment	41.6	20.3
Basic metals	9.0	98.3
Electrical goods	6.3	70.2
Mean for four industries above	26.5	58.6
Industries with decreasing comparative advantage		
Metal products	−7.7	30.0
Other industries	−11.5	—
Paper and printing	−21.4	5.9
Chemicals	−34.7	20.5
Nonmetallic minerals	−42.1	—
Rubber and plastics	−42.7	—
Textiles	−49.1	42.1
Food, beverages, tobacco	−68.6	27.9
Mean for industries above	−32.2	25.3

There are four industries in which Japan's RCAs increased between 1970 and 1982: machinery, transport equipment, basic metals, and electrical goods. Three of these four had TFP growth that was well above average. In basic metals, relative TFP nearly doubled over the period. The next two best performing industries, in terms of relative TFP growth, were machinery and electrical goods. The one anomaly is again transport equipment, and the problem here is likely to be that the relatively good TFP performance of the United States reflects the aircraft component of this industry, whereas Japan's growing export strength is in the motor vehicle component. Nevertheless, average relative TFP growth for the four industries with increasing RCAs (58.6% increase over the period 1965–82) is well above average growth for the industries with declining RCAs (25.3%).

Relative TFP growth was particularly low in chemicals and food, beverages, and tobacco, both industries where Japan's RCA measures dropped substantially between 1970 and 1982. An interesting point to note here is that Japanese TFP was growing relative to U.S. TFP in every industry measured. Nevertheless, industries will tend to lose comparative advantage if their relative TFP growth is lower than the average for all industries. The relationship that we find between Japan's changing comparative advantage and growth of relative TFP is consistent with the view that TFP growth encapsulates the expansion of industry-specific productive factors that contribute to comparative advantage.

Table 7.5 shows the percent changes between 1970 and 1982 for U.S. RCAs. These are divided in our study into three groups: those with increasing, basically stable, or decreasing RCAs. We had already calculated the growth of average TFP for the eight countries other than the United States relative to the United States. (Because of data availability, the time period covered was 1967–79.) This seemed to be the most appropriate measure of the changing relative TFP position of the United States, even though the time period covered by the calculation is a little different from the period covered by the trade data (1970–82). For all twelve industries, the average change in TFP for the eight countries, relative to the United States, was 14.4%. For the five industries in which U.S. RCAs increased, the other countries' TFP convergence on the United States was somewhat slower, increasing on average 12.0% over the period. The relative TFP increase was particularly low in machinery, one of the major U.S. export industries. (It should be noted that, for historical reasons, computing equipment is included in machinery, not in electrical goods.) In textiles and in electrical goods, on the other hand, the relative TFP growth of other countries was relatively rapid, and yet U.S. RCAs increased.

Table 7.5
Percent changes in U.S. revealed comparative advantages (RCAs), 1970–82, and in eight countries' relative total factor productivity (TFP), 1967–79

	Percent change in U.S. RCAs, 1970–82	Percent change in eight countries' TFP relative to the United States, 1965–82
Industries with increasing comparative advantage		
Textiles	48.5	21.4
Electrical goods	14.5	28.3
Nonmetallic minerals	8.7	16.5
Machinery	8.0	6.1
Other industries	6.0	−12.3
Mean for five industries above	17.1	12.0
Industries with stable comparative advantage		
Rubber and plastics	0.9	16.4
Paper and printing	−1.1	12.3
Mean for two industries above	−0.1	14.4
Industries with decreasing comparative advantage		
Chemicals	−3.0	40.0
Food, beverages, tobacco	−10.6	−5.4
Metal products	−15.8	34.7
Transport equipment	−17.3	−5.6
Basic metals	−33.6	20.0
Mean for five industries above	−16.1	16.7

For 3 of the 5 industries in which U.S. RCAs declined substantially, relative TFP growth of other countries was higher than average. In both chemicals and metal products the other countries gained rapidly on the U.S. TFP level. In fact, these were the industries in which other countries' TFP convergence on the United States was most rapid, increasing 40.0% in chemicals and 34.7% in metal products. The relative TFP gain was also large (20.0%) in basic metals. In all three of these industries U.S. RCAs declined. The major anomalies are transport equipment and food, beverages, and tobacco, industries in which the U.S. RCA declined, while U.S. TFP gained on the other countries. The food processing industry, however, is probably the manufacturing industry most subject to government intervention, and there is reason to doubt that the measured decline in U.S. comparative advantage is real rather than managed by the importing countries.

It should also be noted that the declining U.S. comparative advantage in capital-intensive industries like basic metals, transport equipment, and chemicals can also be explained by the more rapid accumulation of capital by other industrial countries. Bowen (1983) demonstrates that this approach has considerable explanatory power. Unfortunately, there is no easy way to test for the relative importance of capital accumulation and industry TFP growth in explaining changing patterns of trade. It is likely that both variables are important. One interesting possibility is that the accumulation of capital in countries like Japan can explain the general shift of their exports toward heavy industries, while relative TFP growth at the industry level determines the particular heavy industries that develop.[6]

A focus on capital accumulation alone leaves certain anomalies. For instance, why does Japan have comparative advantage in basic metals but a disadvantage in the very capital-intensive industry, chemicals? Furthermore, as Japan has accumulated capital, its disadvantage in chemicals has increased. For each country there are similar details that are unlikely to be explained by changes in the aggregate capital-labor ratio. Examination of TFP levels and growth rates for individual industries may clear up some of these anomalies.

This analysis also redirects our attention to the determinants of high levels of TFP. To the extent that they reflect technology-related assets owned by the firm or embodied in technical labor, investment in research and development and training of skilled labor clearly are important ingredients for promoting rapid TFP growth. Furthermore, if many of these assets really are industry-specific, then it is likely that past history, as well as past and current government policy, will have a major effect on the kinds of assets developed, and consequently on the industries that emerge as major exporters. For instance, U.S. concentration of R & D on military-related industries clearly is a major explanation of U.S. comparative advantage in aircraft, large-scale computers, and advanced telecommunications. Japanese industrial policy, on the other hand, has targeted R & D at advanced consumer products, such as automobiles and consumer electronics. Past history is also important in certain industries: large German and U.S. firms that got into the chemical industry early on continue to devote substantial resources to R & D in this industry and to maintain relatively high TFP.

7.4 Conclusions

Our analysis of changing trade patterns among nine industrial countries over the period 1970–86 supports the conclusion arrived at in earlier chapters, that the convergence of aggregate labor and total factor productivity has resulted as countries improved their relative productivity in industries that differed from country to country. Consequently, productivity convergence is stronger in the aggregate than in individual industries. A further result of this development, documented in this chapter, is that the trade patterns of the industrial countries are not converging or becoming more similar. This result is consistent with our conclusion that specialization has continued at the industry level in the advanced industrial countries.

In addition, as suggested in chapter 6, export patterns between the United States and Japan bore a much stronger relation to relative TFP levels in 1982 than in 1970. This is consistent with our finding that by the early 1980s unit cost differences among the industrialized countries were dominated by technological advantage and disadvantage rather than by differences in wage and capital costs.

Consequently, there emerged a clear relationship between the growth of industry TFP and changing comparative advantage for Japan and the United States. The industries with growing comparative advantage in Japan between 1970 and 1982 tended to be those in which Japan's TFP level relative to the United States increased especially rapidly. Correspondingly, the industries in which the United States was losing comparative advantage over this period are those in which other countries, including Japan, were rapidly gaining on or overtaking the U.S. TFP level. It would appear, then, that TFP captures some influence, probably industry-specific, that contributes to comparative advantage. We favor the view that this crucial factor is technology in its various forms: disembodied knowledge, embodied in machinery, or reflected in skilled labor.

8 Productivity Growth in the Newly Industrialized Countries

The (unconditional) convergence phenomenon at the aggregate level has been largely confined to developed countries.[1] As noted in chapter 1, there is no strong evidence of convergence of productivity levels among all countries in the world. Many developing countries, especially in Africa, seem to lag further and further behind the more advanced economies. On the other hand, there is a select group of developing countries whose productivity has been increasing very rapidly. Most notable are the four Asian tigers: Hong Kong, Singapore, South Korea, and Taiwan. But, taking the postwar period as a whole, aggregate growth has also been quite rapid in several other developing countries, both in Latin America (e.g., Brazil, Mexico) and elsewhere in Asia (e.g., Malaysia, Thailand). These rapid developers are often referred to as the newly industrialized countries (NICs).

Lack of comparable industry data made it impossible to include these economies fully in our analysis. But in this chapter we use the available information to provide some evidence of productivity convergence on the U.S. industry level by these NICs. Because of data availability, the analysis was confined to Brazil, Hong Kong, Singapore, South Korea, and Thailand. For all of these countries, labor productivity data at the industry level were taken from the same source utilized in the earlier analysis of developed countries—the United Nations *Yearbook of Industrial Statistics.* The first section of the chapter reviews trends in each economy's industry labor productivity relative to the United States, addressing the same set of questions that we posed for developed countries: Has there been convergence at the industry level? Is it smaller or greater than the convergence at the level of all manufacturing? Have changes in employment mixes played any important role in aggregate convergence?

Capital stock data, on a comparable basis, were not available for all of these countries. However, Dollar (1991) assembled comparable capital stock data for South Korea and West Germany in order to examine the role of capital accumulation and TFP growth in the convergence of Korean productivity levels on those of the developed countries. The second section of the chapter reviews the findings of that study. The third section of the chapter provides evidence concerning what factors permit some developing countries to catch up with the advanced economies while others fell further behind.

8.1 Labor Productivity Convergence at the Industry Level

As we have data for only five NICs, and as each country has a somewhat different industry classification scheme for reporting data, it is easiest to look at each country in turn. We have compiled measures of industry labor productivity (value added per worker) relative to the U.S. level using two alternative approaches. First, we employed PPP exchange rates (from Summers and Heston 1988), as we did with the developed countries. The use of PPP exchange rates, however, almost certainly overestimates NIC relative productivity in manufacturing industries. Relative prices of services tend to be very low in developing countries, with the result that a large correction must be made in the market exchange rate in order to achieve a PPP exchange rate that is appropriate for the entire GDP. Such an exchange rate, however, is likely to provide too much of an exchange rate correction for manufactured goods. Ideally, one should use a PPP exchange rate just for tradables or manufactured products. Lacking this, we used the PPP measures that were available. But we also calculated measures based on official exchange rates. Official rates probably undervalue NIC productivity. True relative productivity almost certainly lies somewhere between the two figures that we report for each year. The problem is not as great as it sounds, though, because the trends over time need not be affected by this bias, and show up clearly in both measures. In the text we discuss the measures derived from official exchange rates, and then present those calculated via PPP exchange rates in appendix tables at the end of the chapter.

Brazil's productivity relative to the United States is shown industry by industry for the years 1963, 1970, 1976, and 1980 in table 8.1.[2] For all manufacturing the relative productivity level in 1963 was .19. Industries are categorized according to the same classification scheme that we employed for developed countries in chapter 3. At the industry level the relative productivity was almost exactly the same as at the level of all manufacturing in 1963: for the eighteen industries disaggregated in table 8.1, the average productivity was .20 of the U.S. level. Furthermore, rela-

Table 8.1
Ratio of Brazilian to U.S. labor productivity for selected years, 1963–80 (index of value added per worker, U.S. = 1.0)

	1963	1970	1976	1980
Manufacturing	.19	.24	.27	.29
Heavy industries	.19	.31	.32	.39
Chemicals	.19	.33	.37	.47
Iron and steel	.18	.28	.27	.31
Nonferrous metals[a]				
Medium industries	.20	.26	.27	.30
Paper products	.20	.23	.25	.34
Printing	.17	.25	.29	.29
Rubber products	.30	.36	.32	.36
Plastic products	.19	.25	.27	.31
Pottery, glass, nonmetal	.12	.16	.24	.19
Metal products, n.e.c.[a]				
Machinery	.15	.25	.26	.26
Transport equipment	.24	.30	.29	.36
Light industries	.22	.25	.29	.31
Textiles	.20	.28	.34	.38
Clothing	.25	.25	.33	.36
Leather products	.21	.25	.26	.27
Footwear[b]				
Wood products	.19	.18	.20	.23
Furniture	.18	.20	.27	.24
Electrical goods	.29	.32	.34	.39
Other industries	.18	.21	.22	.20
Food products	.19	.20	.21	.21
Beverages	.16	.17	.25	.24
Tobacco products	.19	.26	.21	.14
Petroleum, coal products[c]				
Professional goods[d]				
Manufactures, n.e.c.[d]				

Calculated with official exchange rates.
a. Included in iron and steel.
b. Included in clothing.
c. Included in chemicals.
d. Included in plastic products.

Table 8.2
Value added per worker in Brazilian manufacturing for selected years, 1963–80 (index, actual weights 1980 = 100)

	1963	1970	1976	1980
Actual weights	51	70	92	100
1963 weights	51	73	98	113
1970 weights	50	70	93	105
1980 weights	49	69	89	100
U.S. 1986 weights	55	77	99	115

tive productivity was about the same for heavy, medium, and light industries. The productivity level for all manufacturing rose to .24 of the U.S. level in 1970, and then reached .29 of the U.S. level in 1980. At the industry level, average relative productivity was .30 in 1980. Relative productivity for medium and light industries was similar to that of all manufacturing; in heavy industries, on the other hand, relative productivity was a distinctly higher .39 in 1980. In sum, Brazilian productivity in manufacturing converged modestly on the U.S. productivity level between 1963 and 1980, as a result of productivity convergence at the industry level.

Table 8.2 provides evidence about the employment mix in Brazilian manufacturing—how it compares to the United States and how it has changed over time. As noted earlier, value added per worker is higher in some industries than in others, generally as the result of greater use of physical capital or human capital in those industries. Value added per worker in all manufacturing is a weighted average of productivity levels for each industry, in which the weights are actual employment shares. In table 8.2. indexes of value added per worker for manufacturing are calculated employing different hypothetical weights. All of the results are expressed as index numbers, with actual aggregate productivity in 1980 equal to 100.

The results of this exercise indicate that there has been a modest shift in Brazilian employment *away* from high value added industries. This can be seen from the fact that recalculation of the 1963 productivity with 1980 employment shares *reduces* aggregate productivity from 51 to 49. Similarly, recalculating aggregate productivity in 1980 with 1963 weights *increases* aggregate productivity to 113. What is very surprising is that Brazilian 1963 weights appear to be similar to U.S. 1986 weights. When these recent U.S. employment shares are utilized as weights, Brazilian productivity in manufacturing in 1980 is calculated to be 115.

This finding is a very interesting piece of evidence that can be interpreted in a number of different ways. We interpret it as an indication that between 1963 and 1980 Brazil became more involved in international trade, partly because its own trade policy became more open and partly because of the enormous growth of world trade during the 1960s, and to a lesser extent during the 1970s. Compared to developed countries, Brazil's static comparative advantage in manufacturing industries lay in the lower value-added sectors. In 1963 Brazil's employment structure within manufacturing appears to have been similar to the United States. We hypothesize that, by responding to static comparative advantage, Brazil's employment structure became less similar to that of the United States during the following two decades.

The shift of employment from high-value-added to low-value-added activities, holding constant the productivity level in each sector, tends to reduce aggregate productivity. However, if the labor-intensive sectors in which Brazil had comparative advantage are experiencing rapid productivity growth, as a result in part of the expanded market and information that come through international trade, then over time the effect of shifting employment in that direction could be to accelerate productivity convergence. There is some evidence for this hypothesis in the Brazilian data. For instance, Brazil's relative productivity in 1980 was particularly high in a number of labor-intensive industries, such as textiles, clothing, footwear, and electrical goods. Furthermore, while employment has shifted in relative terms away from heavy industries, the latter have, of course, not disappeared completely. As noted, relative productivity in the heavy sector, particularly in chemicals, was very high. This result suggests that Brazil has concentrated its investment in a few areas within heavy industry, and consequently attained a high productivity level.

The analysis of Hong Kong's experience (table 8.3) is hampered by the fact that the data go back only to 1973. Nevertheless, there are some interesting differences from Brazil's experience. First, the productivity level is noticeably lower than in Brazil, only .12 of the U.S. level in all manufacturing in 1973.[3] However, unlike Brazil in 1963, Hong Kong had distinctly higher productivity at the industry level than at the aggregate level. For the twenty-two industries covered, average relative productivity in 1973 was .16; it was especially high in textiles (.27), clothing (.20), and footwear (.18). For manufacturing as a whole, there is little evidence of convergence on the U.S. level between 1973 and 1986.

Hong Kong differs from Brazil in that at the beginning of the period of analysis its employment structure was quite different from that of developed countries, and then changed little between 1973 and 1986. These

Table 8.3
Ratio of Hong Kong to U.S. labor productivity for selected years, 1973–86 (index of value added per worker, U.S. = 1.0)

	1973	1976	1982	1986
Manufacturing	.12	.12	.15	.14
Heavy industries	.19	.20	.19	.17
Chemicals	.11	.12	.13	.11
Iron and steel	.27	.28	.24	.23
Nonferrous metals[a]				
Medium industries	.12	.14	.18	.17
Paper products	.12	.11	.13	.12
Printing	.16	.16	.22	.18
Rubber products	.08	.10	.12	.12
Plastic products	.12	.12	.16	.18
Pottery, glass, nonmetal	.13	.17	.27	.24
Metal products, n.e.c.	.12	.11	.15	.16
Machinery	.09	.14	.18	.15
Transport equipment	.14	.20	.21	.18
Light industries	.19	.21	.24	.22
Textiles	.27	.27	.27	.31
Clothing	.20	.22	.27	.25
Leather products	.18	.24	.23	.24
Footwear	.18	.27	.23	.24
Wood products	.15	.14	.25	.16
Furniture	.20	.18	.24	.19
Electrical goods	.12	.13	.19	.16
Other industries	.18	.35	.24	.22
Food products	.13	.12	.17	.13
Beverages	.24	.35	.26	.28
Tobacco products	.30	.92	.48	.37
Petroleum, coal products	—	—	—	—
Professional goods	.09	.12	.11	.13
Manufactures, n.e.c.	.16	.22	.20	.20

Calculated with official exchange rates.
a. Included in iron and steel.

trends can be seen in table 8.4. In every year covered, Hong Kong's aggregate productivity (value added per worker) is more or less the same, regardless of which year's weights are used for the calculation. On the other hand, use of U.S. 1986 weights consistently increases the measure of aggregate productivity. Our interpretation of these results is that Hong Kong was already very open to international trade in 1973, and hence we do not find the same pattern of change observed in Brazil. (This result may also be attributable to our inability to begin the analysis before 1973.) More important, there is surprisingly little evidence of convergence of industry productivity on U.S. levels.

Table 8.4
Value added per worker in Hong Kong manufacturing for selected years, 1973–86 (index, actual weights 1980 = 100)

	1973	1976	1982	1986
Actual weights	70	74	92	100
1973 weights	70	78	93	103
1982 weights	67	76	92	99
U.S. 1986 weights	78	95	113	116

Table 8.5
Ratio of Korean to U.S. labor productivity for selected years, 1963–86 (index of value added per worker, U.S. = 1.0)

	1963	1970	1976	1982	1986
Manufacturing	.12	.17	.18	.23	.26
Heavy industries	.09	.16	.22	.39	.39
Chemicals	.09	.17	.17	.25	.26
Iron and steel	.12	.18	.30	.67	.58
Nonferrous metals	.07	.13	.20	.26	.33
Medium industries	.09	.13	.15	.20	.25
Paper products	.15	.16	.15	.19	.25
Printing	.12	.14	.16	.26	.29
Rubber products	.07	.10	.11	.11	.14
Plastic products	.07	.10	.10	.14	.19
Pottery, glass, nonmetal	.12	.17	.23	.24	.30
Metal products, n.e.c.	.08	.10	.13	.22	.28
Machinery	.07	.10	.13	.20	.27
Transport equipment	.06	.18	.20	.26	.28
Light industries	.13	.15	.19	.25	.29
Textiles	.12	.15	.23	.26	.23
Clothing	.14	.15	.17	.23	.25
Leather products	.14	.13	.19	.29	.38
Footwear	.11	.18	.20	.20	.31
Wood products	.22	.20	.18	.30	.23
Furniture	.09	.10	.17	.22	.26
Electrical goods	.12	.15	.16	.22	.27
Other industries	.18	.32	.38	.43	.45
Food products	.11	.14	.17	.22	.21
Beverages	.19	.27	.45	.33	.34
Tobacco products	.38	.54	.50	.67	.57
Petroleum, coal products	.04	.34	.41	.49	.67
Professional goods[a]					
Manufactures, n.e.c.[a]					

Calculated with official exchange rates.
a. Included in plastic products.

Table 8.6
Value added per worker in Korean manufacturing for selected years, 1963–86 (index, actual weights 1986 = 100)

	1963	1970	1976	1982	1986
Actual weights	31	48	59	79	100
1963 weights	31	55	81	109	140
1970 weights	29	48	70	93	121
1982 weights	26	41	58	79	104
U.S. 1986 weights	26	42	59	82	108

South Korea's experience is covered by tables 8.5[4] and 8.6; it is remarkably similar to Brazil's. In 1963 Korea's productivity in manufacturing was only .12 of the U.S. level. Light industries (.13) had higher relative productivity than heavy (.09) or medium (.09) industries, but the difference was not great. This relative productivity had increased substantially by 1986, to .26 for all manufacturing. Average relative productivity at the industry level increased even more, to .31. There are also a number of interesting special features of the Korean case. For instance, Korean relative productivity in iron and steel increased an extraordinary amount, from .12 in 1963 to .58 in 1986. To some extent that performance was probably a result of the heavy and chemical industry promotion program of President Park Chung-Hee, which channeled huge amounts of low-cost investment funds into a few targeted industries.[5]

The interesting parallel between Korea and Brazil is that in 1963 both economies had employment structures within manufacturing that were not too different from those of developed countries like the U.S. In fact, use of U.S. employment shares of 1986 to recalculate Korean manufacturing productivity for 1963 results in a *reduction* of measured productivity. Despite Korea's attempts to target a few heavy industries, employment shifted substantially toward labor-intensive industries over the period 1963–86. By 1986 the employment mix has changed so much that recalculation of 1986 productivity with 1963 employment weights *increases* productivity *by 40%*. Even more dramatically than in the case of Brazil, Korea's manufacturing structure appears to have altered between 1963 and 1986 in response to the country's static comparative advantage in labor-intensive sectors.

Singapore (tables 8.7[6] and 8.8) exhibits yet another pattern. It is similar to Hong Kong in that its employment structure has not altered very much between 1963 and 1986, probably reflecting the fact that, like Hong Kong, it was already very open to international trade in 1963. Unlike Hong Kong,

Table 8.7
Ratio of Singapore to U.S. labor productivity for selected years, 1963–86 (index of value added per worker, U.S. = 1.0)

	1963	1970	1976	1982	1986
Manufacturing	.21	.22	.27	.35	.43
Heavy industries	.33	.45	.59	.91	.81
Chemicals	.37	.55	.70	.99	.83
Iron and steel	.29	.35	.48	.82	.78
Nonferrous metals[a]					
Medium industries	.17	.17	.25	.34	.39
Paper products	.10	.11	.13	.24	.44
Printing	.20	.19	.26	.32	.39
Rubber products	.16	.20	.26	.25	.30
Plastic products	.11	.10	.16	.21	.32
Pottery, glass, nonmetal	.22	.16	.37	.60	.33
Metal products, n.e.c.	.19	.21	.24	.36	.44
Machinery	.14	.18	.30	.43	.40
Transport equipment	.23	.22	.25	.30	.47
Light industries	.24	.20	.24	.27	.35
Textiles	.14	.12	.21	.25	.29
Clothing[b]					
Leather products	.24	.12	.21	.25	.29
Footwear[b]					
Wood products	.20	.25	.29	.34	.36
Furniture	.40	.24	.23	.27	.29
Electrical goods	.22	.24	.23	.26	.47
Other industries	.20	.23	.23	.30	.31
Food products	.11	.18	.23	.27	.31
Beverages	.25	.24	.26	.33	.41
Tobacco products	.25	.27	.19	.31	.20
Petroleum, coal products[c]					
Professional goods[d]					
Manufactures, n.e.c.[d]					

Calculated with official exchange rates.
a. Included in iron and steel.
b. Included in textiles.
c. Included in chemicals.
d. Included in plastic products.

Table 8.8
Value added per worker in Singapore manufacturing for selected years, 1963–86 (index, actual weights 1986 = 100)

	1963	1970	1976	1982	1986
Actual weights	33	38	53	70	100
1963 weights	33	41	61	82	100
1970 weights	31	38	57	74	97
1982 weights	31	37	53	70	98
U.S. 1986 weights	33	40	61	82	105

however, Singapore has experienced very impressive productivity convergence over this period. From 21% of the U.S. level in 1963, its relative productivity increased to .43 in 1986. This productivity convergence can be seen in virtually every industry. As in Brazil and Korea, Singapore's relative productivity in heavy industries is unusually high, reaching .81 by 1986. To some extent this reflects the sophisticated petroleum refining operations in Singapore. Refining is included in the "other industries" category for the other countries, but in the Singapore data it is included in chemicals.

The final NIC to be examined is Thailand (tables 8.9[7] and 8.10). It too has shown convergence on the U.S. productivity level in all manufacturing and in individual manufacturing industries.[8] Like Korea, Thailand shows a decline in measured aggregate productivity for 1963 when U.S. employment weights rather than its actual weights are used in the calculation. Unlike Korea, however, the same calculation yields similar results for 1984. This result is somewhat surprising and may indicate that Thailand's economy has not responded to international trade opportunities to the same extent as the other Asian NICs (at least up through 1984).

The results presented here are based on a very small sample of developing countries, hence generalization requires considerable caution. Clearly some developing countries are experiencing very rapid productivity growth and appear to be converging on the developed countries. These NICs have generally begun at a very low level relative to the United States, so that full convergence, if it occurs at all, may well take decades. Even the limited data that we have available are sufficient to make clear that the process of convergence is quite different for the NICs than for the OECD countries in the postwar period. Most important, all of the NICs examined had employment structures within manufacturing that were either already very different from that of the United States in 1963 or became very different during the 1960s and 1970s. In general, the employ-

Table 8.9
Ratio of Thailand to U.S. labor productivity for selected years, 1963--84
(index of value added per worker, U.S. = 1.0)

	1963	1970	1984
Manufacturing	.13	.13	.21
Heavy industries	.10	—	.20
Chemicals	.08	—	.19
Iron and steel	.11	.25	.20
Nonferrous metals[a]			
Medium industries	.12	—	.19
Paper products	.03	.01	.16
Printing	.10	.11	.10
Rubber products	.29	.11	.24
Plastic products	.06	—	.20
Pottery, glass, nonmetal	.15	.10	.28
Metal products, n.e.c.[a]			
Machinery	.07	.17	.11
Transport equipment	.14	.02	.24
Light industries	.11	.12	.23
Textiles	.07	.12	.15
Clothing	.09	.07	.13
Leather products	.18	.18	.64
Footwear[b]			
Wood products	.10	.08	.12
Furniture	.13	.23	.17
Electrical goods	.09	.04	.19
Other industries	.19	.12	.22
Food products	.07	.05	.16
Beverages	.29	.15	.35
Tobacco products	.21	.16	.15
Petroleum, coal products[c]			
Professional goods[d]			
Manufactures, n.e.c.[d]			

Calculated with official exchange rates.
a. Included in iron and steel.
b. Included in clothing.
c. Included in chemicals.
d. Included in plastic products.

Table 8.10
Value added per worker in Thailand manufacturing, 1963 and 1984
(index, actual weights 1984 = 100)

	1963	1984
Actual weights	44	100
1963 weights	44	105
1982 weights	39	96
U.S. 1986 weights	34	88

ment mixes of the NICs in the 1980s were shifted toward labor-intensive industries, so that differences in employment structure, compared to a developed country like the United States, were a major factor accounting for differences in aggregate productivity between the NICs and more advanced economies. It should be remembered that we expected to find this kind of relationship between the United States and the other industrial countries in the early 1960s, but did not.

8.2 Sources of Korean Convergence at the Industry Level

Unfortunately, comparable capital stock data at the industry level were not available for most developing countries. However, there has been a recent study of convergence of Korean labor productivity, capital-labor ratios and TFP on West German levels (Dollar 1991). In this section we review some of the findings from that study. It is dangerous to generalize on the basis of one country's experience, and Korea's experience may not be typical. Nevertheless, the pattern of Korea's convergence provides some interesting evidence and suggests some hypotheses that can be explored further in future work.

Table 8.11 presents the rates at which a number of different Korean variables have been converging on West German levels. Owing to data unavailability, the time period covered is relatively short, from 1966 to 1978. In line with the earlier discussion, it can be seen that aggregate labor productivity for manufacturing has been growing rapidly in Korea, and consequently catching up with the West German level. German productivity growth over this period, it should be noted, was quite good, so that what we are examining here is Korea aiming for a fairly rapidly moving target. The rate of catch-up for manufacturing labor productivity was 3.7%

Table 8.11
Korean convergence on German manufacturing, 1966–78
(percent per annum)

	Labor productivity	Capital intensity	Total factor productivity	Real wages
Manufacturing[a]	3.7	3.3	1.4	4.0
Unweighted averages				
Heavy industries	6.0	7.9	0.2	4.6
Medium industries	3.8	3.4	1.4	4.0
Light industries	2.4	0.2	2.2	4.0
All industries	4.2	4.6	1.1	4.0

a. Calculated from aggregate data for manufacturing.

per annum during the period examined. For aggregate manufacturing, the Korean capital-labor ratio was converging on the German level at an annual rate of 3.3%, while TFP was converging at 1.4% per annum. Both TFP growth and capital accumulation played important roles in Korea's catch-up, although it seems that for aggregate manufacturing capital accumulation was the leading influence. Real wages in Korea grew at a rate of 4% relative to German levels, close to the rate of labor productivity convergence.

Repetition of this analysis for individual manufacturing industries revealed some interesting differences between capital-intensive and labor-intensive sectors.[9] For heavy industries, labor productivity convergence took place at an extremely rapid rate (6.0%), mostly driven by relative capital deepening (at a 7.9% rate). To some extent, this experience during the 1970s reflects the Korean government's deliberate program of channeling investment funds to steel, heavy machinery, and transport equipment. The only economic justification for this kind of targeting is the assumption that there are significant externalities in these sectors: however, the relative TFP growth for heavy industry was a lackluster 0.2%, well below the rate for other industries and for all manufacturing. Hence the TFP data do not provide any evidence of such externalities.

The light industrial sector was almost the mirror image of heavy industry. Labor productivity convergence proceeded at a 2.4% rate, fueled almost completely by technological advance. Relative TFP in the light sector grew at a 2.2% rate. The medium industries had an experience that was about the same as that of manufacturing as a whole.

Table 8.11 also shows the (simple) average rate of convergence for manufacturing industries, which provides an interesting contrast to the results based on the aggregate manufacturing data. At the industry level, labor productivity convergence was at an average rate of 4.2%, distinctly higher than the rate for aggregate manufacturing (3.7%). Similarly, convergence of industry capital-labor ratios was at a rate of 4.6%, compared to 3.3% in the aggregate data. The reason for these discrepancies is that over this period there was a sharp shift of the employment mix in the direction of labor-intensive industries. By adjusting the industrial structure in the direction of comparative advantage (i.e., toward labor-intensive industries), Korea was able to economize on the use of scarce capital and to carry out capital deepening at the industry-level more rapidly than could have occurred had the employment structure remained concentrated in medium and heavy industries.

Table 8.12
Distribution of Korean manufacturing employment, 1966 and 1978 (percent)

	1966	1978
Heavy industries	26.1	23.4
Medium industries	44.6	33.3
Light industries	29.3	43.3

The exact shift in the employment structure is indicated in table 8.12. Between 1966 and 1978, the employment share of light industries increased substantially, from 29.3% to 43.3% of manufacturing. Most of this shift was at the expense of industries of medium capital intensity, though there was also a small decline in the heavy industry employment share, from 26.1% to 23.4%. German employment shares, in contrast, did not change much over this period: 49.1% in heavy industries, 21.8% in medium industries, and 29.1% in light industries for 1978. The light industries that showed the greatest employment growth in Korea were electronic goods and clothing. Thus, if the Korean experience is at all typical, the productivity convergence of the NICs is a considerably more complicated process than what we have observed among OECD countries. Especially for countries that carried out a clear policy of trade liberalization in the late 1950s or early 1960s, the structure of manufacturing has tended to shift in favor of light industries. (This indicates, incidentally, that trade patterns between developing and developed countries can be explained fairly well by a simple HO model: developing countries tend to export more labor-intensive products, whereas developed countries tend to export more capital-intensive items.) As noted before, the shift of labor from capital- to labor-intensive sectors, holding industry-level productivity constant, would by itself reduce aggregate productivity. However, in practice, this employment shift is associated with a number of dynamic factors. First, it enables developing countries to economize on the use of scarce capital so that capital deepening at the industry level can proceed rapidly. This is a simple, intuitive point: with a given amount of investment funds, capital deepening at the industry level will occur much more rapidly if, for example, a country concentrates only on clothing production, rather than on both clothing and steel.

There is also evidence that the export-oriented strategy facilitates technological upgrading in the light sector. In the case of Korea, the relative TFP growth rate of 2.2% for light industries is evidence to support this notion. The electronics industry is probably the best single example of this process. That industry is sometimes included as a heavy industry, on the basis of end use. However, when Korean industries are ranked on the basis of capital intensity, electronics turns out to be one of the most labor-intensive; in fact, it is distinctly more labor-intensive than textiles (though not as labor-intensive as clothing). Dollar and Sokoloff (1990) find that TFP growth for Korean electronics averaged an astounding 10.4% between 1963 and 1979.

It is also plausible that the elements of Korea's experience just described are relevant to other NICs. In particular, we believe that NIC convergence depends heavily on the shift of the employment structure in the direction called for by static comparative advantage, so that for selected light industries these countries are able to achieve rapid capital deepening, realization of economies of scale, and high growth in TFP based on technology borrowed from more advanced economies.

Korea's experience with heavy industries may not be typical, on the other hand. There certainly have been other developing countries that have tried to build up heavy industry behind protective barriers. Almost all of these attempts have yielded poor results in terms of productivity growth, both for the sectors in question and for aggregate manufacturing. Korea's targeting of heavy industries was unusual in several ways, however. First, a few heavy industries were targeted through protection and investment subsidies, but within an overall incentive structure that favored light industry. It should be remembered that employment shifted dramatically in favor of light industries even during a period when heavy industries were allegedly being favored. Second, Korea channeled massive resources into the few heavy industries it selected. As a result, the capital-labor ratio in the steel industry was much higher in Korea than in West Germany in 1978. Korea needed more than twice as much capital per worker to produce about the same value added per worker. In steel, Korea's relative TFP declined between 1966 and 1978. Hence there is substantial evidence suggesting that the heavy and chemical industry program led to inefficient overinvestment in some industries.

On the other hand, Korea's experience with targeting has been more successful than that of most other developing countries. Certainly there were some complete disasters within the Korean program (i.e., petrochemicals and heavy machinery). But even some industries in which TFP performance was unimpressive, such as steel, managed to become successful exporters. Returning to table 8.11, we can see that relative wage growth in Korea was similar among sectors, and close to the average rate of growth of labor productivity at the industry level (4.2%). In heavy industries, for example, relative wages grew at a rate of 4.6%; relative labor productivity in that sector, however, increased at a substantially more rapid rate, 6.0%. It is no surprise that, faced with subsidized investment funds and rapidly declining relative labor costs, Korea moved aggressively into the export market for heavy products like steel and ships, which had traditionally been the preserve of the more developed countries.

In sum, Korea's targeting of heavy industries yielded mixed results: some industries became successful exporters, but at a massive cost. Korea's ongoing export success seems to have depended more on the basic outward orientation of its economy than on policies that have favored specific industries. Finally, it should be emphasized that there is no inherent contradiction between having an outward-oriented strategy that favors light industries and choosing a small number of heavy subindustries to develop. That seems to be a good description of Korea's strategy, and may characterize Brazil's and Singapore's as well.

8.3 Outward Orientation and Productivity Growth

It is crucial to determine why some developing economies are catching up with the developed world, while others stagnate or fall further and further behind. Although a detailed examination of the issue is beyond the scope of this book, nevertheless we have some initial ideas about the factors that permit entrance into the "convergence club." In his classic article on the "advantages of being backward," Gerschenkron (1952) noted that the ability of backward economies to borrow technology from more developed economies was most likely to be possessed by countries that are *not too far behind*. In other words, the technologies created in Western Europe and North America were not likely to be relevant to extremely poor countries.

There is clearly some truth in this idea. The countries that were very poor already in the period immediately after World War II have generally not fared too well in the subsequent decades. On the other hand, according to Gerschenkron's hypothesis, the middle-income countries of Latin America should have had a large advantage over Asian developing economies. In the mid-1950s, Asian developing economies such as Taiwan, Korea, Malaysia, and Thailand were far behind the developed world in terms of per capita income and aggregate productivity. Latin American economies were much closer to the stage of development of the OECD countries and hence should have had better opportunities for advancement. Clearly, being "not too far behind" is not a sufficient condition for joining the convergence club.

Ambramovitz (1986) offered a related, though somewhat different idea: that countries need to possess a "social capacity for development" in order to take advantage of the opportunities inherent in underdevelopment. In our view, the level of education and the extent of literacy are likely to be important contributors to this social capacity. While the Asian economies just named had low per capita incomes in the 1950s, they also had surprisingly high primary school enrollment rates and levels of literacy.

The same can also be said for much of Latin America, however. Argentina and Venezuela are examples of economies that were "not too far behind" the OECD countries at the end of World War II and that also had high levels of education and literacy. Yet neither of these economies has grown very successfully over recent decades.

Another interesting possibility is that these differences in growth performance can be explained to a large extent by differences in trade orientation.[10] Dollar (1992) has constructed an index of outward versus inward orientation, based on distortion and variability of the real exchange rate.[11] His statistical analysis found that Asian developing economies in general were more outward oriented than their Latin American counterparts, and that African developing economies were most inward oriented of all.

Figure 8.1 shows the relationship between per capita GDP growth, 1976–85, and this outward orientation index, for ninety-five developing economies.[12] It can be seen that there is a clear, positive relationship between outward orientation and growth, a relationship that is statistically significant, even when other variables such as investment rate are included in a multivariate regression. Figure 8.1 also identifies a number of NICs, including those whose productivity convergence was discussed in the first section of this chapter: Brazil (BRA), Hong Kong (HK), Korea (KOR), Malaysia (MAL), Singapore (SING), Taiwan (TAI), and Thailand (THAI). All of these NICs fall in the upper right quadrant of the graph—that is, among countries with outward orientation and high growth rates. In particular, all of these economies were found to be in the most open quartile (among the ninety-five developing countries), though Brazil was found to be less open than the Asian NICs. As can be seen in the figure, growth rates for these economies in recent decades have been well above average for the less developed countries (LDCs).

The causal link between outward orientation and growth in these developing economies is likely to be that such an orientation provides more opportunity and incentive to introduce technologies that have not previously been employed there. This can result when domestic firms learn

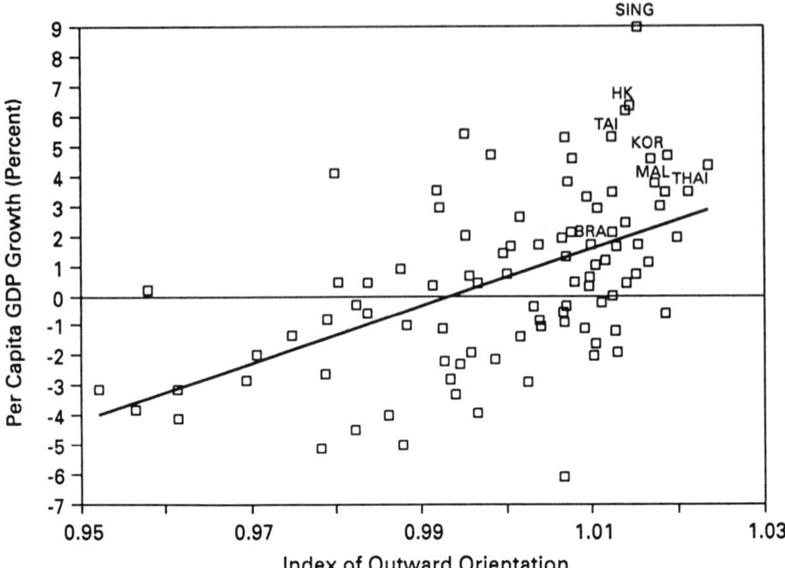

Figure 8.1
Per capita GDP growth and outward orientation of ninety-five LDCs, 1976–1985

about new technologies or when foreign firms introduce new processes or products through direct investment.

Our tentative conclusion is that the combination of education—particularly at the primary and secondary level—and outward orientation of the economy is the incentive regime most likely to generate rapid productivity growth in developing countries. The distinctive feature of the most successful NICs, Singapore, Taiwan, and Korea, is the combination of really excellent educational systems and a strong outward orientation. Hong Kong, in contrast, has done fairly well with its outward orientation, but lags behind the other Asian tigers because its educational system is relatively weak. Similarly, Thailand has done quite well, but remains constrained by a low secondary school enrollment rate (barely more than 25%). In this simple framework, the strong inward orientation of Latin economies such as Argentina, Chile, and Venezuela has hampered their development, despite very good records in the area of education. Brazil and Mexico, in contrast, have had more outward oriented trade regimes, but not such good performance in the area of education.

Many observers have commented on the very high investment and savings rates in the East Asian NICs. We should note that we are inclined to view this as an *endogenous* development, rather than as a significant exogenous explanation of NIC success. For example, both Korea and Taiwan had rather low investment rates in the 1950s, before their significant trade liberalizations. After trade liberalization, their savings and investment rates climbed steadily over a long time period, to reach extraordinarily high levels, around 40% of GDP. In our view, the combination of a well-educated labor force and outward orientation created profitable investment opportunities, which then attracted funds, both from domestic savings and from external sources.

8.4 Conclusions

Some developing economies have been growing extremely rapidly and are catching up with the OECD countries. We think that strong investment in education and outward orientation of their trade regimes are the key factors that distinguish the successful developing countries from those that are falling further and further behind, though more research will be necessary to test that hypothesis.

What we can establish with the limited data at hand is that the pattern of NIC convergence is different from that of more developed economies. In particular, we have found a tendency for the employment mix of the NICs to be shifted toward labor-intensive industries. This was already the situation in the early 1960s, or became so during the 1960s and 1970s. It seems clear that this shift of the employment structure was a response to the static comparative advantage of these economies. That shift enabled the NICs to economize on the use of scarce capital, achieve economies of scale, and borrow technology from more-advanced economies, all of which tended to accelerate productivity growth at the industry level. The productivity convergence at the industry level is similar to what we found for OECD countries. The main difference in the NIC experience is that the employment mix does explain some of the difference in aggregate productivity between the NICs, on the one hand, and fully developed economies like the U.S., on the other.

Another interesting feature of the NIC experience is that, although employment has tended to shift away from heavy industries in relative terms, some of those heavy industries have achieved very high levels of relative productivity. This result is not as paradoxical as it sounds. To produce via modern techniques, the metal and chemical industries require immense amounts of capital. If developing economies attempt to produce a full range of products in the heavy sectors (for example, by means of of a heavy-handed import-substitution strategy), then they will almost inevitably fail to achieve the necessary level of capital intensity. It is the scarcity of capital that, in essence, defines their status as developing countries.

A relatively open trade strategy will result in a large volume of imports of heavy products, and a consequent reduction in domestic production of these items. This is reflected in the shift of the employment mix away from heavy industries that we have documented. The open-trade strategy, however, also makes it possible for the NICs to achieve the extreme capital intensity needed for competitive production in a few subsectors of heavy industry. Thus, Brazil, Korea, and Singapore all appear to have some very high productivity subindustries in metals and chemicals. What really distinguishes the NICs from the OECD countries is not so much that the heavy sector uses less capital per worker in particular industries, as that the heavy sector is relatively small.

Although it is in some ways impressive that the NICs can attain such high productivity in the subindustries of metals and chemicals, it should also be noted that this high relative productivity in heavy industries has very little effect on relative productivity for manufacturing *as a whole*, because employment in those sectors is so minor. In contemporary Korea, for instance, there are far more workers in textiles, clothing, and footwear, than in metals and chemicals. For the Asian NICs in particular, it is the rapid productivity convergence in labor-intensive industries that has been the main driving force behind productivity convergence for all manufacturing.

Appendix Table 8.A1
Ratio of Brazilian to U.S. labor productivity for selected years, 1963–80 (index of value added per worker, U.S. = 1.0)

	1963	1970	1976	1980
Manufacturing	.42	.53	.60	.64
Heavy industries	.42	.68	.71	.87
Chemicals	.42	.73	.82	1.05
Iron and steel	.41	.62	.60	.69
Nonferrous metals[a]				
Medium industries	.43	.57	.61	.67
Paper products	.44	.50	.55	.76
Printing	.37	.55	.64	.65
Rubber products	.67	.80	.72	.81
Plastic products	.41	.56	.59	.69
Pottery, glass, nonmetal	.28	.35	.53	.43
Metal products, n.e.c.[a]				
Machinery	.33	.55	.58	.57
Transport equipment	.53	.66	.65	.79
Light industries	.49	.54	.65	.70
Textiles	.43	.62	.75	.85
Clothing	.56	.55	.73	.80
Leather products	.46	.55	.58	.60
Footwear[b]				
Wood products	.42	.40	.45	.51
Furniture	.40	.43	.61	.54
Electrical goods	.64	.70	.75	.87
Other industries	.39	.46	.50	.44
Food products	.41	.44	.47	.47
Beverages	.35	.37	.55	.54
Tobacco products	.42	.58	.48	.32
Petroleum, coal products[c]				
Professional goods[d]				
Manufactures, n.e.c.[d]				

Calculated with PPP exchange rates.
a. Included in iron and steel.
b. Included in clothing.
c. Included in chemicals.
d. Included in plastic products.

Appendix Table 8.A2
Ratio of Hong Kong to U.S. labor productivity for selected years, 1973–86 (index of value added per worker, U.S. = 1.0)

	1973	1976	1982	1986
Manufacturing	.22	.22	.27	.26
Heavy industries	.34	.36	.33	.31
Chemicals	.19	.22	.23	.20
Iron and steel	.49	.49	.43	.41
Nonferrous metals[a]				
Medium industries	.22	.25	.32	.30
Paper products	.21	.19	.24	.22
Printing	.29	.28	.39	.32
Rubber products	.15	.19	.21	.22
Plastic products	.22	.22	.29	.32
Pottery, glass, nonmetal	.24	.30	.48	.44
Metal products, n.e.c.	.21	.19	.27	.29
Machinery	.16	.25	.33	.27
Transport equipment	.24	.36	.37	.32
Light industries	.33	.37	.43	.40
Textiles	.48	.49	.49	.55
Clothing	.36	.40	.48	.44
Leather products	.32	.44	.41	.43
Footwear	.33	.48	.41	.44
Wood products	.26	.25	.44	.30
Furniture	.35	.32	.43	.33
Electrical goods	.21	.23	.33	.28
Other industries	.33	.62	.44	.40
Food products	.24	.22	.31	.23
Beverages	.43	.63	.46	.50
Tobacco products	.53	1.65	.86	.66
Petroleum, coal products				
Professional goods	.16	.22	.20	.23
Manufactures, n.e.c.	.28	.40	.35	.37

Calculated with PPP exchange rates.
a. Included in iron and steel.

Appendix Table 8.A3
Ratio of Korean to U.S. labor productivity for selected years, 1963–86 (index of value added per worker, U.S. = 1.0)

	1963	1970	1976	1982	1986
Manufacturing	.20	.29	.31	.41	.46
Heavy industries	.16	.29	.39	.69	.69
Chemicals	.17	.30	.29	.45	.46
Iron and steel	.20	.32	.53	1.18	1.02
Nonferrous metals	.12	.24	.36	.45	.58
Medium industries	.16	.23	.26	.36	.44
Paper products	.26	.29	.26	.33	.43
Printing	.21	.24	.28	.45	.51
Rubber products	.12	.17	.20	.20	.25
Plastic products	.12	.18	.18	.25	.34
Pottery, glass, nonmetal	.21	.30	.40	.42	.52
Metal products, n.e.c.	.14	.18	.22	.39	.48
Machinery	.13	.17	.23	.34	.47
Transport equipment	.11	.32	.34	.46	.50
Light industries	.24	.27	.32	.43	.51
Textiles	.21	.27	.40	.46	.58
Clothing	.25	.27	.30	.40	.44
Leather products	.24	.24	.33	.51	.66
Footwear	.20	.31	.34	.36	.54
Wood products	.39	.34	.32	.53	.40
Furniture	.16	.17	.29	.38	.46
Electrical goods	.20	.27	.28	.38	.48
Other industries	.32	.56	.67	.75	.79
Food products	.19	.25	.30	.39	.37
Beverages	.34	.47	.79	.58	.60
Tobacco products	.67	.94	.87	1.18	1.01
Petroleum, coal products	.07	.59	.73	.86	1.17
Professional goods[a]					
Manufactures, n.e.c.[a]					

Calculated with PPP exchange rates.
a. Included in plastic products.

Appendix Table 8.A4
Ratio of Singapore to U.S. labor productivity for selected years, 1963–86 (index of value added per worker, U.S. = 1.0)

	1963	1970	1976	1982	1986
Manufacturing	.26	.28	.34	.44	.55
Heavy industries	.42	.58	.75	1.15	1.03
Chemicals	.47	.71	.89	1.25	1.06
Iron and steel	.37	.45	.61	1.04	.99
Nonferrous metals[a]					
Medium industries	.22	.22	.31	.43	.49
Paper products	.12	.14	.17	.30	.55
Printing	.25	.24	.33	.41	.50
Rubber products	.21	.25	.33	.31	.38
Plastic products	.14	.13	.21	.27	.41
Pottery, glass, nonmetal	.28	.21	.47	.77	.42
Metal products, n.e.c.	.25	.27	.30	.46	.56
Machinery	.18	.23	.38	.55	.51
Transport equipment	.29	.28	.32	.38	.59
Light industries	.30	.26	.30	.35	.44
Textiles	.17	.16	.27	.32	.36
Clothing[b]					
Leather products	.31	.22	.29	.30	.44
Footwear[b]					
Wood products	.25	.31	.37	.44	.46
Furniture	.51	.30	.29	.35	.36
Electrical goods	.28	.31	.29	.33	.59
Other industries	.26	.29	.29	.39	.39
Food products	.14	.23	.29	.34	.40
Beverages	.32	.31	.33	.42	.52
Tobacco products	.32	.34	.24	.40	.26
Petroleum, coal products[c]					
Professional goods[d]					
Manufactures, n.e.c.[d]					

Calculated with PPP exchange rates.
a. Included in iron and steel.
b. Included in textiles.
c. Included in chemicals.
d. Included in plastic products.

Appendix Table 8.A5
Ratio of Thailand to U.S. labor productivity for selected years, 1963–84
(index of value added per worker, U.S. = 1.0)

	1963	1970	1984
Manufacturing	.31	.32	.51
Heavy industries	.23	—	.48
Chemicals	.19	—	.46
Iron and steel	.27	.61	.50
Nonferrous metals[a]			
Medium industries	.29	—	.47
Paper products	.07	.02	.39
Printing	.24	.27	.25
Rubber products	.71	.28	.59
Plastic products	.15	—	.51
Pottery, glass, nonmetal	.37	.25	.69
Metal products, n.e.c.[a]			
Machinery	.17	.43	.28
Transport equipment	.34	.04	.60
Light industries	.27	.30	.58
Textiles	.17	.29	.36
Clothing	.22	.19	.32
Leather products	.44	.44	1.59
Footwear[b]			
Wood products	.25	.20	.30
Furniture	.32	.56	.43
Electrical goods	.23	.09	.48
Other industries	.47	.30	.55
Food products	.18	.12	.39
Beverages	.72	.37	.88
Tobacco products	.52	.40	.37
Petroleum, coal products[c]			
Professional goods[d]			
Manufactures, n.e.c.[d]			

Calculated with PPP exchange rates.
a. Included in iron and steel.
b. Included in clothing.
c. Included in chemicals.
d. Included in plastic products.

9 Conclusions, Implications, and Speculations

9.1 The Sources of Aggregate Convergence among Industrialized Countries

Our main task has been the investigation of the sources of the convergence of aggregate labor productivity observed among industrialized countries in the world. We have considered three possible sources. (1) convergence of labor productivity in individual industries; (2) specialization by countries in industries that differ from one country to another, with modest leads in labor productivity held by the specializing countries; and (3) shifts in employment distribution, toward sectors with high value added per worker.

We first examined data for manufacturing industries from 1963 to 1986 (chapter 3). We found that between the early 1960s and the early 1970s productivity catch-up on the industry level played the dominant role. Indeed, after the early 1970s, convergence of labor productivity within industries slowed down considerably (and that of TFP essentially halted). After 1973, convergence continued to occur at the aggregate level, though at a modest pace, while at the industry level there was clear evidence of specialization, with different countries emerging as productivity leaders in different industries. The third candidate mechanism, the shift of employment toward high-productivity sectors, played almost no role at all.

Chapter 4 investigated the source of the labor productivity convergence observed on the individual industry level, considering two possible sources: (1) convergence in degree of sophistication of technology (as measured by TFP) or (2) convergence in capital-labor ratios. Until the early 1970s, technology catch-up was found to play the major role, and TFP differences among countries narrowed considerably. This period was also characterized by a strong interaction effect (complementarities) between the growth in capital intensity and that of TFP. However, from the mid-1970s onward, as the advantages of backwardness exhausted themselves, convergence in capital intensity became the dominant influence.

We also found that variation in technology levels, capital intensity, and labor productivity levels was consistently greater at the individual industry level than at the aggregate manufacturing level. These results lend support to our hypothesis that specialization of countries in different industries, particularly since the mid-1970s, has played a critical role. The greater similarity in overall productivity levels than in those of the representative industry is attributable to the fact that countries excel in different industries, so that on average among countries aggregate productivity levels are closer than industry productivity levels. The same is true for capital intensity. Countries have chosen different industries for their main investment in new technology, which explains the emergence of countries other than the United States in leadership roles in terms of both technology and labor productivity.

The results were remarkably similar results when we compared productivity levels of the major nonmanufacturing sectors among the industrialized countries of the world (chapter 5). There was strong evidence of convergence in labor productivity levels for the total economy in these countries during the 1970s and 1980s, and a somewhat weaker trend at the sectoral level. Capital intensity also showed convergence at the sectoral level, but the dispersion in technology levels generally remained unchanged. Also, when looking across the ten major sectors, we found a much more varied pattern of sector leadership in the 1980s than among individual manufacturing industries, which the United States still generally dominated.

It is also true that the manufacturing sector, which is the most open in trade and investment, consistently showed the least variation in productivity levels among all the sectors of the industrialized economies. Dispersion in productivity levels was particularly high in sectors that are insulated from international trade—such as utilities and community, social, and personal services. Resource-based sectors, such as agriculture and mining, also displayed medium to high levels of intercountry dispersion. The results support the argument that international trade plays a crucial role in the convergence process.

We also found strong convergence in real wages for both total manufacturing and for individual manufacturing industries (chapter 6). This process was as strong after 1973 as before. The results also show a weak tendency toward profit rate equalization among countries on the industry level. On the other hand, differences in unit costs did not exhibit any tendency to diminish over time, because of the strong correlation between real wages and the average productivity level within a country. During the 1960s, unit-cost differences between countries were dominated by real-wage differences, but by 1982 the variation in TFP levels was the dominant factor.

This result is consistent with the finding that comparative advantage between the United States and Japan (as developed from export patterns) depended primarily on technological advantage in the 1980s (chapter 7). There was also a clear relationship between relative TFP growth by industry and country and changing trade patterns. Trade patterns among industrialized countries, on the other hand, showed no tendency toward greater similarity, despite the convergence in aggregate TFP, but remained divergent. This result reinforces the evidence of country specialization at the industry and subindustry level.

The world dominance of American capitalism of the 1950s and early 1960s is over, not because the United States performed poorly, but because other nations caught up (both in terms of technology and capital investment). U.S. preeminence in all manufacturing industries of the world economy was, however, historically unique. Even when the United Kingdom enjoyed overall productivity leadership in the late nineteenth century, it was not uniformly dominant in all industries. At that time, the United States had major strengths in machine tools; light machinery, such as cameras and typewriters; a broad range of electrical equipment; and industrial machinery, such as boilers and printing presses, while Germany was the pioneer in many chemical products (see Rosenberg 1963; Nelson and Wright, forthcoming). The U.S. dominance in the early postwar period reflected the wartime destruction of the capital stock in Europe and Japan as well as the development of major new technologies in the United States.

American preeminence has given way to an era of technological equals and rivals. Today's situation is characteristic of more normal times, with international competition and an international division of labor. The world economy is now characterized by growing international specialization and differentiation: different nations are the productivity leaders in different industries. Yet, the converse of this is that the U.S. economy has not entered a period of secular decline, but rather has taken a position of first among equals.

An Update

To show that stories of the demise of the U.S. economy are still premature, we present some updated comparisons of manufacturing pro-

Table 9.1
Output per hour in manufacturing for twelve OECD countries, 1985 and 1990 (index, 1985 = 1.00)

	1985	1990
Belgium	1.00	1.21
Canada	1.00	1.02
Denmark	1.00	1.00
France	1.00	1.17
Germany	1.00	1.12
Italy	1.00	1.13
Japan	1.00	1.23
Netherlands	1.00	1.09
Norway	1.00	1.10
Sweden	1.00	1.05
United Kingdom	1.00	1.23
United States	1.00	1.19
Unweighted average	1.00	1.13

Source: U.S. Department of Labor, Bureau of Labor Statistics, Office of Productivity and Technology, December, 1991.

ductivity growth for twelve OECD countries through 1990 (see table 9.1). According to the latest U.S. Bureau of Labor Statistics data, productivity growth in U.S. manufacturing was well above average among OECD countries between 1985 and 1990. Output per hour increased by 19% over this period, and U.S. growth was surpassed only by Japan (23%), the United Kingdom (23%), and Belgium (21%). The increase in German manufacturing productivity was well below that of the United States, at 12%.

We also have updated data on industry and sector level productivity among the world's three major economies—Germany, Japan, and the United States—through 1988 (table 9.2). Using national accounting data from the three countries and basing the relative productivity calculations on GDP in current prices per person engaged in production, we find very little evidence of major relative declines in U.S. sectoral productivity. Among the 9 major sectors of the economy, Japanese productivity increased relative to the United States in 3 and declined in 2 (in the other 4 there was little change); while relative German productivity increased in 3 and declined in 5. Among the 12 manufacturing industries, Japanese productivity gained on the United States in only 3 and declined in 7, whereas German productivity gained in only 1 and declined in 8. If anything, the United States has not only remained strong in manufacturing, but has expanded its lead over its close rivals. (Calculations were also performed using corresponding industry GDP data in constant prices, with very similar results.)

Table 9.2
Relative labor productivity levels for Japan, Germany, and the United States by major sector and industry, 1985 and 1988

	Japan/U.S.		Germany/U.S.	
	1985	1988	1985	1988
Agriculture, forestry, and fisheries	0.19	0.20	0.30	0.35
Mining	0.21	0.22	0.18	0.11
Construction	0.65	0.84	0.65	0.72
Manufacturing	0.63	0.59	0.61	0.54
Stone, clay, and glass products	0.61	0.58	0.64	0.67
Primary metal and fabricated metal products	0.74	0.72	0.56	0.52
Machinery, except electrical	0.52	0.38	0.43	0.30
Electric and electronic equipment	0.73	0.63	0.71	0.57
Transport equipment	0.60	0.54	0.56	0.47
Instruments and related products	0.65	0.48	0.59	0.53
Food and kindred products	0.68	0.79	0.49	0.51
Textiles	0.42	0.41	0.75	0.73
Paper and allied products	0.64	0.68	0.55	0.51
Chemicals and allied products	1.03	0.94	0.60	0.53
Petroleum and coal products	1.45	1.16	1.27	0.91
Others	0.57	0.62	0.76	0.78
Transportation and communication	0.50	0.50	0.51	0.47
Electric, gas, and sanitary services	0.96	0.85	0.55	0.46
Wholesale and retail trade	0.55	0.56	0.58	0.58
Finance and insurance	1.11	1.22	1.46	1.31
Other services	0.72	0.79	0.94	1.01
Total	0.64	0.66	0.67	0.65

Source: National Income and Product Accounts, Japan, Germany, and the United States. Figures are based on GDP by industry in current prices, deflated by the country GDP deflator to 1985 prices, and converted to U.S. dollars using the 1985 PPP exchange rate. Employment is persons engaged in production.

9.2 High-Value-Added Sectors

Some have argued that U.S. success during the early postwar period was due to the concentration of its production in the so-called high-value-added industries; and that other countries' gains relative to the United States were due to an increasing concentration of their output or employment in these industries. We found absolutely no evidence of this. There is almost no correlation between sectoral value added per employee and the employment mix (chapters 3 and 5) for the United States or for any other industrialized country; little correlation was found between the capital-labor intensity of a sector and its employment distribution (chapters 4 and 5); and none between the growth of overall labor productivity, either within all manufacturing or the total economy, and shifts in employment mix (chapters 3 and 5). Rather, the high overall value added per employee and the growth of value added per worker was attributable almost exclusively to gains in productivity at the industry level.

The evidence showed that there has been no deindustrialization of the United States relative to other OECD countries. Indeed, the latest figures from the OECD *Indicators of Industrial Activity* indicate that the U.S. proportion of total OECD manufacturing output remained unchanged between 1985 and 1990, at 37%. The evidence suggests rather strongly that the richest nations are not so for the "mercantilist" reason that their workers are employed in the most productive industries. Countries do not forge ahead or catch up by stealing jobs in high-value-added industries from others, nor do they fall behind by losing jobs in high-value-added industries.

Indeed, the forces of "unbalanced growth" suggest that employment tends to shift out of high productivity growth industries or sectors almost in step with its rate of labor productivity growth. Sectors with high productivity growth generally slough off labor. In a closed economy this occurs because there is not much substitution in domestic consumption among the products of different industries (even as the price of the high-productivity-growth industries falls). In an open economy there is a greater possibility that employment shares may shift toward the high-productivity-growth sectors, provided the exports of those industries can be continually expanded. But, even in the export-oriented economies of Japan and Korea, this was not the case; employment shifts were dominated by relative productivity growth movements. Thus, the "high-value-added strategy" is generally a losing battle: it is almost impossible to maintain labor force shares in high-productivity-growth sectors, let alone to expand them (see chapter 6 of Baumol, Blackman, and Wolff 1989 for a further discussion of the unbalanced-growth effect).

9.3 The Role of Strategic Sectors

Some have argued that certain industries of the economy are more important than others in the overall growth of an economy. These have been dubbed "strategic sectors." One thinks first off of the early usage of the term in the context of the development literature. Hirshman (1958), for example, argued that to promote economic development among less developed countries, it was important to install industries that had large interindustry linkages, both forward and backward. The idea was that once such an industry was in operation within an economy, it would stimulate the development of both local suppliers (backward linkages) and new local customers or users of the product (forward linkages). Sectors with high linkages were thus thought to be strategic elements in the attempt to stimulate wholesale industrialization of a backward economy.

The current usage has more to do with the diffusion of new technologies over a broad spectrum of industries. Here, too, the role of interindustry linkages is crucial. However, whereas the early literature simply emphasized the presence of such linkages, the modern parlance focuses on *technological spillovers* among sectors. There are many historical examples of this. One is the interplay between developments in the machine tool industry and stitching machines in the shoe industry (see Thompson 1989). Another example is the development of the automobile industry during the first half of this century, and concomitant advances in steel, glass, rubber, electrical equipment, radios, and machine tools.

It is true that today countries form groups of specialized industries, particularly through forward and backward linkages. For example, in the United States, computers, software, and telecommunications are closely connected; in Italy, ceramic tiles and related machinery; in Germany, printing presses and paper machines; and in Japan, consumer electronics and electronic components. Two recent studies (Wolff and Nadiri 1991; Bartelsman, Caballero, and Lyons 1991) have documented close connections between the rate of technical advance of individual industries and that of their suppliers and users.

Yet, it is not clear that promoting strategic sectors is a "magic potion" for economic success. There is no evidence that one industry (microchips, for example) or set of industries (computers and related industries, for example) is inherently superior to another. Indeed, the results of our analysis indicate that different countries have achieved high productivity levels by specializing in very different industries. Even among the NICs, the emphasis on heavy, capital-intensive industry has produced relatively little advantage, as the experience of Korea (steel) and Singapore (petroleum refining) attest; despite promotion of selected heavy sectors, their successes have been mainly in the labor-intensive industries.

In fact, there is no apparent reason why manufacturing is intrinsically superior to any other sector. This notion is reminiscent of the Physiocrats, who portrayed agriculture as the economy's only productive sector (see, for example, Quesnay 1968). For them, agriculture was the source of all value, and manufacturing was a derivative sector. A similar notion seems to haunt the push for industrialization. Yet some advanced countries have achieved notable successes in nonmanufacturing sectors, such as agriculture

(Australia), natural gas and petroleum (the Netherlands and Norway), banking (Germany), and computer software (the United States).

What is the vehicle of technological spillovers—geographical proximity and travel distance (or time) between supplying and using plants? Some have suggested that there are agglomeration effects, with clusters of related industries producing sizable spillovers through geographic proximity. Others have put forward the notion of a "food chain," with technological advance in one industry immediately dependent on that of its (geographically) close supplier. Yet, in this age of electronic mail and fax machines, it is not clear that geography is vital for the transmission of new technology among industries. It is not evident that spillovers even depend on *domestic* manufacture. Many of the early examples of industrial spillovers in the United States (such as the automobile industry) occurred in the days of limited international trade. Today it seems possible for them to occur even if one country manufactures inputs (such as microchips in Japan) and another the corresponding outputs (such as computers or software in the United States).

In fact, recent econometric evidence of ours and others (also noted in the Introduction) shows that trade openness, particularly *import* openness, is a major contributor to the growth of country productivity. Multinational businesses also play a vital role in the spillover process (see, Blomstrom and Wolff 1989 for the case of Mexico). These results suggest that geographical proximity between the developers of new technology and the eventual users and adopters of such is not essential. Technological spillovers can still take place even if the locations where an invention occurs, where the new products are manufactured, and where the new products are used are separated by thousands of miles.

Industrial Policy

Many have argued against the idea of an industrial policy on the grounds that the U.S. government should not be in the business of picking winners and losers. Yet the United States does have an implicit industrial policy, supported through a wide range of subsidies (agriculture, for example), and import protection (automobiles and clothing, for example). The Department of Defense also has an unofficial industrial policy, supporting industries which it considers vital for the national interest. Most of these produce military products.

Unfortunately, the federal government now generally supports the laggard industries, such as autos and steel, in its trade policy. If the tool is trade policy, then, politically, the United States is almost forced to favor declining industries. That is, the government supports those industries that compete against technologically superior imports, and this has the effect of pulling down our aggregate TFP. We do *not* favor government intervention in the form of protectionism. This type of policy might work for a relatively backward economy, such as Japan in the 1950s (the "infant industry" argument), but not for an advanced economy.

Moreover, the pattern of military spending provides direct and indirect support to specific sectors of the economy, such as the aircraft industry. Indeed, Jean-Claude Derian (1990) has recently argued that the Department of Defense in the United States essentially plays the role of MITI (the Ministry of International Trade and Industry) in Japan, promoting selected industries. Unfortunately, the success of this approach for general economic growth has been constricted for two reasons. First, commercial spillovers from military suppliers are somewhat limited, and there is evidence that such spin-offs and applications have lessened in recent years (see, for example, Nelson and Wright, forthcoming). Second, promoting industries that produce military hardware creates tremendous pressure on these companies to export their wares. This can produce undesirable military consequences, as the 1991 Gulf War attests.

We argue against targeting specific industries. On the other hand, we are not advocating laissez-faire; rather, we are recommending that the government provide the general wherewithal to allow individual firms and industries to develop advanced technology and remain competitive in the international sphere. This should take the form of education and training for individuals, and the promotion of research, either through the government's own laboratories or through providing the necessary financial support to firms, universities, and nonprofit institutions.

9.4 The Role of R & D

Another important development in the past two decades is that other countries besides the United States have become major creators of technology. Japan and Germany are probably the best examples. Thus the United States is no longer the productivity leader in every industry. However, even here, if one country gains an edge through a technological advance, before long the other large countries are likely to imitate this development. What is different today from the early postwar period is that other countries no longer invariably borrow from the United States. Today, U.S. firms often learn new technologies from their foreign competitors (from Japan in automobiles, for example).

It is, perhaps, not surprising that the major export successes of the United States—aircraft, munitions, medical equipment, pharmaceuticals, and agricultural products (see chapter 2)—are in fields where the U.S. government has heavily subsidized, funded, or provided R & D. The first two are heavily defense-funded; the third and fourth benefit immensely from the National Institutes of Health and general funding for medical research; and the last from agricultural research, partly through land grant state universities. Successes were also achieved in the NASA space program (and its spillover into satellite communications). Military R & D is also related to U.S. successes in large-scale computers and advanced telecommunications.

However, somewhat paradoxically, many studies have found that both the social and private return to government-funded R & D has been zero, if not negative (see, for example, Griliches 1980, 1986; Lichtenberg 1984; and Wolff and Nadiri 1991). The facts suggest that government-funded R & D does have payoffs, but that the funding pattern is so distorted by defense needs, that overall it does not generate positive returns.

We believe that R & D is particularly important to promote. There are three problems associated with firm-level R & D. First, it is a high fixed-cost activity, which can dissuade the individual firm from undertaking it. Second, there is duplication of effort if many firms undertake the same or similar projects. Third, there are difficulties in "appropriating" the returns to R & D (see Nelson and Wolff 1991, for example) and there is thus a strong incentive to be a follower in an industry.

Economists have long recognized that these externalities involved in the production of commercially valuable knowledge are inevitable—and even to some extent desirable. For this reason, direct and indirect support for R & D promotes our national welfare and may greatly enhance our competitive position in the future. Such subsidies can take the form of tax breaks for R & D or direct government assistance to the research effort. Governments of all the major economies—including the United States—provide these kinds of subsidies. In Japan, government support has tended to favor the development and use of new technologies for consumer products, and has met with notable successes in automobiles, consumer electronics, and medium-range mainframe, high-quality personal, and laptop computers.

The end of the Cold War provides the United States the opportunity to adjust the direction of its publicly supported research away from military hardware and toward industrial and consumer items. It is not essential, nor even desirable, that we try to compete with other countries in lines that they are supporting with substantial funding, such as semiconductors or high-definition TV (HDTV). It makes more sense to us that future research be directed at applications where the likelihood of commercial and international success is strong.

9.5 Interplay between Technological Advance and Investment

The results of chapters 4 and 6 and elsewhere (Wolff 1991) suggest that there are positive complementarities between capital investment and technological progress. This is especially true in times of rapid productivity catch-up. As we noted, it is not possible to separate out the direction of causation, and the evidence suggests that it goes both ways. In particular, the prospect of technical advance appears to be an important stimulus to investment. That is to say, the demand for investment seems to depend partly on the opportunity for the introduction of new technology.

Recently, many observers have focused on the supply side of investment as a lever for promoting new capital formation. Among their proposals are expanded investment tax credits, more rapid write-off of new investment, reduced capital gains taxation, and the like. Although these may be worthy instruments, we expect that they will prove to be ineffective *by themselves*, unless there is a corresponding demand for new investment. Here, the major pull is the availability of new technology. We feel that investment policy must be designed in *conjunction* with R & D policy and that, again, a substantial federal program in commercial R & D would be beneficial, not only in developing new technology, but also in stimulating new investment.

Reduction of the federal deficit is another important policy objective. By pure arithmetic, if the deficit is high, then, ceteris paribus (consumption and the trade deficit remaining constant), private investment will be low. A reduction in the federal (and state and local) deficit will free up funds for capital investment; it may also lower the interest rate and hence the cost of capital. However, it should be stressed that the way in which the deficit is reduced is also crucial to the long-term growth of the U.S. economy. If the deficit is reduced by decreasing military spending and other "unproductive uses" (see Wolff 1987), then it will be effective in promoting growth. However, the government—federal, state, and local—also provides productive investments; most notably, infrastructure, education, and training.

If these are thereby reduced, then an overall reduction in the budget deficit may actually prove to be *harmful* to growth.

9.6 The New Comparative Advantage

The results of chapter 7 support our argument that, at least among industrialized nations, comparative advantage is rooted in technological superiority. Because real wages among this select group of countries have reached a position of parity or near parity (chapter 6), comparative advantage has become tantamount to *absolute* advantage, and trade has become more and more based on leadership in TFP. A comparison of U.S. and Japanese trade documents the strong correlation between export patterns and technology superiority. Competitiveness is really about absolute advantage, since it allows a country to compete with high real wages and a high standard of living.

This trend toward export specialization is striking because it has occurred at a time when other differences between industrial economies have been disappearing. The gap between low-productivity and high-productivity countries within OECD has been shrinking, as has the relative capital intensity of their production. But the differences in trade patterns remain sharp, as countries specialize in areas where their technology is advancing most rapidly. For example, Japan's exports have surged in electrical goods and basic metal products, industries which have scored large productivity gains relative to the United States and other industrialized countries. The United States has also has been emphasizing specialities in which its productivity advantage remains large—aircraft, large-scale computers, and scientific and medical equipment—precisely those industries for which export demand has been growing.

The strong productivity growth in U.S. manufacturing during the late 1980s, as documented in table 9.1, not surprisingly was accompanied by a similar surge in U.S. exports. According to 1991 OECD figures (*Foreign Trade by Commodities*, April 1991), U.S. commodity exports to the world increased by 81% between 1985 and 1990, and those to other OECD countries doubled. Over the same period, U.S. world commodity imports grew by only 44%, so that the U.S. overall (commodity) trade deficit fell substantially (more recent IMF data indicate that it fell even more during 1991, reaching a net deficit of only 73 billion dollars, its lowest in a decade). Thus, superior performance in technology does appear to have direct pay-offs in trade patterns.

A Future in Services

Although the United States has continued to remain strong in manufacturing (particularly as the data for 1990 attest), it also has some very strong comparative advantages in services. Casual observation suggests that some of the leading sectors in terms of exports are university education (particularly, foreign graduate students); amusements (particularly films and television programs); medical services; communications; financial services; business services (including advertising and legal services); and computer software.

Unfortunately, consistent and reliable data on trade in services are quite weak. However, we have made some calculations based on export figures from U.S. input-output tables for 1963–82. Over this period, total U.S. exports (in current dollars) increased by a factor of 17.8. In comparison total manufacturing exports grew by a factor of 9.6. By far the fastest growing export was banking, financial services, and insurance, which increased by a factor of 166.4 (though from an admittedly small base). Other large increases were recorded by communications (34.7) and business services (22.7).

These results raise the possibility of continued U.S. specialization in high-end services, perhaps because new technologies are becoming more and more information-based. Baumol, Blackman, and Wolff (1989, chapter 7) documented this trend for the United States. They found that between 1960 and 1980 knowledge workers (defined as producers of knowledge, including scientists and engineers) were the fastest growing occupational group, at 3.5% per year, followed by data workers (defined as users of knowledge, including secretaries and clerks) at 3.1% per year. In contrast, noninformation employment grew at 1.1% per year (see also Reich 1991).

If the U.S. experience is a harbinger for the rest of the world, these results suggest that other industrialized nations will fast be moving toward information economies. Manufacturing, on the other hand, will lose its importance as a source of employment in the world economy, as earlier happened to agriculture. This is likely to be true even for the hardware side of the information economy, particularly computers, since the major employment and output growth will be in the production, not of computers, but of software. In other words, as computers become more powerful and hence cheaper, the major source of revenue and employment will be the provision of the necessary software to operate the computer hardware effectively. Thus, in general, information-based services are likely to occupy an increasingly larger share of world output and also of world trade.

9.7 A Guide for Developing Countries

Does our analysis provide any lessons for developing countries to follow? We feel there are lessons for at least the middle-income countries, including the NICs. Their main mission, so to speak, is to change from relatively backward countries, whose comparative advantages are rooted in low wages, to more developed countries, whose comparative advantages are lodged in superior productivity and high wages (this is our definition of *competitiveness*).

We found that what distinguished the NICs from other less developed countries was the strong educational base of their labor force and the outward orientation of their trade policy (chapter 8). We showed that their pattern of catch-up to the most advanced countries was different from the convergence process among the advanced countries. In particular, there was a noticeable tendency for their employment mix to shift toward labor-intensive industries. It seems clear that this shift was a response to the static comparative advantage of these economies; it also enabled them to make better use of relatively scarce capital, achieve economies of scale, and borrow technology from more advanced economies, all of which tended to accelerate productivity growth at the industry level.

Although many of these countries undertook early on the strategy of encouraging heavy industries (Korea in steel, Brazil in chemicals, and Singapore in petroleum refining), this was not the locus of their success. It is true that some were able to achieve very high levels of labor productivity and TFP in these industries. However, their employment shares in these industries were so small as to have very little impact on the productivity of the manufacturing sector as a whole. For the Asian NICs, in particular, it has been specialization in labor-intensive industries and rapid productivity convergence in these industries that has been the main source of catch-up in overall productivity.

It is also important to note that the high capital formation of the NICs is much more likely to have been a *consequence* of investment opportunities (high expected TFP and profitability) than a cause. There is no cultural basis for the high savings rate of Japan or Korea (see Baumol, Blackman, and Wolff 1989, chapter 8, for a discussion of Japan). Indeed, as we saw for the advanced countries (chapter 6), it is more likely the pull of expected gains in technology and productivity, rather than a large push of available savings, that is at the heart of their rapid capital accumulation.

9.8 What Will the Future Hold?

What we seem likely to see in the future is aggregate productivity levels of OECD countries that remain close together, while different countries' technological advances and investments are concentrated in different industries and subindustries. The situation in the early postwar period, when the United States dominated the world economy in productivity overall and in almost every manufacturing industry, was unusual and the convergence process is, in part, a return to normalcy. It is highly unlikely that the United States or, for that matter, *any other country* (including Japan), will dominate all industries. International specialization implies that countries can put the bulk of their resources in their high-productivity industries, resulting in further industry specialization in the future. Will divergent industry productivity performance lead to convergence or divergence of aggregate productivity levels in the future? How can the U.S. position in this international division of labor be bolstered?

There is nothing automatic about the process of convergence. The sources of productivity growth for individual industries are innovation, rapid absorption of foreign technology, and investment. The continued U.S. TFP lead in many manufacturing industries suggests that the United States is performing satisfactorily, at least as regards the former. Lackluster U.S. savings and investment, however, and the fact that other OECD countries have overtaken the United States in terms of capital abundance raise some concerns about America's ability to maintain its position among the advanced countries.

That other countries are catching up with the United States should not necessarily be viewed as evidence of U.S. decline. With ever-increasing economic integration among OECD countries, it is inevitable that a large productivity lead cannot be sustained. This conclusion, however, does not mean that America should be complacent about economic growth. It seems unlikely to us that any one industrial country will lag far behind the others in this period, but it is certainly possible to lag modestly behind (or to decline in relative terms, as the United Kingdom has) if a nation's innovation and investment do not proceed at a pace comparable to those of its rivals. Furthermore, the United States continues to be the largest economy in the world; hence its own growth is likely to have significant spillover effects on the other industrial economies (as well as on developing countries in the Third World). A strong U.S. performance in innovation and investment is not going to produce the kind of leadership that America enjoyed in the 1950s; but it would ensure continuance of its present position as first among equals.

We believe that the United States must concentrate on three areas: (1) new technology, (2) the availability of an appropriately educated and trained labor force, and (3) new investment in those spheres. We thus favor general government involvement in supporting and funding R & D, improving education, and bolstering investment rates. Recent developments in the (former) Soviet Union and Eastern Europe have now provided an opportunity for the redeployment of government resources away from military programs and towards schooling and R & D. Indeed, the dislocation effects of reduced government defense spending will release exactly the trained manpower needed for a major R & D effort in the high-technology industries. Moreover, a general reduction in government spending can also provide the capital to finance the new investment sustained growth will require. But the availability of increased savings will not, in itself, lead to the new investment required; the new investment must also be stimulated by the availability of new technology in which to invest.

Consumers all benefit from international specialization in terms of their standard of living. The trade balance is a result of comparative, not absolute, advantage in productivity. However, if productivity growth is low, the equilibrating mechanism will operate through a decline in the exchange rate and real wages (compare the United Kingdom). On the other hand, if productivity growth is high, the equilibrating mechanism will entail a rising exchange rate and increasing real wages (as the experience of Japan and Germany attests). For the United States to maintain its competitiveness in the international arena, it is essential to pursue the second of these paths.

Appendix: Data Sources and Methods

I. United Nations, *Yearbook of Industrial Statistics*: Detailed industry classification (chapters 2 and 3)

Industry number	Industry name
311/2	Food products
313	Beverages
314	Tobacco
321	Textiles
3211	Spinning, weaving, and related products
322	Wearing apparel
323	Leather and leather products
324	Footwear
331	Wood products
332	Furniture, fixtures
341	Paper and paper products
3411	Pulp, paper, and related products
342	Printing, publishing
351	Industrial chemicals
3511	Basic chemicals excluding fertilizers
3513	Synthetic resins, and related products
352	Other chemical products
3522	Drugs and medicines
353	Petroleum refineries
354	Petroleum and coal products
355	Rubber products
356	Plastic products, n.e.c. (not elsewhere classified)
361	Pottery, china, and related products

362	Glass and products
369	Nonmetal products, n.e.c.
371	Iron and steel
372	Nonferrous metals
381	Metal products
382	Machinery, n.e.c.
3825	Office, computing, and related equipment
383	Electrical machinery
3832	Radio, televisions, and related products
384	Transport equipment
3841	Shipbuilding and ship repair
3843	Motor vehicles
385	Professional goods
390	Other industries
3	Manufacturing

II. Dollar-Wolff data base (chapters 4, 6, and 7)

A. Eurostat (NACE) codes for manufacturing industries

13	Ferrous and nonferrous metals
15	Nonmetal minerals and products
17	Chemicals
19	Finished metal products, except machinery and transportation equipment
21/23	Machinery
25	Electrical goods
28	Transport equipment
36	Food, beverages, and tobacco products
42	Textiles, clothing, footwear, and leather goods
47	Paper and printing
49	Rubber and plastics
48	Other manufacturing

B. Employment data availability by country and industry

Belgium:	All industries except 19, 21–23, 25, 28: 1963–84.
Canada:	All industries: 1963: 1965–84.
France:	All industries: 1963, 1965–84.

Germany: All industries: 1965–83.
Italy: All industries: 1967–82.
Japan: All industries: 1963, 1965–83.
Netherlands: All industries except 13, 17, 21–23, 49: 1963, 1965–84.
United Kingdom: All industries: 1963, 1965–83.
United States: All industries: 1963, 1965–83.

Source: United Nations, *Yearbook of Industrial Statistics*, various years.

C. Value added data availability by country and industry

Belgium: All industries except 19, 21–23, 25, 28: 1963, 1965–83.
Canada: All industries, 1963, 1965–84.
France: All industries: 1963, 1965–84.
Germany: All industries: 1965–82.
Italy: All industries: 1963, 1965–82.
Japan: All industries: 1963, 1965–83.
Netherlands: All industries except 13, 17, 21–23, 49: 1963, 1965–82.
United Kingdom: All industries: 1963, 1968, 1970–83.
United States: All industries: 1963, 1965–83.

Source: United Nations, *Yearbook of Industrial Statistics*, various years.

D. Capital stock data availability by country and industry

Belgium: Industries 13, 15, 17, 36, 47, 48, 49: 1963–84; industry 42: 1963–72, 1973–84; total manufacturing: 1963–71, 1974–83.
Canada: All industries, 1963–82 and 1984.
France: All industries, 1963–84.
Germany: All industries, 1963–84.
Italy: All industries, 1963–84.
Japan: All industries except 15 and 49: 1965–84; industry 15: 1975–84.
Netherlands: Industries 15, 25, 28, 36, 42, 48: 1963–83; industry 19: 1963–71, 73–84; industry 47: 1963–76, 1978–84; total manufacturing: 1963–71, 1974–77, 1979–83.

United Kingdom:	Industries 13, 15, 21–23, 25, 28, 36, 48, 49: 1963–83; industries 17, 19, 42, 47, and total manufacturing: 1963–71, 1973–83.
United States:	All industries: 1963–84.

Sources:

Belgium:	Eurostat worksheets.
Canada:	For 1983 and 1984, Statistics Canada, Science, Technology and Capital Stock Division, *Fixed Capital Flows and Stocks*, September, 1987; other years are from Statistics Canada worksheets.
France:	Eurostat worksheets.
Germany:	Eurostat worksheets.
Italy:	Eurostat worksheets.
Japan:	Economic Planning Agency, Department of National Accounts, Economic Research Institute, *Gross Capital Stock of Private Enterprises, 1965–86*, February, 1988.
Netherlands:	Eurostat worksheets.
United Kingdom:	Eurostat worksheets.
United States:	Musgrave, John C., "Fixed Reproducible Tangible Wealth in the United States: Revised Estimates," *Survey of Current Business*, vol. 66, no. 1, January, 1986, pp. 51–75; and Musgrave, John C., "Fixed Reproducible Tangible Wealth in the United States, 1982–1985," *Survey of Current Business*, vol. 66, no. 8, August, 1986, 36–39.

E. Employee compensation data availability by country and industry

Belgium:	All industries except 19, 21–23, 25, 28: 1963, 1965–82.
Canada:	All industries: 1963, 1965–84.
France:	Not available.
Germany:	All industries: 1965–83.
Italy:	All industries: 1968–82.
Japan:	All industries: 1963, 1965–83.
Netherlands:	All industries except 13, 17, 21–23, 49: 1963, 1965–82.
United Kingdom:	All industries: 1963, 1965–83.
United States:	All industries: 1963, 1965–83.

Source: United Nations, *Yearbook of Industrial Statistics*, various years.

F. Industry wage share calculations

Belgium:	All industries except 19, 21–23, 25, 28: 1963, 1965–82.
Canada:	All industries: 1963, 1965–82.
France:	Not available.
Germany:	All industries: 1965–82.
Italy:	All industries: 1968–82.
Japan:	All industries: 1963, 1965–82.
Netherlands:	All industries except 13, 17, 21–23, 49: 1963, 1965–82.
United Kingdom:	All industries: 1963, 1968, 1970–82.
United States:	All industries: 1963, 1965–82.

Source: United Nations, *Yearbook of Industrial Statistics,* various years.

Industry wage shares for each country were calculated as the ratio of employee compensation to value added, averaged over all the years between 1963 and 1982 for which the relevant data are available. The two exceptions are: (1) for France, the international average wage share is used for each industry; and (2) for NACE 49 in Belgium, because the calculated wage share exceeded one, the wage share for Belgian manufacturing as a whole is used.

III. OECD data base for manufacturing (chapters 2 and 4)

All data are from the OECD International Sectoral Database on Microcomputer Diskette.

A. Manufacturing industry codes

1 Food, beverages, and tobacco
2 Textiles
3 Wood and wood products
4 Paper, printing, and publishing
5 Chemicals
6 Nonmetal mineral products
7 Basic metal products
8 Machinery and equipment
9 Other manufactured products

B. Employment data availability by country and industry

Australia:	Total manufacturing: 1970–85.
Belgium:	All industries except 3: 1970–85.
Canada:	All industries: 1970–85.
Denmark:	All industries: 1970–85.
Finland:	All industries: 1970–85.
France:	All industries except 3: 1970–85.
Germany:	All industries: 1970–85.
Italy:	All industries: 1970–85.
Japan:	All industries except 3, 1970–85.
Netherlands:	All industries: 1970–85.
Norway:	All industries: 1970–85.
Sweden:	All industries: 1970–85.
United Kingdom:	All industries except 3: 1970–85.
United States:	All industries: 1970–85.

C. GDP data availability by country and industry

Australia:	Total manufacturing: 1970–85.
Belgium:	All industries except 3: 1970–85.
Canada:	All industries: 1970–85.
Denmark:	All industries: 1970–85.
Finland:	All industries: 1970–85.
France:	All industries except 3: 1970–85.
Germany:	All industries: 1970–85.
Italy:	All industries, 1970–85.
Japan:	All industries except 3: 1970–85.
Netherlands:	All industries except 3: 1970–85.
Norway:	All industries: 1970–85.
Sweden:	All industries: 1970–85.
United Kingdom:	All industries except 3: 1970–85.
United States:	All industries: 1970–85.

D. Capital stock data availability by country and industry

Australia:	Total manufacturing: 1970–85.
Belgium:	All industries except 3, 1970–85.
Canada:	All industries: 1970–85.
Denmark:	All industries: 1970–85.

Finland: Total manufacturing: 1970–85.
France: All industries except 3: 1970–85.
Germany: All industries: 1970–85.
Italy: All industries except 9: 1970–85.
Japan: All industries except 3: 1970–85.
Netherlands: All industries except 3: 1970–83; total manufacturing: 1984–85.
Norway: All industries: 1970–85.
Sweden: All industries: 1970–85.
United Kingdom: All industries except 3: 1970–85.
United States: All industries: 1970–85.

E. Employee compensation data availability by country and industry

Australia: Total manufacturing: 1970–85.
Belgium: All industries except 3: 1970–85.
Canada: All industries: 1970–85.
Denmark: All industries: 1970–85.
Finland: All industries: 1970–85.
France: All industries except 3: 1970–85.
Germany: All industries: 1970–85.
Italy: All industries: 1970–85.
Japan: All industries except 3: 1970–85.
Netherlands: All industries except 3: 1970–85.
Norway: All industries: 1970–85.
Sweden: All industries: 1970–85.
United Kingdom: All industries except 3: 1970–85.
United States: All industries: 1970–85.

F. Documentation of industry wage share calculations

Country-specific average wage shares were calculated for each industry on the basis of the longest time span for which data on employee compensation and GDP were available. Exceptions are: (1) for industry 8 in the Netherlands, because the calculated wage share exceeded one, the wage share for the Netherlands' manufacturing sector as a whole is used; (2) for industry 9 in Sweden, because the calculated wage share exceeded one, the wage share for Sweden's manufacturing sector as a whole is used; and (3) for industries with missing employee compensation data, the international average wage share was used.

The international average wage share was computed for each industry as an unweighted average of country-specific industry average wage shares, except as indicated below:

1	Food, beverages, and tobacco:	All countries except Australia.
2	Textiles:	All countries except Australia.
3	Wood and wood products:	All except Australia, Belgium, France, Japan and the United Kingdom.
4	Paper, printing, and publishing:	All countries except Australia.
5	Chemicals:	All countries except Australia.
6	Non-metal mineral products:	All countries except Australia.
7	Basic metal products:	All countries except Australia.
8	Machinery and equipment:	All countries except Australia and the Netherlands
9	Other manufactured products:	All except Australia and Sweden.

IV. OECD data base for the major sectors of the economy (chapter 5)

All data are from the OECD International Sectoral Database on Micro-computer Diskette.

A. Major sector codes

AGR. Agriculture
MIN. Mining and quarrying
MAN. Manufacturing
EGW. Electricity, gas, and water ("utilities")
CST. Construction
RET. Wholesale trade, retail trade, restaurants, and hotels
TRS. Transport, storage, and communication
FNI. Finance, insurance, and real estate
SOC. Community, social and personal services
PGS. Producers of government services.

B. Employment data availability by country and sector

Data are available for all industries from 1970 to 1985, except

Belgium: Data missing for MIN., 1970–85.

France: Data missing for MIN., 1970–85.
Italy: Data missing for MIN. and FNI., 1970–85.

C. GDP data availability by country and sector
Data are available for all industries from 1970 to 1985, except

France: Data missing for MIN., 1970–85.
Italy: Data missing for MIN. and FNI., 1970–85.
Netherlands: Data missing for FNI., 1970–85.
United Kingdom: Data missing for MIN., 1970–72.

D. Capital stock data availability by country and sector
Data are available for all industries from 1970 to 1985, except

France: Data missing for MIN., 1970–85.
Italy: Data missing for MIN. and FNI., 1970–85.

E. Employee compensation data availability by country and sector
Data are available for all industries from 1970 to 1985, except

Belgium: Data missing for MIN. and FNI., 1970–85.
France: Data missing for MIN. and FNI., 1970–85.
Italy: Data missing for MIN. and FNI., 1970–85.

F. Documentation of sector wage share calculations
Country-specific average wage shares were calculated for each industry on the basis of the longest time span for which data on employee compensation and GDP were available. Exceptions are (1) for both Germany and Japan, the adjusted wage share for agriculture exceeded unity, so that the adjusted international average wage share was used instead; (2) for the Netherlands, the international adjusted average wage share was used for the transport, storage, and communication sector, since its adjusted wage share exceeded unity; and (3) for industries with missing employee compensation data, the international average wage share was used.

The international average wage share was computed for each sector as an unweighted average of country-specific industry average wage shares, except as indicated below:

Mining and Quarrying (MIN.): All countries except Belgium, France and Italy.

Finance, Insurance, and Real Estate (FNI.): All countries except Belgium, France and Italy.

Total Economy: All countries except Belgium and France.

V. U.N. world trade classification by commodity code (chapter 2)

00 Live animals
01 Meat and preparations
02 Dairy products and eggs
03 Fish and preparations
04 Cereals and preparations
05 Fruit and vegetables
06 Sugar and preparations; honey
07 Coffee, tea, cocoa, spices
08 Animal feeding stuff
09 Miscellaneous food preparations
10 U.N. Special code
11 Beverages
12 Tobacco and manufactures
20 U.N. special code
21 Hides, skins, furs undressed
22 Oil, seeds, nuts, kernels
23 Rubber, crude and synthetic
24 Wood, lumber, and cork
25 Pulp and waste paper
26 Textile fibers
27 Crude fertilizer, minerals, n.e.c.
28 Metalliferous ores, scrap
29 Crude animal, vegetable matter, n.e.c.
30 U.N. special code
32 Coal, coke, briquettes
33 Petroleum and products
34 Gas, natural and manufactured
35 Electric energy
40 U.N. special code
41 Animal oils and fats

42 Fixed vegetable oil, fat
43 Processed animal, vegetable oil, and related products
50 U.N. special code
51 Chemical elements, compounds
52 Coal, petroleum and related chemicals
53 Dyes, tanning, color products
54 Medicinal and related products
55 Perfume, cleaning and related products
56 Fertilizers manufactured
57 Explosives, pyrotechnic products
58 Plastic materials and related products
59 Chemicals, n.e.c.
60 U.N. special code
61 Leather, dressed fur, and related products
62 Rubber manufactures, n.e.c.
63 Wood, cork manufactures, n.e.c.
64 Paper, paperboard and manufactures
65 Textile yarn, fabric and related products
66 Nonmetal, mineral manufactures, n.e.c.
67 Iron and steel
68 Nonferrous metals
69 Metal manufactures, n.e.c.
70 U.N. special code
71 Machinery, nonelectric
72 Electrical machinery
73 Transport equipment
80 U.N. special code
81 Plumbing, heating, lighting equipment
82 Furniture
83 Travel goods, handbags
84 Clothing
85 Footwear
86 Instruments, watches, clocks
89 Miscellaneous manufactured goods, n.e.c.
90 U.N. special code
91 Mail not classed by kind
93 Special (estimates)

94 Zoo animals, pets
95 War firearms, ammunition
96 Coin, nongold, noncurrent
712 Agricultural machinery
714 Office machines
715 Metalworking machinery
724 Telecommunications equipment
726 Electro-medical, X-ray equipment
732 Road motor vehicles
734 Aircraft
735 Ships and boats

Notes

Chapter 1

1. Other recent studies of the convergence phenomenon include Matthews, Feinstein, and Odling-Smee (1982), and Baumol, Blackman, and Wolff (1989). To a large extent the literature on international convergence was spurred by Maddison's (1982) publication of aggregate data for the industrialized countries. In a related literature, Barro and Sala-i-Martin (1992) have shown that there has been a strong tendency for real per capita income levels of U.S. states to converge over the past century.

2. Aggregate labor productivity should be measured by value added per hour of labor input. GDP per capita is not exactly the same thing, although it will generally be a good proxy for aggregate labor productivity in international comparisons; it would have to be adjusted for the share of the population in the labor force and the number of hours worked per year in order to be the correct measure. These data are from Summers and Heston (1988).

3. The leading proponents of this view are Bluestone and Harrison (1982).

4. This selection-bias issue is analyzed in detail in Romer (1986), de Long (1988), and Baumol and Wolff (1988).

5. This literature investigates whether there is an inverse relationship across countries between the level of per capita GDP at the beginning of a period and its growth rate during the period, after controlling for other variables. Several studies have reported such an inverse relationship after controlling for investment; these include Kormendi and Meguire (1985), who use a sample of 47 countries drawn from the *International Financial Statistics* for the period 1950–77; Hess (1989) for a sample of 66 LDCs over the 1970–85 period; Barro (1991) for the Summers-Heston sample over the 1960–85 period; and Dowrick and Nguyen (1989) for a sample of 24 OECD countries (1950–81) and for the Summers-Heston (1984) sample over the same period. Barro (1991) also finds that education and trade openness are important control variables.

6. Lawrence (1984) reaches a similar conclusion.

7. Magaziner and Reich (1982, p. 343), for example, argue that a "rational industrial policy ... must seek to facilitate the movement of capital and labor into businesses

that permit higher value added per employee." Cohen and Zysman (1987, pp. 234–243), in their book *Manufacturing Matters,* similarly argue that in order to maintain America's competitiveness the government should develop an industrial policy, targeted at specific subindustries, with the broad goal of shifting the industrial mix toward high-productivity activities.

8. Increasing returns and imperfect competition form the basis for international trade in the "new trade theories" developed in recent years. See Helpman and Krugman (1985) for a coherent theory of trade based on these ideas. Traditional trade theory based on factor endowments can explain exchanges among countries that have different basic factor supplies; the new trade theories, on the other hand, help account for the vast amount of trade in fundamentally similar products among advanced economies whose factor supplies differ little. Grossman and Helpman (1991) integrate the new trade theories into the analysis of economic growth. Their work is particularly concerned with endogenous innovation and its effects both on long-term growth and on the pattern of international specialization and trade.

9. Multinational corporations, which are primarily found in manufacturing, also spread new technology to many countries, another factor contributing to stronger convergence in manufacturing than in other sectors.

10. Michael Porter's (1990) book, *The Competitive Advantage of Nations,* in particular, examines the institutional structure for innovation and competition among firms in a range of industrialized and newly industrialized countries. Although we document the general trend for countries to specialize in different areas and show the implications of this for productivity convergence, Porter's book focuses on the firm and subindustry level and examines some of the factors that have led to successful innovation and expansion. Other recent work on national systems of innovation includes Nelson (1982) and Amsden (1989).

Chapter 2

1. Japan does not use the wood and wood products classification for its output, so that no shares are reported.

2. The 1985 figures are not commented on here, because they look a bit suspicious. According to the U.N. figures, total world exports of petroleum and petroleum products declined from 266 to 139 billion dollars between 1982 and 1985, while the OECD figures showed a slight increase. It is likely that the problem is due to missing data for several countries in 1985.

3. It is not clear from the data how much of the aircraft exports consisted of military aircraft, but we assume that it is not an insignificant portion.

Chapter 3

1. Our earlier article, Dollar and Wolff (1988), examined convergence of industry labor productivity up through 1982. This chapter updates that work to 1986.

2. The basic model was developed in Heckscher (1919) and Ohlin (1933). It was formalized in a series of papers by Samuelson, notably Samuelson (1953).

3. Leamer (1984) discusses the conditions under which factor-price equalization holds, and also demonstrates that certain implications of factor-price equalization are borne out empirically for a large group of countries in 1958 and 1975.

4. Exposition is also easiest if the number of factors equals the number of goods. However, this highly unrealistic assumption is not necessary to generate the basic results. In particular, the number of goods can be greater than the number of factors, and still there can be an equilibrium with factor-price equalization. With more goods than factors, the pattern of trade *in goods* is not uniquely defined; nevertheless, it remains true that countries tend to be implicit exporters of their relatively abundant factors through their trade in goods. For details, see Chang (1979) and Vanek (1968).

5. Using value added rather than gross output introduces biases if materials prices change significantly and countries differ in their dependence on materials. This concern is more relevant for studies of aggregate labor productivity, since inter-country variation in the use of materials at the industry level is likely to be small. We have made productivity calculations using U.S. input-output data for 1958 and 1977 in order to compare the value added measure with the gross output one. Using an eighty-five-industry breakdown, we calculated both the annual rate of growth of value added (in 1972 dollars) per worker and that of gross output (in 1972 dollars) per worker over the period. The correlation coefficient between the two series is 0.80. Thus, value added per worker at the industry level appears to be a good proxy for gross output per worker.

6. See Ward (1985) for an explanation of how these PPP exchange rates are calculated. PPP exchange rates were not available for Australia and Sweden. In the case of Sweden, we assumed that the market exchange rate maintained PPP between this country and its close trading partner Germany. For Australian data we used the market exchange rate. If data were available, it would be preferable to deflate the output measures with industry-specific deflators, then convert to a common currency with PPP exchange rates for tradeable goods. Unfortunately, neither industry-level deflators nor PPP exchange rates for tradeables were available for all of our countries. The use of the PPP exchange rate for GDP could introduce some bias into our work. We have minimized the potential bias by using own-country price deflators to convert data into 1983 prices and then using the PPP exchange rate for that single year to convert to a common currency. The choice of exchange rate will thus affect the estimated level of productivity relative to the U.S. level, *but any bias would be proportionately the same in all years.* With this approach, the choice of exchange rate should not have a large effect on the pattern of convergence. Furthermore, we compare our results to those of others who have employed a different methodology; use two separate data sets constructed through different approaches (mostly in chapter 4); and use both PPP and market exchange rates in the analysis of developing countries (chapter 8). These different forms of sensitivity analysis have convinced us that the use of PPP exchange rates for GDP does not introduce any particular bias.

7. The hours data are from Maddison (1982) and do not correspond exactly to the years that we report. Hence we used 1960 hours data for 1963; 1970 hours data for 1970; 1978 hours data for 1976; and 1979 hours data for 1982.

8. Note that, as in almost all productivity comparisons, we have used average productivity rather than marginal productivity. The latter would also be interesting to compare among nations, if information were available to do so, because we could determine whether productivity levels of newly added production units were similar among countries. However, average productivity figures are also of interest in and of themselves, since they more directly relate to movements in per capita income.

9. The convergence is slightly weaker if value added per worker rather than value added per work hour is used, although the difference is not large.

10. That the 1982 recession was in fact more severe in the United States can be seen in measures of capacity utilization for manufacturing. In Germany, France, Italy, and Japan, for example, capacity utilization declined an average of 8% between 1979 and 1982; in the United States the decline was 17%.

11. Again, the results are essentially the same if value added per worker rather than value added per work hour is the measure of productivity.

12. Another major effort to make international comparisons of productivity at the industry level is the International Comparison of Output and Productivity (ICOP) project at the University of Groningen, under the direction of Angus Maddison. Their approach relies mainly on the industrial censuses of each country, adjusted to a national accounts basis, using both national accounts and input-output data. The main advantage of their approach is the computation of industry-specific (their so-called industry of origin) price indices which allow direct output comparisons at the industry level between two countries. As detailed in Maddison and van Ark (1989), these price indices are derived from production censuses by dividing gross value of output by corresponding quantities. The Maddison-van Ark approach is particularly advantageous, since it does not rely on general PPP conversion indices, which are based on expenditure data rather than on production data.

Despite the difference in methodology, our results for total manufacturing are surprisingly similar:

Value added per hour worked (index, U.S. = 100)

	ICOP 1985	**Dollar-Wolff 1985**
Japan	76	65
France	54	56
Germany	66	66
United Kingdom	44	54
United States	100	100

The ICOP sources are Szirmai and Pilat (1990) for Japan and the United States, and van Ark (1990) for France, Germany, and the United Kingdom. Unfortunately, differences in sectoring schemes do not allow a direct comparison of productivity estimates on the detailed industry level.

13. Not surprisingly, a chi-square test finds that industry employment shares are significantly different across countries, both in 1963 and in 1982. However, since the chi-square is very sensitive to the total number of observations, it is not possible to use it to determine whether the employment shares were more or less similar in 1982 than in 1963. Also, chi-square tests reveal that employment shares differ significantly for each country between 1963 and 1982. Hence our results should be interpreted not as evidence that there has been no change in the employment mixes of industrial countries, but rather as evidence that the changes cannot be characterized as a shift from low-productivity to high-productivity industries.

14. Baldwin (1971), for instance, finds that in the 1960s the U.S. was exporting from high-productivity industries and importing goods produced in low-productivity industries.

15. See, for example, Norsworthy and Malmquist (1983).

16. In a formal model, the absence of factor-price equalization is an endogenous result. Basically, differences in aggregate factor endowments are too great to be compensated for simply by variation in industry mix. Such an equilibrium will be accompanied by incomplete specialization: i.e., there will be some, but not complete, overlap in the range of goods produced in different countries.

Chapter 4

1. See Bowen (1983) and Wolff (1991) for evidence on the latter.

2. We also used the U.S. average wage share for the calculations; its value differs so little from the international average wage share that the results are not reported. See also the Appendix for exceptions to these rules and for the years of data availability by industry and country.

3. Eurostat industry codes (NACE) numbers are shown in parentheses.

4. It would be preferable to use gross output, together with a third input, materials, in the TFP measure but the requisite data are not available.

5. The PPP indices were obtained from Ward (1985). It would be more desirable to deflate the output measures with industry-specific price deflators and then convert to a common currency with PPP exchange rates for tradable goods. However, the necessary data are not available.

6. The ideal labor input measure would be hours worked. Unfortunately, such data are not available on the industry level. However, data on average hours worked per year are available by country from Maddison (1982). Adjustment by these data does not significantly alter the results.

7. See the Appendix for details.

8. It should be noted that countries differ in their assumptions with regard to the service life and scrapping behavior of various capital components. Canada, for example, uses longer service lives than the United States for buildings and many types of capital equipment in its calculation of gross capital stock. Differences in

assumptions may distort international comparisons of TFP. Unfortunately, there is no way of correcting for these differences without worksheet data on annual capital flows by industry.

9. The results are almost identical for the two seven-country samples shown in panels B and C of table 4.1. Moreover, results from the OECD data base indicate that the coefficient of variation of labor productivity levels declined from 0.19 in 1970 to 0.15 in 1985 and the average labor productivity relative to the United States increased from 0.68 to 0.73. The 1985 figures for labor productivity are almost identical to those for TFP.

10. The food, beverages, and tobacco industry does not fit easily into this three-way division because of several anomalies and, as a result, is tabulated separately.

11. Our results on Japanese TFP compare rather well to those reported by Nakamura (1989).

12. The importance of capital accumulation as a source of Japanese productivity growth has been well documented. See, for example, Jorgenson and Nishimizu (1978), Norsworthy and Malmquist (1983, 1985), Kendrick (1984), Bronfenbrenner (1985), and Jorgenson, Kuroda, and Nishimizu (1985).

13. As noted above, Statistics Canada uses a lower scrapping rate and longer lifetimes in computing gross capital stock, which may bias upward its estimate of the Canadian capital stock relative to the other countries.

14. This result actually accords quite well with our casual observation that European economies have streamlined their light industries, while the United States has tended to continue its reliance on cheap immigrant labor.

15. According to the OECD data, by 1985 other countries had far surpassed the United States in capital intensity in the light industries; were ahead of the United States in the medium industries; and had reached equality with the United States in the heavy industries. However, as with the first set of results, the dispersion in capital-labor ratios was greatest among heavy industries and smallest among medium industries.

16. Actually, the first term on the right hand side of equation 4.6 also reflects the correlation of a country's employment mix (s_i^h) with the relative capital intensities of its industries. However, this latter effect is found to be insignificant. We can rewrite equation 4.6 as:

$\mathrm{DEV}(\kappa^h) \equiv \kappa^h - \bar{\kappa} = \Sigma_i \bar{s}_i \mathrm{DEV}(\kappa_i^h) + \Sigma_i \kappa_i^h \mathrm{DEV}(s_i^h)$. The results were very similar to those shown in panel A of table 4.4. Using the unweighted averages for $\bar{s}_i$ and $\bar{\kappa}_i$, we obtained:

	$\Delta\kappa^h$	$\Delta\kappa_i^h$	Δs_i^h
1972	11.6	12.6	−1.0
1979	15.8	16.9	−1.1
1985	16.6	18.7	−2.1

17. The unweighted average for the 1979–85 period is a bit misleading, since the aggregate capital-labor ratio in 5 of the 11 countries actually declined relative

to the United States. If we compare the unweighted average value of absolute changes in $\kappa^h[\Sigma_h|\Delta\kappa^h|/n]$ to the corresponding unweighted average $[\Sigma_h|\Sigma_i s_i^h(\Delta\kappa_i^h)|/n]$, we find that 95% of the change in aggregate capital intensity was due to changes in industry-level capital-labor ratios.

18. Though there are differences in industry classification between the Dollar-Wolff data base and the OECD data base, we have tried for illustrative reasons to line up the two classification schemes as closely as possible in panel B of this table.

19. It is, perhaps, not coincidental that the post-1970 period is also associated with the rapid introduction of computerization among manufacturing industries. Many commentators have suggested that there are sizable adjustment costs associated with this new technology. See, for example, David (1991).

Chapter 5

1. Results based on the ratio of GDP to the number of employees also show overall productivity convergence occurring from 1970 to the early 1980s. However, the rate of convergence is slower according to these data, and this, in turn, largely reflects a smaller initial dispersion in labor productivity levels among the countries. Moreover, according to these statistics, the United States lost its overall leadership position in 1977. Australia led in 1979 and Norway led in 1983 and 1985. Indeed, in 1985, Australia ranked second and the United States third, with Germany a very close fourth.

2. It is also interesting to note that, once these two sectors are excluded, the United States led in overall labor productivity in 1985. The reason is Norway's large oil deposits. Norway ranked only fifth when the sectors were left out.

3. For these calculations, we use the (unadjusted) international average wage share, because we are interested here in measuring the relative contribution of capital-labor growth to labor productivity growth and do not want the results affected by country differences in capital shares, $(1 - \alpha)$.

4. This calculation is based on the unweighted average growth rates for labor productivity, TFP, and the capital-labor ratio. We also computed the unweighted average across sectors of the percentage contributions to labor productivity growth of the latter two components. On the basis of this calculation, TFP growth accounted for 22% of labor productivity growth and capital-labor growth for 78%.

5. By construction, the overall productivity level in 1970 with 1970 employment weights is identical to actual 1970 productivity. We also experimented with weights of other years. For example, we fixed the 1985 employment weights to determine whether productivity levels in earlier years would be greater than their actual levels. Our findings are almost identical to those reported below.

Chapter 6

1. The relation is not exclusive, since differences in factor proportions between countries may also partly account for differences in unit costs.

2. See chapters 3 and 4 and the Appendix for details on the data.

3. The ideal wage measure would be hourly compensation. Unfortunately, data on hours worked are not available on the industry level. However, data on average hours worked per year are available by country from Maddison 1982. Adjustment by these data did not significantly alter our comparisons of average employee compensation among countries.

4. We also made the same set of calculations reported below on the basis of the OECD database. The data, as noted in chapter 4, are available only from 1970 to 1985. Results for the 1970–85 period are quite similar to those shown below for the 1970–83 period on the basis of the Dollar-Wolff data base, but are not shown due to space limitations.

5. In 1972 the coefficient of variation in overall labor shares among the eight countries was 0.09.

6. For convenience, we will use the term "real wages" as a shorthand for real employee compensation.

7. The results are as equally pronounced for panels B and C, which show the summary statistics for the same sample of countries over time.

8. Also see Gittleman and Wolff (1991) for confirming evidence that industry wage differentials are highly correlated among OECD countries.

9. See, for example, Smith 1965; Ricardo 1981; Marx 1967, vol. 3; Bain 1951; Stigler 1963; and Hirshleifer 1976.

10. See, for example, Glick and Ehrbar 1988a, 1988b for a discussion of several of these issues.

11. By the way, this finding also casts doubt on the usual presumption that capital costs are significantly lower in Japan than in the United States. Although gross profitability is not the same as the cost of capital, the two are usually closely related.

12. The pattern is identical for the summary statistics in panels B and C, which are based on constant country samples over time.

13. Technically, r is the ratio of (current) profits to gross capital in real terms. As a result, it differs from the profit rates shown above in tables 6.4 through 6.6, which are defined as the ratio of current profits to gross capital in current prices.

14. In the simple case of unit labor costs, ULC is given by $\omega(L/Y)$. Thus, unit labor costs vary directly with the wage rate and inversely with labor productivity (Y/L).

15. The sign of the correlation coefficient with the TFP level is negative, since high productivity levels are associated with low unit costs.

16. A similar analysis was conducted of the correlation between unit costs and profit rates. The two factors were generally uncorrelated and no trend was evident.

17. We also used lagged TFP growth instead of its concurrent value for two other reasons. The first is to avoid the likely simultaneity bias between TFP growth and

capital accumulation. The second is that investment may have a negative effect on contemporaneous productivity growth because of adjustment and learning costs associated with new capital.

18. Results were very similar for crude TFP growth (equation 4.1).

19. Results in the last column, based on three-year averages for the variables, are very similar to those in column three.

Chapter 7

1. Nakamura's (1989) study of Japan, Germany, and the United States also found that by the late 1970s input prices were quite similar among these three countries, so that the "relative TFP level has become the principal determinant of sectoral cost advantage and disadvantage among the three countries..." (p. 713).

2. The year 1982 was chosen for this discussion because the TFP data that are linked to the trade data in the next section end in 1982. Choosing 1986, alternatively, would not require any significant change in this discussion of trade patterns.

3. The TFP results are based on the Dollar-Wolff data base.

4. Relative TFP growth rates may provide a superior indicator of changing comparative advantage than relative TFP levels for two reasons. First, comparing TFP levels across countries is sensitive to the choice of price deflators and PPP exchange rates and the assumptions of service lives used to construct the capital stock estimates. If there are biases in the TFP level estimates, there is a good chance that these biases are relatively stable over time, so that relative TFP growth rates are more likely to be accurately measured than relative TFP levels. Second, other factors, such as trade restrictions, clearly influence the composition of trade. Again, if these factors are relatively stable over time, there may be a stronger relationship between relative TFP *growth* and changing RCAs than between relative *levels* at a given point in time.

5. Our data indicated some large and improbable changes in Japanese TFP between 1965 and 1970, and hence we feel that the changes between 1965 and 1982 are better indicators of trends than the changes from 1970 to 1982.

6. Leamer's classic (1984) empirical study of trade patterns for over 100 economies found that actual patterns could be explained fairly well by an endowment-based model with ten factors, including capital, several types of natural resources and land, and three skill classes of labor. It should be noted, however, that in that study manufacturing was disaggregated into only four industry classifications. Furthermore, the model was considerably more successful at explaining trade in primary products than trade in manufactures. Those results are consistent with the argument that the broad pattern of exports—primary versus secondary goods, heavy versus light manufactures—can be explained by general factor endowments, but the *specific* pattern of exports of manufactures at a more disaggregated level depends on industry-specific factors captured in the TFP measure.

Chapter 8

1. It is helpful to distinguish between what researchers in this area have recently been calling "unconditional" and "conditional" convergence. The former is characterized by the notion that all nations of the world will eventually attain the same level of per capita income or average productivity in the long term. The latter view, in contrast, maintains that, given other characteristics such as the country's investment rate and educational attainment, countries with lower initial per capita income (or productivity) will experience more rapid growth rates of per capita income (or productivity). In other words, countries with the same or similar investment rates, educational attainment, and the like, will eventually approach the same level of per capita income (or productivity).

Almost all studies have concluded that unconditional convergence is a very weak force, explaining very little about relative rates of productivity growth among all nations of the world. See, for example, Baumol, Blackman, and Wolff 1989, appendix to chapter 5. However, almost all studies have found that conditional convergence is a very strong force, explaining between 40% and 70% of the variation in growth rates of countries at all levels of development, depending on the other variables and sample of countries employed. See, for example, Baumol, Blackman, and Wolff 1989, chapter 9; Barro 1991.

2. Corresponding figures on the basis of the PPP exchange rates are shown in appendix table 8.A1.

3. Corresponding figures on the basis of the PPP exchange rates are shown in appendix table 8.A2.

4. Corresponding figures on the basis of the PPP exchange rates are shown in appendix table 8.A3.

5. See World Bank (1987) for a description of the Heavy and Chemical Industry program and an analysis of the program's results.

6. Corresponding figures on the basis of the PPP exchange rates are shown in appendix table 8.A4.

7. Corresponding figures on the basis of the PPP exchange rates are shown in appendix table 8.A5.

8. There are many anomalies in the Thai data for 1970, as can be seen in table 8.9. Hence our discussion is confined to the beginning (1963) and end (1984) years covered by this data source.

9. It is important to note that Dollar's (1991) study of Korean convergence does not employ the same classification scheme for industries utilized in the first section of this chapter. A broader definition of "heavy" industry was employed, including nonmetal products (n.e.c.), transport equipment, and machinery, in addition to metals and chemicals. In that study, medium industries consist of paper, glass, printing, textiles, plastic products, and metal products (n.e.c.). Light industries are wood products, furniture, electrical goods, pottery, rubber products, leather products, clothing, footwear, and manufactures (n.e.c.). Food, beverages, tobacco, and

petroleum/coal products were not covered in this study. As noted, the classification scheme employed in this chapter is the same as that employed for developed countries in chapter 3, which was based on capital intensity rankings within German industry. Dollar's study of Korea ranked industries according to Korean capital intensity in 1978.

10. This notion has been put forward by Balassa (1978) and Krueger (1980), among others.

11. The distortion index measures the extent to which a country's price level is high or low, relative to its endowments. The price levels reported by Summers and Heston (1988) are regressed, cross-sectionally, on country characteristics. A large positive or negative residual is taken as an indication of inward or outward orientation—that is, a higher or lower price level than can be justified by the country's endowments.

12. The data to construct this figure are reported in Dollar 1992.

References

Abramovitz, Moses. 1986. "Catching Up, Forging Ahead, and Falling Behind." *Journal of Economic History,* June, vol. 46, pp. 385–406.

Amsden, Alice H. 1989. *Asia's Next Giant: South Korea and Late Industrialization.* New York: Oxford University Press.

Bain, Joseph S. 1951. "Relation of Profit Rate to Industry Concentration: American Manufacturing, 1936–1940." *Quarterly Journal of Economics,* vol. 65, pp. 293–324.

Balassa, Bela. 1965. "Trade Liberalization and 'Revealed' Comparative Advantage." *The Manchester School,* May, vol. 33, pp. 99–123.

Balassa, Bela. 1978. "Exports and Economic Growth: Further Evidence." *Journal of Development Economics,* June, vol. 5, pp. 181–189.

Baldwin, Robert E. 1971. "Determinants of the Commodity Structure of U.S. Trade." *American Economic Review,* March, vol. 61, pp. 126–146.

Barro, Robert J. 1991. "Economic Growth in a Cross Section of Countries." *Quarterly Journal of Economics,* May, vol. 105, pp. 407–443.

Barro, Robert J., and Xavier Sala-i-Martin. 1992. "Convergence." *Journal of Political Economy,* vol. 100, April, pp. 223–251.

Bartelsman, Eric J., Ricardo J. Caballero, and Richard K. Lyons. 1991. "Short- and Long-Run Externalities." NBER Working Paper no. 3810, August.

Baumol, William J. 1986. "Productivity Growth, Convergence, and Welfare: What the Long-Run Data Show." *American Economic Review,* December, vol. 76, pp. 1072–1085.

Baumol, William J., and Edward N. Wolff. 1988. "Productivity Growth, Convergence, and Welfare: Reply." *American Economic Review,* December, vol. 78, pp. 1155–1159.

Baumol, William J., Sue Anne Batey Blackman, and Edward N. Wolff. 1989. *Productivity and American Leadership: The Long View.* Cambridge: MIT Press.

Blomstrom, Magnus, and Robert E. Lipsey. 1989. "The Export Performance of U.S. and Swedish Multinationals." *Review of Income and Wealth,* September, series 35, pp. 245–264.

Blomstrom, Magnus, and Edward N. Wolff. 1989. "Multinational Corporations and Productivity Convergence in Mexico." NBER Working Paper no. 3141, October.

Bluestone, Barry, and Bennett Harrison. 1982. *The Deindustrialization of America: Plant Closings, Community Abandonment, and the Dismantling of Basic Industry*. New York: Basic Books.

Bowen, Harry P. 1983. "Changes in the International Distribution of Resources and Their Impact on U.S. Comparative Advantage." *Review of Economics and Statistics*, August, vol. 65, pp. 402–415.

Boyer, Robert, and Pascal Petit. 1981. "Employment and Productivity in the EEC." *Cambridge Journal of Economics*, vol. 5, pp. 47–58.

Bronfenbrenner, Martin. 1985. "Japanese Productivity Experience." In William J. Baumol and Kenneth McLennan, eds., *Productivity Growth and U.S. Competitiveness*. New York: Oxford University Press.

Chang, W. W. 1979. "Some Theorems of Trade and General Equilibrium with Many Goods and Factors," *Econometrica*, May, vol. 47, pp. 709–726.

Coe, David, and Gerald Holtham. 1983. "Output Responsiveness and Inflation: An Aggregate Study." *OECD Economic Studies*, no. 1, Autumn.

Cohen, Stephen S., and John Zysman. 1987. *Manufacturing Matters: The Myth of the Post-Industrial Economy*. New York: Basic Books.

David, Paul A. 1989. "Computer and Dynamo: The Modern Productivity Paradox in a Not-Too-Distant Mirror." in *Technology and Productivity: The Challange for Economic Policy* OECD, 1991, 315–48.

Deardorff, Alan. 1984. "Testing Trade Theories and Predicting Trade Flows." In Ronald Jones and Peter Kenen, eds., *Handbook of International Economics*, vol. 1. Amsterdam, the Netherlands: Elsevier Science Publishers.

de Long, Bradford. 1988. "Productivity Growth, Convergence, and Welfare: Comment." *American Economic Review*, December, vol. 78, pp. 1138–1154.

Derian, Jean–Claude. 1990. *America's Struggle for Leadership in Technology*, Cambridge: MIT Press.

Dickens, W. T., and L. F. Katz. 1987. "Interindustry Wage Differences and Industry Characteristics." In K. Lang and J. Leonard, eds., *Unemployment and the Structure of Labor Markets*. Basil Blackwell.

Dollar, David. 1991. "Convergence of Korean Productivity on West German Levels, 1966–1978." *World Development*, February/March, vol. 19, pp. 263–273.

Dollar, David. 1992. "Outward–Oriented Developing Economies Really Do Grow More Rapidly: Evidence from 95 LDCs, 1976–85." *Economic Development and Cultural Change*, April, vol. 40, pp. 523–544.

Dollar, David, and Kenneth Sokoloff. 1990. "Patterns of Productivity Growth in South Korean Manufacturing Industries, 1963–1979." *Journal of Development Economics*, October, vol. 33, pp. 309–327.

Dollar, David, and Edward N. Wolff. 1988. "Convergence of Industry Labor Productivity among Advanced Economies, 1963–82," *Review of Economics and Statistics*, November, vol. 70, pp. 549–558.

Dollar, David, Edward N. Wolff, and William J. Baumol. 1988. "The Factor-Price Equalization Model and Industry Labor Productivity: An Empirical Test across Countries." In Robert Feenstra, ed., *Empirical Methods for International Trade*, Cambridge: MIT Press.

Dowrick, Steve, and Duc-Tho Nguyen. 1989. "OECD Comparative Economic Growth, 1950–85: Catch-Up and Convergence." *American Economic Review*, December, vol. 79, pp. 1010–1031.

Gerschenkron, Alexander. 1952. "Economic Backwardness in Historical Perspective." In Bert F. Hoselitz, ed., *The Progress of Underdeveloped Areas*. Chicago: University of Chicago Press.

Gittleman, Maury, and Edward N. Wolff. 1991. "International Comparisons of Inter-Industry Wage Differentials." Mimeo. New York University.

Glick, Mark, and Hans Ehrbar. 1988a. "Profit Rate Equalization in the U.S. and Europe: An Econometric Investigation." *Economic Journal of Political Economy*, Special Issue, vol. 4, pp. 179–201.

Glick, Mark, and Hans Ehrbar. 1988b. "Structural Change in Profit Rate Differentials: The Post World War II U.S. Economy." *British Review of Economic Issues*, Spring, vol. 10, pp. 81–102.

Griliches, Zvi. 1980. "Returns to Research and Development Expenditures." 1980. In John W. Kendrick and Beatrice Vaccara, eds., *New Developments in Productivity Measurement*. New York: National Bureau of Economic Research.

Griliches, Zvi. 1986. "Productivity, R & D, and Basic Research at the Firm Level in the 1970's." *American Economic Review*, March, vol. 76, pp. 141–154.

Grossman, Gene M., and Elhanan Helpman. 1991. *Innovation and Growth in the Global Economy*. Cambridge, Mass.: MIT Press.

Heckscher, Eli. 1919. "The Effect of Foreign Trade on the Distribution of Income." *Ekonomisk Tidskrift*, vol. 21, pp. 497–512. Reprinted as chapter 13 in A.E.A. *Readings in the Theory of International Trade*. Philadelphia: Blackiston, 1949.

Helpman, Elhanan, and Paul R. Krugman. 1985. *Market Structure and Foreign Trade: Increasing Returns, Imperfect Competition, and the International Economy*. Cambridge: MIT Press.

Hess, Peter. 1989. "The Military Burden, Economic Growth, and the Human Suffering Index: Evidence from the LDCs." *Cambridge Journal of Economics*, vol. 13, pp. 497–515.

Hirschman, Albert 0. 1958. *Strategy of Economic Development*. New Haven: Yale University Press.

Hirshleifer, Jack. 1976. *Price Theory and Applications*. Englewood Cliffs, N.J.: Prentice Hall.

Hooper, Peter, and Kathryn A. Larin. 1989. "International Comparisons of Labor Costs in Manufacturing." *Review of Income and Wealth,* December, series 35, pp. 335–356.

Japan Economic Planning Agency. 1988. Department of National Accounts. Economic Research Institute. *Gross Capital Stock of Private Enterprises, 1965–1986.* February.

Jorgenson, Dale W., Masahiro Kuroda, and Mieko Nishimizu. 1985. "Japan-U.S. Industry-Level Productivity Comparison, 1960–1979." Paper presented at the U.S.-Japan Productivity Conference. Cambridge, Mass., August.

Jorgenson, Dale W., and Mieko Nishimizu. 1978. "U.S. and Japanese Economic Growth, 1952–1974: An International Comparison." *Economic Journal,* vol. 88, pp. 707–726.

Kendrick, John W., ed. 1984. *International Comparisons of Productivity and Causes of the Slowdown.* Cambridge, Mass.: Ballinger.

Kormendi, Roger C., and Philip G. Meguire. 1985. "Macroeconomic Determinants of Growth: Cross-Country Evidence." *Journal of Monetary Economics,* vol. 16, pp. 141–163.

Kreuger, Alan B., and Lawrence H. Summers. 1987. "Reflections on the Inter-industry Wage Structure." In Kevin Lang and Jonathan S. Leonard, eds., *Unemployment and the Structure of Labor Markets.* New York: Basil Blackwell, pp. 17–47.

Krueger, Anne. 1980. "Trade Policy as an Input to Development." *American Economic Review,* May, vol. 70, pp. 288–292.

Lawrence, Robert Z. 1984. *Can America Compete?* Washington, D.C.: Brookings Institution.

Leamer, Edward. 1984. *Sources of International Comparative Advantage,* Cambridge: MIT Press.

Lichtenberg, R. Frank. 1984. "The Relationship between Federal Contract R & D and Company-Financed R & D." *American Economic Review,* May, vol. 74, pp. 73–78.

Maddison, Angus. 1982. *Phases of Capitalist Development.* Oxford: Oxford University Press.

Maddison, Angus, and Bart van Ark. 1989. "International Comparisons of Purchasing Power, Real Output and Labour Productivity: A Case Study of Brazilian, Mexican, and U.S. Manufacturing, 1975." *Review of Income and Wealth,* March, series 35, pp. 31–56.

Magaziner, Ira C., and Robert B. Reich. 1982. *Minding America's Business: The Decline and Rise of the American Economy.* New York: Harcourt Brace Jovanovich.

Marx, Karl. 1967. *Capital,* vols. 1 and 3. New York: International Publishers.

Matthews, R. C. O., C. H. Feinstein, and J. C. Odling-Smee. 1982. *British Economic Growth, 1856–1973.* Calif.: Stanford, Stanford University Press.

Mokhtari, Manouchehr, and Farhad Rassekh. 1989. "The Tendency Toward Factor Price Equalization among OECD Countries." *Review of Economics and Statistics*, vol. 71, no. 4, November, pp. 636–642.

Mueller, Dennis C. 1986. *Profits in the Long Run*. Cambridge: Cambridge University Press.

Musgrave, John C. 1986a. "Fixed Reproducible Tangible Wealth in the United States: Revised Estimates." *Survey of Current Business*, January, vol. 66, pp. 51–75.

Musgrave, John C. 1986b. "Fixed Reproducible Tangible Wealth in the United States, 1982–1985." *Survey of Current Business*, August, vol. 66, pp. 36–39.

Nakamura, Shinichiro. 1989. "Productivity and Factor Prices as Sources of Differences in Production Costs between Germany, Japan, and the U.S." *The Economic Studies Quarterly*, March, vol. 40, pp. 701–715.

Nelson, Richard, ed. 1982. *Government Support of Technical Progress: A Cross-Industry Analysis*. New York: Pergamon Press.

Nelson, Richard R., and Edward N. Wolff. 1991. "Factors Behind Cross-Industry Differences in Technical Progress." Mimeo, September. New York University.

Nelson, Richard R., and Gavin Wright. N.d. "The Rise and Fall of American Technological Leadership: The Postwar Era in Historical Perspective." *Journal of Economic Literature*. Forthcoming.

Norsworthy, J. R., and David H. Malmquist. 1983. "Input Measurement and Productivity Growth in Japanese and U.S. Manufacturing." *American Economic Review*, December, vol. 73, pp. 947–967.

Norsworthy, J. R., and David H. Malmquist. 1985. "Recent Productivity Growth in Japanese and U.S. Manufacturing." In William J. Baumol and Kenneth McLennan, eds., *Productivity Growth and U.S. Competitiveness*. New York: Oxford University Press, pp. 58–69.

Organization for Economic Cooperation and Development. 1980. *Main Economic Indicators, 1960–1979*, Paris, June.

Ohlin, Bertil. 1933. *Interregional and International Trade*. Cambridge: Harvard University Press.

Porter, Michael. 1990. *The Competitive Advantage of Nations*. New York: Free Press.

Quesnay, François. 1968. *Economical Table*. New York: Bergman Publishers.

Reich, Robert. 1991. *The Work of Nations*. New York: Knopf.

Ricardo, David. 1981. *On the Principles of Political Economy and Taxation*, Cambridge: Cambridge University Press.

Romer, Paul. 1986. "Increasing Returns and Long-Run Growth." *Journal of Political Economy*, vol. 94, pp. 1002–1037.

Rosenberg, Nathan. 1963. "Technological Change in the Machine Tool Industry, 1840–1910." *Journal of Economic History*, December, vol. 23, pp. 414–443.

Samuelson, Paul A. 1953. "Prices of Factors and Goods in General Equilibrium." *Review of Economics Studies*, vol. 21, pp. 1–20.

Smith, Adam. 1965. *The Wealth of Nations*. New York: Random House.

Statistics Canada. 1987. Science, Technology and Capital Stock Division. *Fixed Capital Flows and Stocks*, September. Ottawa, Canada.

Stigler, George. 1963. *Capital and Rates of Return in Manufacturing Industries*, Princeton, N.J.: Princeton University Press.

Summers, Robert, and Alan Heston. 1984. "Improved International Comparisons of Real Product and its Composition, 1950–1980." *Review of Income and Wealth*, series 30, pp. 207–262.

Summers, Robert, and Alan Heston. 1988. "A New Set of International Comparisons of Real Product and Prices: Estimates for 130 Countries, 1950–1985." *Review of Income and Wealth*, March, series 34, pp. 1–26.

Szirmai, Adam, and Dirk Pilat. 1990. "Comparisons of Purchasing Power, Real Output, and Labour Productivity in Manufacturing in Japan, South Korea, and the U.S.A., 1975–1985." *Review of Income and Wealth*, March, series 36, pp. 1–32.

Thompson, Ross. 1989. *The Path to Mechanized Shoe Production in the United States*. Chapel Hill: University of North Carolina Press.

van Ark, Bart. 1990. "Comparative Levels of Manufacturing Productivity in Post-war Europe: Measurement and Comparisons." *Oxford Bulletin of Economics and Statistics*, vol. 52, pp. 343–374.

Vanek, J. 1968. "The Factor Proportions Theory: The N-Factor Case." *Kyklos*, October, vol. 21, pp. 749–754.

Ward, Michael. 1985. *Purchasing Power Parities and Real Expenditures in the OECD*. Paris: Organization for Economic Cooperation and Development.

Wolff, Edward N. 1987. *Growth, Accumulation, and Unproductive Activity: An Analysis of the Post-War U.S. Economy*. Cambridge: Cambridge University Press.

Wolff, Edward N. 1991. "Capital Formation and Productivity Convergence over the Long Term." *American Economic Review*, June, vol. 81, pp. 565–579.

Wolff, Edward N., and M.I. Nadiri. 1991. "Spillover Effects, Linkage Structure, and Research and Development." Mimeo. New York University.

World Bank. 1987. *Korea: Managing the Industrial Transition*. Washington, D.C.

Index

HETERICK MEMORIAL LIBRARY
3 5111 00385 5081